A SIMPLIFIED GUIDE TO FORTRAN PROGRAMMING

DANIEL D. McCRACKEN

A SIMPLIFIED GUIDE TO FORTRAN PROGRAMMING

JOHN WILEY & SONS, INC.
NEW YORK LONDON SYDNEY TORONTO

This book was set in Caledonia with Trade Gothic display by Graphic Arts, Inc. and printed by Halliday Lithographers, Inc. The designer was Madelyn Waxman. The drawings were designed and executed by The Wiley Illustration Department.

Cover art was computer generated and photographed by Bob Blarsky of Dolphin Productions, Inc., a subsidiary of TAV.

Malcolm Easterlin handled the editing and Joan E. Rosenberg supervised production.

Library of Congress Cataloging in Publication Data:

McCracken, Daniel D.
  A simplified guide to Fortran programming.
  Includes bibliographical references.
  1. FORTRAN (Computer program language)   I. Title.

QA76.73.F25M32   001.6′424   74-876
ISBN 0-471-58292-1

Printed in the United States of America

10 9 8 7 6 5 4 3 2 1

To
Harold R. McArthur
Wilfrid W. Newschwander
*At Central Washington State College,
they taught me teaching*

PREFACE

This book might have been titled "Fortran Without Mathematics." It is for the person who needs to learn about computing using Fortran, but whose math preparation is limited to high school algebra—and maybe even that is not strong or recent. It is of no importance whether the lack of math background is because of level or subject specialization. That is, the college freshman will find the book useful regardless of his field, and the graduate student who happens not to know much math will find that the tone is not condescending just because the math level is simple.

Each chapter except the final one is based on one or more example programs that present the programming concepts in the framework of meaningful applications. These examples are drawn from a variety of areas familiar to all students: a simple pay calculation, the conversion of a distance in miles to kilometers, and the calculation of simple statistics describing grades on an examination, among many others. In fact, more than half of the book consists of examples. All programs have been run on a computer, and actual computer output is displayed for all of them.

There are nine case studies at the end of the text, to provide a broader insight into typical applications of computers and to give further examples of common programming techniques. Some are quite simple and others are moderately difficult. Each case study is identified so that the reader will know where in the text it will be meaningful.

There is a brief summary section at the end of each chapter. This is followed by a series of review questions, both to reinforce the central concepts and to give the reader an idea what he may need to restudy, with answers to all questions immediately following. Finally, there are lots of exercises, with answers to half of them given at the back of the book. Most of the exercises are suitable for running on a computer.

The concept of an algorithm is introduced at the very beginning, and there is emphasis at various points on practical demonstrations of how algorithms are developed. The concept of structured programming, which is of such growing importance, is utilized in writing programs to the extent that the characteristics of Fortran make possible; the resulting simplification of the understanding of programs is remarkable.

People learn programming by writing programs. This book recognizes that fact by providing plentiful exercises, a chapter (Chapter 5) that goes through the writing of a program in step-by-step fashion, and a set of term problem suggestions. The first complete program appears on page 3, and some of the exercises at the end of the first chapter can (and should) be run on the computer by the student. Every experienced instructor knows that the sooner students see complete programs, no matter how simple, and begin writing and running them themselves, the quicker they begin to develop a real understanding of what the subject is all about.

It is a pleasure to give well-deserved credit to the varied contributions of my primary reviewers: Gora Bhaumik, California State University, Fullerton; Mrs. Joyce Fodor, University of Wisconsin; Mrs. Susan Jaedecke, University of Denver; Jerry L. Ray, Educational Service Unit 3, State of Nebraska; and Jonathan D. Wexler, State University of New York, Buffalo. I am also indebted to the following people who reviewed the manuscript at various stages during its development and made many valuable suggestions for improvements: Ray P. Carreon, Fullerton (California) Junior College; J. Daniel Couger, University of Colorado; Donald W. Duman, Southern Connecticut State College; John Friedrich, San Antonio College; Milton Johnson, Oregon State University; Cliff Kirkhart, California State University, San Jose; Arthur Kraft, Ohio University; Marvin Kushner, Manhattan Community College; Kenneth McCallister, Federal City College; R. A. Rademacher, Colorado State University; William Riddle, University of Michigan; Al Stehling, San Antonio College; and Charles L. Van Gordon, Millersville State College, Pennsylvania. Mrs. Phyllis Dennen, Miss Cindy McCracken, and Miss Virginia McCracken did the typing and served in various other important ways in the production of the book.

All programs were tested and run using the time sharing services of National CSS, Inc., Stamford, Connecticut, and it is a pleasure to acknowledge their cooperation and assistance. The index was prepared using the National CSS system and the program on pages 212–214.

Daniel D. McCracken
Ossining, New York, 1974

CONTENTS

APPENDICES

CHAPTER ONE
GETTING STARTED PROGRAMMING WITH FORTRAN

What is programming all about?

Computer programming is a human activity. A person who has a problem that he wants the computer to help him solve must develop a procedure consisting of a sequence of the elementary operations that the computer is capable of carrying out. The procedure must then be expressed in a language that the computer can "understand." Fortran is such a language, and one of the most widely used.

It is worth pausing to emphasize that *people* have problems, whereas computers follow *procedures*. A computer cannot "solve a problem," no matter how many Sunday supplements say so. When we have a problem that we want to use a computer to help solve, we must first devise a precise method of solving it. The method chosen must, in principle, be something a person could do, if given enough time. In other words, it must be absolutely clear at every stage exactly what is to be done, and what is to be done next. Such a rigorously specified sequence of actions for solving a problem is called an *algorithm*. An algorithm can be expressed in many ways: in English, in a graphical form called a flowchart, or as a computer program, among others. If the algorithm is not expressed as a computer program in the first place, and usually it is not, the next step is to write a computer program that carries out the processing actions required by the algorithm.

In this book we talk both about devising algorithms and about writing computer programs, although the concentration is on programming. At the beginning it is necessary to focus on the Fortran language, so that we will have a way of "expressing ourselves" to the computer when we turn to problems that require more time to be spent on devising and expressing appropriate algorithms.

A simple program

Let us begin the study of Fortran programming by considering a simple example of a program, one where the processing required is so short and easily stated that the algorithm is a matter of a few sentences.

The task is simply to compute a worker's pay for a week. The number of hours worked and the hourly rate will be read from a data card. We are then to print a line giving the hours, the rate, and the pay. Even though this

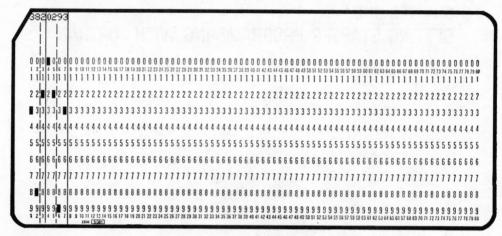

FIGURE 1.1. A data card, punched with values of 382 representing 38.2 hours worked, and 0293 representing $2.93 per
hour.

job is small, it will let us see a complete Fortran program in action, exhibit-
ing some important and fundamental programming concepts.

The data card

A representative data card is shown in Figure 1.1, where we see vertical
lines marking off groups of columns. Columns 1 through 3 contain punches
representing the number of hours worked, to tenths of an hour. The dotted
line between columns 2 and 3 indicates the location of an assumed decimal
point, which is not punched; we shall have to inform the computer to treat
the numbers in columns 1-3 *as if* there were a decimal point, which we shall
see how to do shortly. We see punches in columns 1-3 representing a sample
value of 38.2 hours worked. In like manner columns 4-7 contain a value of
0293 representing a pay rate of $2.93 per hour; we shall have to tell the com-
puter to assume a decimal point followed by two digits, as indicated by the
dotted line.

   The numbers at the top of the card were printed there by the card punch
at the same time that the holes were punched. The computer is able to read
punches only; the printing is only for our benefit. Naturally, the computer
cannot read the lines drawn on the card, either. One of the things we have
to do with our Fortran program is to tell the computer how the numbers are
punched on the card.

   Let us now turn to the program shown in Figure 1.2 to see how this is
done.

Fortran statements

A Fortran program consists of *statements*. In this program each statement
occupies just one line, so this program consists of seven statements. Blanks
within a Fortran statement are ignored except for a case considered in Chapter Three.

```
       READ (5, 100) HOURS, RATE
100    FORMAT (F3.1, F4.2)
       PAY = HOURS * RATE
       WRITE (6, 200) HOURS, RATE, PAY
200    FORMAT (1X, F8.1, F7.2, F10.2)
       STOP
       END
```

FIGURE 1.2. A simple but complete program for finding a
worker's pay given hours worked and pay rate.

The READ statement

The first statement begins with the word READ, which is a Fortran command
for the computer to read data. The 5 within parentheses specifies that the data
values come from a card reader; it is possible sometimes to read data from
magnetic tape or disk, or other devices, although we shall have little occasion to do so in this book. The 100 in parentheses refers to the *statement
number* of a FORMAT statement, which immediately follows the READ.
After the parentheses are listed the names by which we want to refer to the
data values that are to be read: the obvious choices of HOURS and RATE
have been used. The selection of names is one part of the job of the programmer. We might have used X and Y, or TIME and DOLLAR, or many other
choices for names. The computer does not "know" that HOURS has something
to do with payroll calculations—it simply reads a number from a card and
stores it away for later use under whatever name you have specified. When
we later call for the value by writing HOURS in a multiplication formula,
for example, the computer retrieves the number that it has stored under
the name HOURS.

The FORMAT statement

The FORMAT statement is used to describe to the computer how the data
values are arranged on the card. There has to be a description in the FORMAT
statement for each data value that we are going to read from the card. Since
there are two data values (HOURS and RATE), there must be two *field descriptors* in the FORMAT. The field descriptors are enclosed in parentheses.
A *field*, for our purposes, can be thought of simply as a group of columns that
holds a value; our two fields are therefore columns 1-3 (for HOURS) and
columns 4-7 (for RATE). The first data name in the READ statement, HOURS,
goes with the first field descriptor in the FORMAT, the F3.1, and the second
name, RATE, goes with the second field descriptor, F4.2. In the field descriptors the F stands for the way the numbers are punched; as we shall see
later, other letters are used in some cases. The first number after the F tells
how many columns there are in the field altogether, and the second number
after the F tells how many columns there are after the assumed decimal
point in the card field. Thus F3.1 means a three-column field having one digit
after the assumed decimal point, so that the digits 382 stand for 38.2 hours.
Likewise, F4.2 means four columns with two digits after the assumed decimal
point, so that the punches 0293 stand for 02.93 dollars per hour.

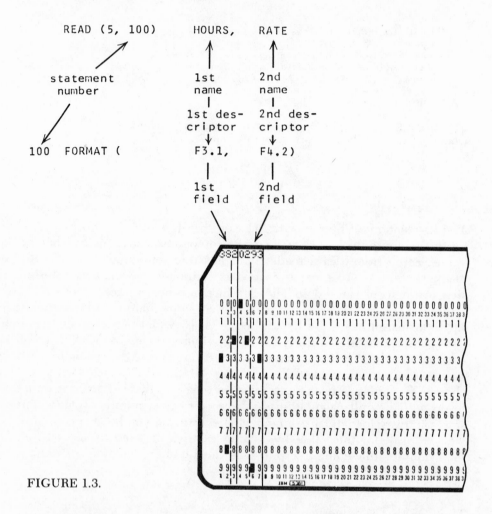

FIGURE 1.3.

Variables

In Fortran any value that is given a name, like HOURS or RATE in the first statement, or PAY in the third statement, is called a *variable*. The term is borrowed from mathematics. Don't look for hidden meanings! The term does not mean, for instance, that values "vary" arbitrarily during program execution. What it does mean is that we have the power to *make* values vary if we write statements calling for such action. In this program, once a value has been read from a card into the computer's storage under the name HOURS, it does not change at all through the subsequent execution of the rest of the program.

The assignment statement

Now that values have been read from a card and stored in the computer under the names HOURS and RATE, we are ready to multiply these two values together to get the worker's pay for the week. In Fortran this is done with an *assignment statement*, which is a command to "assign" a value to a variable. The name of the variable that is to have a value assigned to it is placed on the left of the equal sign, and on the right is a formula that expresses the computation that is to be performed to get that value. The fact that formulas can be written on the right-hand side of an assignment statement was the original basis for the choice of the name Fortran, which comes from the words FORmula TRANslation.

The use of the equal sign in the Fortran assignment statement is somewhat unfortunate, since it sometimes misleads beginners into thinking that an assignment is an equation. If card punches generally had the left-pointing arrow (←) available, we would prefer to use it instead of the equal sign since it better symbolizes the idea of assigning to the variable named on the left the value of the expression on the right.

In the statement

```
PAY = HOURS * RATE
```

the asterisk is a Fortran command to multiply the values of HOURS and RATE. Later we shall see examples of three other *arithmetic operators*, as they are called: a plus sign (+) for addition, a minus sign (−) for subtraction, and a slash (/) for division. There are numerous other considerations having to do with assignment statements that are taken up at appropriate later times.

We are now ready to print a line giving the results. Most of the programming ideas are quite similar to those in reading a card, but there are a few differences.

The WRITE statement

The Fortran command that calls for information to be sent from the computer to an output device, such as a printer, is WRITE. Within parentheses we specify the output device, using a 6 in our case to designate a printer. The FORMAT statement number is 200 this time, corresponding to the number of the statement that follows. Since the format in which we want to print the values is different from the format in which the input values appeared on the card, and since there are three values to print whereas only two were read, there has to be a separate FORMAT. In the WRITE statement we specify the names of the variables for which values are to be printed, and list them in the same order as we wish the numbers to be printed: HOURS first, then RATE, and finally PAY.

In the FORMAT statement there is a field descriptor for every variable name in the WRITE, as before, but we begin with a descriptor that does *not* go with any variable name. The first field descriptor in any FORMAT for printing should always be a *carriage control* specification. We shall study later the various choices for controlling the spacing of lines on the printer; for now note that writing 1X as the first field descriptor will cause ordinary single spacing.

The first field descriptor that is associated with a variable name is the F8.1, which goes with HOURS. The 8 says that we want eight printing positions on the printer, and the 1 says that there should be one digit after the decimal point. On output, the decimal point does actually print, and it counts as one of the eight printing positions. Extra spaces have been allowed for readability. The hours figure read from the card has three digits. Adding one printing position for the decimal point makes four, and since the field descriptor assigns eight printing positions, there will be four blanks inserted to the left of the number. In this case a negative value makes no sense, but if the value were negative the minus sign would print immediately to the left of the number and take up a printing position. On printing we must always allow space for the decimal point and the minus sign, if any, together with any blanks provided for easier readability.

The F7.2 field descriptor goes with RATE. It will cause the pay rate to be printed with a decimal point followed by two digits—in other words, as a dollars and cents amount. Extra space has again been allowed for improved readability.

Rounding

The PAY figure has been allocated ten spaces (with the 10 in F10.2) and two decimal places (with the 2). Actually, the multiplication produces a number with three digits after the decimal point, as we can see by writing out the computation in the form that is usual for paper-and-pencil work:

$$\begin{array}{r} 38.2 \\ \times\ 2.93 \\ \hline 111.926 \end{array}$$

Fortran will *round off* the result in preparing it to print with two digits after the decimal point. That is, if the digit dropped is five or greater it will increase the last digit printed by one. Thus 111.926 will print as 111.93. The 2 is increased to 3 because the digit dropped was five or greater.

The STOP statement

The STOP statement is a Fortran command that says we are ready to stop processing when this step is reached. Here, the STOP is at the end of the program, but there will be occasions when we want to stop at other places in the program, perhaps because of errors in data, for instance. In other words, the STOP may not always come at the end of the program.

The END statement

The END says that no more program statements follow. The last statement in a Fortran program must always be an END. The distinction between STOP and END will become clearer later. Both are required, but they will not always occur together this way.

The program deck

The most common way to give our program to the computer is to punch it on cards, one card for each line of the program. An introduction to this subject is given in Appendix 1. The data card is placed behind the Fortran program cards, and a few *control cards* are added at the beginning of the deck and elsewhere; these tell the computer system such things as the programmer's name and account or class number, that it is a Fortran program, and other matters. These control cards are different at different computer centers; your instructor or computer center will tell you how to prepare and use them.

The results

We can now submit the deck to the computer center and ask that it be run on the computer. If there are no errors in the program and if the deck is properly made up, we will get back a printed line like this:

    38.2   2.93   111.93

We see that the values for HOURS (38.2) and RATE (2.93) have been printed correctly, as has the product of the two, 111.93. To see how the spacing of the characters (digits and decimal points) along the line has been handled, let us show the output again, with printing positions identified:

```
              10        20        30
|||||||||||||||||||||||||||||||||||||
   38.2    2.93    111.93
```

Now we can observe that the HOURS value has indeed been allocated eight positions, as specified in the FORMAT statement 200 that went with the WRITE: four blanks at the beginning, two digits, a decimal point, and the final digit. Likewise RATE has seven positions and PAY has ten. There is no convincing way to exhibit one line of printing so as to prove that it was single spaced, as directed by the 1X, but we do see at least that the 1X does not correspond to a printing position in the line but rather was interpreted as the carriage control character.

This program is rather severely limited in that it is only able to process the data on one card. We shall see later how to get around this restriction to carry out more typical calculations. For now, to see how another set of data might appear, we would have to run the entire program again, substituting a different data card. Suppose we do so, with a card that specifies 39.1 hours and a rate of $10.41 per hour:

    39.1   10.41   407.03

The product of 39.1 and 10.41, keeping all the digits, is 407.031. No rounding was required this time.

The pattern of a simple Fortran program

The outline of the program we have just seen is adaptable to any small calculation. Let us summarize the actions.

1. The READ causes data to be read from a card. List the names of all the variables that are to receive values from the card, separating them from each other by commas. The names are of the programmer's choosing, subject

to a few simple rules listed in the next chapter. Within parentheses write a 5 to specify a card reader; at some computer centers this number might be different—your instructor or computer center will tell you if it is. The FORMAT statement number within parentheses in the READ statement must be the one that the programmer has chosen to be the FORMAT associated with the READ.

2. The FORMAT that is referenced by the READ tells Fortran how the data values are punched on the card. There must be one field descriptor for every variable name in the READ. In each field descriptor we tell how many columns there are in the field containing the number and how many digits there are after an assumed decimal point.

In many calculations the programmer will prefer to punch an actual decimal point in the input field on the card. When this is done the actual decimal point overrides whatever the field descriptor says, and the decimal point specification in the field descriptor is therefore immaterial. We could write a field descriptor of F9.0, for instance, which specifies nine columns, then punch a data value with an actual decimal point and a fractional part. The zero in the field descriptor then has no effect. (Note: the same thing is not true for WRITE FORMATs, where an actual decimal point is always placed where the F field descriptor says to place it.)

Punching an actual decimal point is more common in scientific and engineering calculations; leaving the decimal point assumed (and therefore described in the FORMAT) is more common in business and statistical applications. But the choice is entirely up to you; this kind of decision is part of the work of programming.

3. The actual calculation, whatever it may be, is specified by one or more assignment statements, or by various other Fortran statements that we shall study in due course. To be completely accurate, it should be noted that it is not even necessary to do *any* calculation: values can be read from cards and simply printed in a suitable format.

We take up more facts about Fortran calculation facilities and techniques in the next chapter.

4. A WRITE statement causes printing of whatever we wish. This will ordinarily include some or all of the input data, so that a person reading the printout can tell what the values were, plus the computed results. The output values will be printed in the same order in which the names of the variables in the WRITE statement are listed. The WRITE statement may or may not include all the variables listed in the READ statement, as the programmer wishes, and the WRITE statement may (and usually will) include variables not listed in the READ statement.

5. A FORMAT statement must be specified in the WRITE, to control the form and spacing of the output. The first field descriptor in the FORMAT associated with the WRITE should always specify the desired line spacing of the printed output; for the time being use a 1X descriptor, which will cause single spacing.

6. A STOP says to terminate processing.

7. An END says that there are no more statements in the program.

REVIEW QUESTIONS

(Answers to all review questions appear following the questions. Try to answer the questions before looking at the answers, but the answers are there for your benefit. If you cannot answer most of the questions without looking, it might indicate that you should go over the text material again.)

Note. Questions 1-7 refer to Figure 1.2.

1. What does the READ statement in our program do?
2. In the first FORMAT statement, the one with the statement number 100, which field descriptor goes with the variable named HOURS?
3. How many columns are there in the RATE field, and what in the program specifies that?
4. In the assignment statement PAY = HOURS ∗ RATE, what does the asterisk do? Why is this called an "assignment" statement?
5. Why is the field descriptor for HOURS different in the two FORMAT statements? Could it have been the same?
6. What in the program says that the printed output should be single spaced? What is this called?
7. Must there be an END statement in every program? Must it be the last statement?
8. Find the two errors in this version of our program:

```
        READ (5, 100) HOURS, RATE
100     FORMAT F3.1, F4.2
        PAY = HOURS * RATE
        WRITE (6, 200) HOURS RATE PAY
200     FORMAT (1X, F8.1, F7.2, F10.2)
        STOP
        END
```

ANSWERS

1. The READ causes a card to be read, and two numbers from it are stored in the computer under the names HOURS and RATE.
2. The F3.1. Since HOURS is the *first* variable name in the list of variables in the READ, the *first* field descriptor in the associated FORMAT goes with it.
3. There are four columns, which is the meaning of the 4 in the field descriptor F4.2.
4. The asterisk specifies multiplication. This is called an assignment statement because it results in assigning a value to the variable named on the left of the equal sign, PAY.
5. The two field descriptors are different because the form in which the number is to be printed is not the same as the form in which it is punched on

the card. They could not be the same in this case because an extra space has to be allowed for the decimal point to be printed, whereas the decimal point is *assumed* on the card.

6. Single spacing is called for by the 1X in the second FORMAT. This is called the carriage control character.

7. Yes. Yes.

8. Parentheses around the field descriptors in the first FORMAT are missing and the required commas between variable names in the WRITE statement are missing. Fortran requires strict adherence to punctuation rules.

EXERCISES

Answers to starred exercises appear at the back of the book.

*1. Write a field descriptor describing a card field having six columns, with an assumed decimal point between the third and fourth columns.

2. Write a field descriptor describing a card field having nine columns, with an assumed decimal point between the next-to-last and the last columns.

*3. Write a field descriptor describing a card field ten columns wide, in which an actual decimal point is punched.

4. Write a field descriptor describing a card field twelve columns wide, in which an actual decimal point is punched.

*5. A card contains a number in columns 1-4, with an assumed decimal point between columns 3 and 4. Write a READ statement and an associated FORMAT statement that will cause such a card to be read and the number assigned to a variable named PRICE. You may use any statement number of five or fewer digits that you please, so long as the same number appears on the FORMAT and within parentheses of the READ.

6. A card contains a six-digit number in columns 1-6, with two digits after an assumed decimal point, and another number in columns 7-10, with one digit after an assumed decimal point. Write a READ-FORMAT combination to read the card, assign the first value to a variable named RATE, and the second to a variable named TIME.

*7. Suppose that, in some program, you have already read a card giving values to variables named REG and OTIME. (Fortran variable names cannot be more than six characters in length, as discussed in the next chapter; these names are meant to suggest "regular earnings" and "overtime earnings.") Write an assignment statement that will cause these two values to be added and their sum assigned to the variable named EARN.

8. Assume that prior statements in a program have given values to variables named PRICE and QUANT, either by a READ statement or by

assignment statements. Write an assignment statement to multiply these values and give that value to a variable named ORDER.

*9. Consider the value read from a card in Exercise 5. Write a WRITE statement and an associated FORMAT statement to print that number in nine printing positions, with one digit after an actual decimal point. Be sure to include the carriage control field descriptor.

10. Consider the two numbers read from a card in Exercise 6. Write a WRITE-FORMAT combination to print the value of RATE in 10 printing positions, with its two decimal places, and the value of TIME in 12 printing positions including the decimal point and the one digit after it.

*11. You are to write a complete Fortran program to read two numbers from a card, perform a simple calculation, and print both the original values and the computed result, as follows.

Columns 1-7 of the card contain a value that is to be read into a variable named COST; the number has two digits after an assumed decimal point. Columns 8-13 of the card contain a value for a variable named DEPREC (for "depreciation"), which also has two digits after the decimal point. Read the values, subtract DEPREC from COST and assign the value to VALUE, then print all three according to this table:

COST   12 printing positions, with two digits after the decimal point
DEPREC 11 printing positions, with two digits after the decimal point
VALUE   12 printing positions, with two digits after the decimal point

12. Write a complete Fortran program to read two values, perform a calculation, and print input and result as follows:

Columns 1-5 of a card contain a value of HEIGHT, which has one digit after an assumed decimal point, and columns 6-9 contain a value for WIDTH, also with one digit after an assumed decimal point. After reading the card, multiply the two numbers together to get AREA, then print all three in this format:

HEIGHT 10 printing positions, with one digit after the decimal point
WIDTH   9 printing positions, with one digit after the decimal point
AREA   14 printing positions, with one digit after the decimal point

Notice that when two numbers are multiplied together, each of which has one decimal place, the product has two decimal places. The printing format specified thus calls for rounding the product to one decimal place. You do not have to take any special action to cause this rounding; writing an appropriate field descriptor will cause it to happen.

CHAPTER TWO
THE ASSIGNMENT STATEMENT

Introduction and problem statement

Any time we perform a calculation in Fortran—and calculation of one type or another is, after all, the basic purpose of most Fortran applications—we use the assignment statement. Recall that an assignment statement has the name of a variable on the left of the equal sign and some sort of formula on the right. The assignment statement is a command to carry out the calculation expressed by the formula on the right and to assign the computed value to the variable named on the left. In this chapter we shall learn more about the assignment statement, especially about the kinds of things that can be written on the right.

Our illustrative program this time will involve a simple computation from general science: the conversion of a temperature expressed in degrees Centigrade to degrees Fahrenheit. The conversion is accomplished by multiplying the Centigrade temperature by 1.8 and adding 32, so if we use the obvious variable names of C and F for the two temperatures the formula is:

$$F = 1.8 \ C + 32.0$$

Temperatures are commonly expressed in terms of Centigrade degrees in countries that employ the metric system, and in almost all scientific work. The boiling point of water is 100° Centigrade and 212° Fahrenheit; the freezing point of water is 0° C and 32° F. (You might like to check that these figures are correct according to the conversion formula.) "Officially," the word *Centigrade* has been replaced by *Celsius*, but the change has not entirely caught on.

We assume that a student has performed a series of experiments that involve taking temperatures expressed in degrees Centigrade. There are many such experiments, and the student wants the computer output to include an identification of which experiment each temperature reading is for. He has assigned a three-digit number to each reading, which is called the *experiment number*. The temperature itself can vary, in his experiments, between 100° C and 700° C, and he has read the temperatures to tenths of a degree.

The program is required to read a card containing an experiment number and a temperature in degrees Centigrade, then compute the equivalent temperature in degrees Fahrenheit, and finally write a line containing the experiment number and both forms of the temperature.

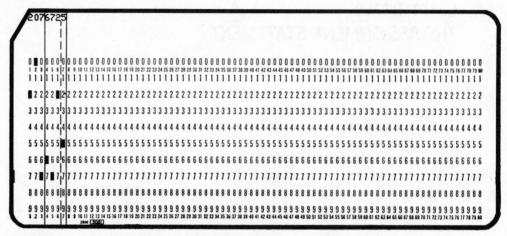

FIGURE 2.1.   A data card for the temperature conversion program, with an experiment number of 207 in columns 1-3 and a temperature of 672.5 in degrees Centigrade in columns 4-7.

The experiment number is punched in columns 1-3 and the temperature in columns 4-7 with an assumed decimal point between columns 6 and 7. Figure 2.1 shows a representative data card, on which the experiment number is 207 and the temperature is 672.5° C. The line of output is to contain the experiment number in printing positions 1-3, the temperature in degrees Centigrade in positions 4-13, and the temperature in degrees Fahrenheit in positions 14-23.

The program

The program to carry out these specifications is shown in Figure 2.2. It contains new features that can be studied with profit.

Comments

First, we see that the first six lines all begin with the letter "C" in column 1. These are *comment lines*. They are for our benefit in identifying and explaining the program to anyone who needs to understand it. They are consid-

```
C CENTIGRADE TO FAHRENHEIT CONVERSION
C VARIABLE NAMES
C     C - DEGREES CENTIGRADE
C     F - DEGREES FAHRENHEIT
C     NUMBER - EXPERIMENT NUMBER
C
      READ (5, 10) NUMBER, C
  10  FORMAT (I3, F4.1)
      F = 1.8 * C + 32.0
      WRITE (6, 20) NUMBER, C, F
  20  FORMAT (1X, I3, F10.1, F10.1)
      STOP
      END
```

FIGURE 2.2.   A program to convert a temperature in degrees Centigrade to a temperature in degrees Fahrenheit.

ered to be a part of the program, but they are not statements. They do not command the computer to do anything as do the statements that follow. Here we have used comments to give an identification of the program and to state the meanings of the three variables that are used. The decision of how to use comments is up to the programmer, and we shall see other ways of using them as we proceed through the book.

Integer and real quantities

The READ statement calls for data values to be read from the card for the variables named NUMBER and C. This brings us to an important distinction between two types of values in Fortran: *integer* and *real*. An integer value is one that *never* has a decimal point, which is to say that it is a whole number and never has a fractional part. We might have an experiment number (NUMBER) like 128 or 201 or 13, but we would never have an experiment number like 23.9. The temperature, on the other hand, might very well have a fractional part: temperatures of 112.9 degrees or 56.1 degrees are perfectly meaningful. A Fortran variable that is able to take on a value that includes a fractional part is called *real*. (The term is borrowed from mathematics; the full implications of it are not important to us.)

Variable names

Fortran imposes a rule on the naming of variables to permit it to distinguish between integer and real variables. A Fortran integer variable name must begin with one of the letters I, J, K, L, M, or N. This initial letter may be followed by any desired letters or digits, up to a maximum of six characters altogether. It must be emphasized that only letters and digits are permitted. All of these would be acceptable names for Fortran integer variables:

```
N
LAST
NUMERO
K7
M2KK7
JOHN23
```

On the other hand, these would not be acceptable names of Fortran integer variables:

```
QUANT        (begins with a wrong letter)
INFINITY     (contains more than six characters)
NAME-2       (contains a character other than a letter or digit)
```

The name of a Fortran real variable must begin with any letter *except* I, J, K, L, M, or N; the initial letter may be followed by any desired letters or digits, up to a maximum of six characters altogether. (Letters and digits only, as before.) All of these would be acceptable names for Fortran real variables:

```
ANYONE
ANY1
X2REAL
QUANT
Z
```

These would not be acceptable names of Fortran real variables:

7X   (does not begin with a letter)
MAX   (begins with a wrong letter)
QUANTITY   (contains more than six characters)

The choice of variable names is entirely under the control of the programmer, within the restrictions imposed by the initial letter requirement and the limitation to a maximum of six characters. It is recommended that variable names be chosen to suggest what they stand for, as we do in our illustrative programs.

The FORMAT statement that is associated with the READ has the statement number 10 this time, to show that the choice of statement numbers is also under the programmer's control. A statement number may be any number of from one to five digits, and may appear anywhere in the first five positions of the Fortran statement but only within the first five positions.

The I field descriptor

The first field descriptor in this FORMAT is of a new type: instead of beginning with the letter F, as before, it begins with I. This designates the card field as containing an integer quantity, that is, one that never contains a decimal point—actual or assumed. The I field descriptor is used, naturally enough, for quantities that are to become the values of integer variables. In our case we are saying that the experiment number, NUMBER, is punched in three columns. Since there is no decimal point location to specify, this field descriptor contains only one number, namely the number of columns in the field. If an integer value has fewer digits than there are columns in the field in which it is punched, the number must be punched at the *right* side of the field.

The second field descriptor, F4.1, is familiar from the previous chapter: it describes a field of four columns that has one digit after an assumed decimal point.

Constants

The next statement is the assignment statement that does the actual conversion from Centigrade to Fahrenheit and assigns the newly computed value to the variable named F. The first thing we observe is the presence of two quantities that appear *as numbers*, not having names but representing themselves. Such quantities are called *constants*. A number that is written without a decimal point is called an integer constant and one that is written with a decimal point is called a real constant.

(The *exponent notation* is available for writing real constants that are too large or too small for writing conveniently with the form discussed above. See Appendix 3 if you are concerned with applications involving such numbers.)

Every Fortran imposes limits on the size of numbers that can be written as real and integer constants or assigned to real or integer variables. You will have to find out what the limits are for your system. Generally speaking, they are quite large, and only in unusual circumstances or as the result of errors do we encounter them.

Here are some acceptable integer constants:

```
0
6
+400
1234
10000
-2000
```

The following are not acceptable integer constants:

```
12.78               (decimal point not allowed in integer)
-10,000             (comma not allowed in any constant)
1234567890000       (too large in most Fortrans)
```

Here are some acceptable real constants:

```
0.0
0.1
.1
6.0
6.
-20000.0
-0.0002783
+15.083
```

The following are not acceptable real constants:

```
12,345.6        (comma not allowed)
+234            (no decimal point)
```

Mixed mode

Most versions of Fortran permit real and integer quantities to be "mixed" in the same expression. This is called *mixed mode*. Since not all Fortrans have this feature and since there are pitfalls in using it, we shall generally avoid using mixed-mode arithmetic.

As an example of what is meant by mixed mode, we could have written the assignment statement in the program in the form

```
F = 1.8 * C + 32
```

instead of

```
F = 1.8 * C + 32.0
```

as we have done.

The assignment statement

It is now time to consider the assignment statement in somewhat more detail. We recall that there is always the name of a single variable on the left-hand side of the equal sign and that the function of the assignment statement is to "assign" a value to this variable. If the variable has never had a value before this, neither as a result of a READ nor as the result of a previously executed assignment statement, the effect of the assignment statement is to give the variable a value for the first time. If, on the other hand, the variable did previously have a value, the effect is to discard the previous value and give the variable the new value specified by the right-hand side of the statement.

Expressions

Up to now we have called what is written on the right-hand side a formula, but the more precise term used in Fortran is *expression*. Often the expression does call for arithmetic operations, as in the HOURS * RATE we saw in the last chapter or the multiplication and addition specified in this example. But an expression can also be just one variable, or just a constant. We frequently write things like

    X = 1.0

for instance, to give a variable a starting value that is able to be modified later in the program.

It is now time to look more closely at what kinds of things can be done with an expression in an assignment statement.

Let us review the four arithmetic operators and their meanings:

    +   means add
    -    means subtract
    *   means multiply
    /   means divide

To these we add a fifth operator—that for exponentiation (raising to a power):

    **   means "raise to a power"

The double asterisk is considered to be one operator. If we write

    SPEED**2

the meaning is "raise the value of the variable named SPEED to the second power," that is, multiply SPEED by SPEED. If we write

    X**4

the meaning is "raise the value of X to the fourth power," which has the same meaning, mathematically and in Fortran, as if we wrote

    X*X*X*X

If we write

    Y**0.5

we mean "raise Y to the 0.5 power," which, mathematically and in Fortran, means to take the square root.

Integer division

The division of two integer quantities is done according to a rule that must always be carefully considered: any remainder is simply dropped. There is no rounding. For instance, the division 7/4 produces a quotient of 1 and a remainder of 3. *The quotient is not rounded up to 2.* If the same quantities in real form are divided, as in 7.0/4.0, the result is 1.75, which is closer to 2 than 1, but this fact has no bearing on the outcome of the integer division.

This is not the result of caprice or oversight on the part of the designers of Fortran. For the relatively unusual situations where integer division is needed at all, it makes sense. The point of bringing it up here is mostly to warn against the hazards of doing it unintentionally, where ignoring the remainder is often not what the programmer really wanted.

Hierarchy of operators

The question now arises: When an expression contains more than one operator, in what order are the operations to be carried out? For example, does the statement

```
F = 1.8 * C + 32.0
```

mean to multiply 1.8 and C, then add 32.0 to the result, or does it mean to add C and 32.0, then multiply the sum by 1.8? The answer is to be found in the *operator hierarchy rule*, which specifies the order in which operations in an expression are carried out:

1. Exponentiations, if any, are done first.
2. Multiplications and divisions are done next.
3. Additions and subtractions are done last.
4. A series of operations at the same hierarchy level are carried out from left to right.

Thus the expression in our program says to perform the multiplication before the addition, just as in normal mathematical notation.

Parentheses

All of this assumes that we are willing to accept these normal hierarchy rules — but sometimes we are not. Perhaps the formula we are trying to express requires that an addition or subtraction be done *before* a multiplication or division. This is easily handled by the use of parentheses in a way quite similar to usual mathematical notation. For example, consider the problem of converting a Fahrenheit temperature to Centigrade, which, using the same symbols as before, is given by

$$C = \frac{F - 32.0}{1.8}$$

We definitely cannot write the assignment statement

```
C = F - 32.0 / 1.8
```

because according to the operator hierarchy rule that would mean to divide 32 by 1.8 and subtract the quotient from F — which is hardly what we want. Instead we write

```
C = (F - 32.0) / 1.8
```

Now, the parentheses force the subtraction to be done first. Just as in mathematics, parentheses in Fortran specify that operations inside parentheses be done before operations outside parentheses. If there are parentheses within parentheses, the innermost operations are done first.

An excellent maxim in writing expressions is: *when in doubt parenthesize*. For example, if there is any question whatsoever in your mind whether

    F = 1.8 * C + 32.0

means

    F = (1.8 * C) + 32.0

or

    F = 1.8 * (C + 32.0)

(and of course the former is correct), then use parentheses. In fact, some instructors will direct you *always* to write parentheses, as above, to try to minimize the chances of mistakes. A prime example of the wisdom of such a policy is almost any application of rule 4 above, that operations at the same level of hierarchy are carried out from left to right. According to this rule,

    A / B * C

means

    (A / B) * C

and not

    A / (B * C)

but the chances of misunderstanding and uncertainty are so great that it would be much better practice to use the parentheses even where they are not required by the Fortran rules.

Cautions

One aspect of mathematical notation that is *not* permitted is sometimes a stumbling block for beginners: the asterisk for multiplication must never be omitted. We cannot write AB to stand for A*B, because Fortran would assume that AB was just another variable name—one happening to have two letters in it. We cannot even write

    (A + B)(C + D)

when we mean

    (A + B) * (C + D)

Neither can we write

    2 SUM

to stand for two times the value of the variable named SUM. Both of these latter might seem to be plausible, but they are not permitted.

It is never permitted to have two operators side by side. We cannot write

```
A * -B
```

for instance; if this operation is necessary we should write

```
A * (-B)
```

or, what gives the same result mathematically,

```
- A * B
```

When a quantity is raised to a power that is a whole number, like 2 or 3, we have a choice of writing the exponent as an integer or a real constant, that is, of writing

```
X**3
```

or

```
X**3.0
```

Using the integer form is better, since it is usually a lot faster. (The real form forces Fortran to use a combination of a logarithm and an antilogarithm, the latter also being called the exponential function.)

Type conversions

Only one other thing needs to be said about arithmetic assignment statements, concerning the occasional situation — intentional or not — where the expression on the right is of the integer type and the variable on the left is real, or vice versa. When this occurs, the calculation called for by the expression is done in the form implied by the type of the variables and constants, and the result is converted to the form of the variable on the left. The only precaution is that when a real value is converted to integer, the fractional portion is simply discarded, just as in integer division. Thus if we write

```
K = 5.0 / 3.0
```

the calculation would be done in the usual fashion, leading to an approximation of the form 1.6666666, but the entire fractional part would be discarded in converting this result to integer form: the value assigned to K would be one.

This is only a precaution that the reader need not be unduly concerned about. There will not be many occasions when this sort of thing need be done on purpose.

The assignment statement is of fundamental importance in using Fortran effectively. Table 2.1 presents some further examples of typical assignment statements, together with equivalent mathematical forms. Variable names have been chosen to be identical to or suggestive of the symbols used in the formulas, but any other names following the real/integer-naming convention would have been acceptable.

The examples in Table 2.2 are presented to emphasize the importance of writing expressions and statements according to the rules of Fortran. Each of the statements in Table 2.2 contains at least one error, of a type frequently made by beginners.

TABLE 2.1

K = 12	$k = 12$
J = 4*K - 6*K1*K2	$J = 4k - 6\,k_1\,k_2$
K = K + 1	$k_{new} = k_{old} + 1$
AREA = 0.5 * B * H	$\text{area} = \frac{1}{2}\,bh$
AREA = (A + B + C - 3.14159) * R**2	$\text{area} = (a + b + c - \pi)\,r^2$
AREA = 3.1416 * (R1 + R2) * (R1 - R2)	$\text{area} = \pi\,(r_1 + r_2)\,(r_1 - r_2)$
AVERAG = SUM / N	$\text{average} = \dfrac{\text{sum}}{N}$
X = A**2 - 2.0*A*B + B**2	$X = a^2 - 2ab + b^2$
P = (X/Y)**N * (1.0 - X/Y)	$P = (x/y)^n\,(1 - x/y)$

TABLE 2.2

Y = 2.X + A	* missing
3.14 = X - A	Left side must be a variable name
A = ((X + Y)A**2	Parenthesis and * missing
X = 1,624,009.*DELTA	Commas not permitted in constants
-J = K**2	Variable on left must be written without sign
BX6 = 1./-2.*A**6	Two operators side by side
A*X + B = Q	Left side must be a single variable name

Back to the program

With the temperature in degrees Fahrenheit now computed, we are ready to print the line of output. The WRITE statement contains nothing new, and the associated FORMAT is not unusual either. We see that the same field descriptor, I3, has been used for writing the experiment number as was used on input. Since an integer number has no decimal point and since the value was not changed by the program, we can use the same field descriptor for output as for input. Naturally, if we wished to allow extra space for readability—if this were not the first number on the line, for instance—we could have written I5 or I12 or whatever we might wish. The field descriptors for the two temperatures involve nothing new. Likewise, the STOP and END are as before.

The line of output from this program, assuming the data card displayed earlier, is this:

```
207      672.5     1242.5
```

We see that a temperature of 672.5° C corresponds to a temperature of 1242.5° F.

Summary of the important facts about the assignment statement

1. The Fortran assignment statement takes the form

variable = expression

It is a command to evaluate the expression written on the right, and to assign that value to the variable named on the left. Any previous value associated with the variable on the left is destroyed by this action.

2. The symbols for the arithmetic operations are:

+	means add
-	means subtract
*	means multiply
/	means divide
**	means raise to a power

3. Two operation symbols must never be written together, side by side.

4. Parentheses are used, as in ordinary mathematical notation, to indicate groupings. When there are parentheses within parentheses, the expression within the inner parentheses is evaluated first.

5. When the hierarchy of operations is not specified by parentheses, the "strength" of the operators is as follows: all exponentiations, if any, are done first, then all multiplications and divisions, and finally all additions and subtractions.

6. Within a sequence of consecutive additions and/or subtractions, or multiplications and/or divisions, in which the order of operations is not completely specified by the use of parentheses, the meaning is that of left to right evaluation.

7. If you don't like to learn rules like those just stated, follow the precept *when in doubt parenthesize.*

8. In integer division, remainders are completely ignored. Thus, 99/100 is zero.

9. When the expression on the right of the equal sign contains any real quantities, the value of the entire expression will be real. Only if nothing but integer quantities appears on the right will the value of the expression be integer. If the expression on the right and the variable on the left are of different types, the expression is evaluated according to the type of the expression on the right, then converted to the form of the variable on the left. In converting from real to integer, any fractional part is dropped, as in integer division.

10. If you are following the rules strictly, the only "mixing" of integer and real quantities within an expression that is legal is to raise a real quantity to an integer power. If you are taking advantage of the ability in your Fortran to use mixed mode, just watch out for subexpressions involving only integer quantities, in which there is a division. Rude shocks await the unwary.

REVIEW QUESTIONS

1. How are integer and real constants distinguished?

2. Why is each of the following incorrect as an integer constant?

    ```
    12,000    3.4    6.0
    ```

3. Are the following correct as integer constants?

    ```
    -12000    987654321
    ```

4. Are the following correct as real constants?

    ```
    41    9,300,000,000    -96.7    +96.7
    ```

5. Which of the following are acceptable names for integer variables, which are acceptable names for real variables, and which are unacceptable as names of either type?

    ```
    G      GAMMA      GAMMA421      I     IJK     J79-1      LARGE      R(2)19
    BT07TH     ZCUBED      ZSQUARED     12AT7     2N173      B6700
    CDC6600    S/370      IBM370       DELTA     KAPPA      EPSILON
    EPSILN     A1.4       A1POINT4     A1P4      AONEP4     FORTRAN
    ALGOL      PL/I       SNOBOL
    ```

6. State in words the meaning of each of the following expressions. For example, an acceptable answer for $A + B$ would be "the sum of the values of the variables named A and B."

    a. X * Y
    b. HOURS - 40.0
    c. K
    d. 3.14159
    e. ANGLE / 6.2832
    f. C ** 2
    g. (POINT1 + POINT2) / 2
    h. (A + F) / (X + 2.0)

7. In each of the following you are given a mathematical expression and what a student intended as a corresponding Fortran expression. Point out an error in each of the student's attempts.

    a. $j \cdot k$ JK

    b. $\dfrac{s+t}{2}$ S + T / 2

    c. $\dfrac{4}{u+v}$ 4.0 / U + V

    d. a^{n+2} A ** N + 2

    e. $\dfrac{a \cdot b}{c \cdot d}$ A*B/C*D

    f. $m \times n$ M X N

    g. $\left(\dfrac{a+b}{c}\right)^2$ (A + B)**2 / C

8. Each of the following arithmetic assignment statements contains at least one error. Identify the errors.

    a. `-V = A + B`
    b. `4 = K`
    c. `V - 3.96 = X**1.667`
    d. `Z*X**2 + Y*X + W`
    e. `Z2 = A*-B + C**4`
    f. `X = Y + 2.0 = Z + 9.0`
    g. `R = 16.9X + AB`

9. Generally speaking, as we saw in the first chapter, the same field descriptor cannot be used both for input and output of the same real quantity. Yet this is possible for integer quantities; why?

10. Suppose we write a statement such as

    `READ (5, 123) TIME, DIST`

or

    `AREA = 3.14159 * R**2`

but put a *C* in column 1 of that line. What will Fortran do with the statement?

11. Identify all the errors in this version of the program of this chapter.

```
C CENTIGRADE TO FARHENHIET CONVERSION
C VARIABLE NAMES
C      C - DEGREES CENTIGRADE
C      F - DEGREES FAHRENHEIT
C      NUMBER - EXPERIMENT NUMBER
C
       READ (5, 15) NUMBER, C
   15  FORMAT (I3, F4.1)
       F = 1.8 C + 32
       WRITE (6, 20) NUMBER, C, F
   20  FORMAT (1X, I3, F10.1, F10.1)
       STOP
```

ANSWERS

1. Real constants always contain a decimal point; integer constants never do.

2. 12,000 is illegal because of the comma. 3.4 is illegal because of the decimal point. 6.0 is also illegal, considered as an integer constant, but it is correct as a real constant. Note that 6.0 is not correct as an integer constant even though *mathematically* 6 and 6.0 are the same number. They are stored and processed differently in Fortran.

3. Both are correct (minus signs certainly are allowed), but the second number would be too large for some computers. For every Fortran there is a maximum size for integer constants; you will have to find out what it is for your system.

4. 41 is incorrect for lack of a decimal point. 9,300,000,000 is incorrect because of the commas and lack of a decimal point and might present a problem anyway in some Fortrans because of limits on the number of digits in a real constant. The exponent form is available for representing

large numbers like this; see Appendix 3 if you are concerned with such applications. −96.7 and +96.7 are both acceptable; although it is not usual to write the plus sign for positive constants, it is permitted.

5. Names of real variables: G, GAMMA, BT07TH, ZCUBED, B6700, DELTA, EPSILN, A1P4, AONEP4, ALGOL, SNOBOL. Names of integer variables: I, IJK, LARGE, IBM370, KAPPA. Unacceptable names: GAMMA421 (too long), J79-1 (contains a character other than a letter or digit), R(2)19 (ditto), ZSQUARED (too long), 12AT7 (does not begin with letter), 2N173 (ditto), CDC6600 (too long), S/370 (contains a character other than a letter or digit), EPSILON (too long), A1.4 (contains a character other than a letter or digit), A1POINT4 (too long), FORTRAN (too long), PL/I (contains a character other than a letter or digit).

6. a. The product of the values of the variables named X and Y.
   b. The value of the variable named HOURS, minus the constant 40.0.
   c. The value of the variable named K.
   d. The constant 3.14159.
   e. The value of the variable named ANGLE, divided by the constant 6.2832.
   f. The square of the value of the variable named C.
   g. One-half of the sum of the values of the variables named POINT1 and POINT2.
   h. The sum of the values of the variables named A and F, divided by the sum of the value of the variable named X and the constant 2.0.

7. a. Asterisk missing.
   b. Parentheses around S + T missing; means $s + t/2$ as written.
   c. Parentheses around U + V missing; means $4/u + v$ as written.
   d. Parentheses around N + 2 missing; since by the operator hierarchy rules all exponentiations are performed first, the expression as written means $a^n + 2$.
   e. Needs parentheses around C*D to force the D to be in the denominator. Means $\frac{a \cdot b}{c} \cdot d$ as written.
   f. X cannot be used as a multiplication sign! Write M * N.
   g. Needs parentheses to force the exponentiation to be done last. Write

   `((A + B) / C) ** 2`

8. a. The variable on the left must not be written with a sign.
   b. The left side must be a variable.
   c. The left side must be a single variable. The Fortran assignment statement is not an equation that the computer solves.
   d. Not an assignment statement at all—no equal sign.
   e. Contains two successive operators, in A * −B.
   f. Contains two equal signs, which is not permitted.
   g. Some operator is needed between 16.9 and X. The writer of such an expression would presumably be thinking that multiplication is assumed here as in ordinary mathematical notation. If he likewise meant AB to stand for A * B he has another error, but Fortran would not so identify it because AB is a legal variable name.

9. If the real quantity has an assumed decimal point whereas the printed

output has an actual decimal point, extra space in the output must be allowed accordingly. Since integer quantities never have decimal points this problem cannot arise.

10. Something of a trick question, perhaps: if there is a C in column 1 Fortran does not treat the line as a statement at all, but a comment. The fact that what appears on the line would be a legal Fortran statement if it did not have a C in column 1 is completely immaterial.

11. First, two changes that are not errors. The misspelling of Fahrenheit in the first line is indeed an error to you and me, but Fortran would never worry about it; comment lines are simply reproduced as written when the program is listed. Second, the change in the statement number for the first FORMAT would have no effect, since the READ was changed correspondingly. The two errors are a missing asterisk in the assignment statement, and a missing END. The absence of a decimal point in the constant 32 makes the assignment statement expression mixed mode, which would be an error in some systems.

EXERCISES

1. Write Fortran expressions corresponding to each of the following mathematical expressions.

   *a. $x + y^3$
   b. $(x + y)^3$
   *c. x^4
   d. $a + \dfrac{b}{c}$
   *e. $\dfrac{a + b}{c}$
   f. $a + \dfrac{b}{c + d}$
   *g. $2x - 3y$
   h. $(h/2)^2$

2. Write arithmetic assignment statements to do the following.
   *a. Multiply the current value of the variable named OTIME by one-half; make this result the new value of a variable named BONUS.
   b. Add the value of the variable named REGULR to the value of the variable named BONUS; assign this value to a variable named GROSS.
   *c. Add the values of the variables named X, Y, and Z, then divide the sum by 3. Assign the quotient to the variable named AVER.
   d. Add the values of variables named S and T and square the sum. Assign the value to the variable named R.
   *e. Make the value of the variable named SQRT2 equal to the square root of 2. Don't look up the value, or try to compute it by hand; write an expression involving only constants.
   f. Make the value of a variable named CONST4 equal to one-half

of the square of pi. Assume you know that pi is approximately 3.141593, but do not try to do the rest of the calculation by hand: write an appropriate expression involving only constants.

*g. Increase the present value of a variable named D by 2.0 and replace the present value of D with the result. The result may look strange — it will convince you that an assignment statement is *not* an equation! — but it is quite legal, and things like it will find wide usefulness in later chapters.

h. Multiply the present value of a variable named E by 1.1 and replace the present value of E with the result.

*i. Add the values of the variables named X and Y, subtract 2 from the sum, and take the square root of the result. Assign this computed value to a variable named CALC.

j. Make the value of Q equal to the fourth root of a variable named Z. (The fourth root can be found by raising a number to the 0.25 power.)

Note. In exercises 3-12 you are asked only to write assignment statements, since that is the focus of the chapter. You are free, however, to devise data cards and suitable READ, WRITE, and FORMAT statements to permit writing complete programs that you may run.

*3. Previous statements have given values to the following variables:

GROSS   Total earnings for the week
FICA   FICA tax
FIT   Federal income tax
SIT   State income tax
USSAV   U. S. savings bonds
UF   United Fund

Write a statement to subtract all of the deductions from GROSS, and assign the difference to CHECK.

4. Previous statements have given values to the following variables, in an inventory control application:

OH   The number of a certain item on hand
PREVOH   The number on hand at the end of the last updating of the inventory record
RECPT   The number received from suppliers
RETURN   The number returned by customers
ADJ   An adjustment, based on an actual count or the discovery of a prior error
ISSUE   The number issued to customers

The number on hand now can be found by adding receipts, returns and adjustments to the previous on hand, and subtracting the number issued. Write an assignment statement to do this arithmetic and assign the result to OH.

*5. If the dimensions of a rectangular box are given by the values of X, Y, and Z, then the volume and surface area can be computed from

$$\text{VOLUME} = XYZ$$
$$\text{AREA} \quad = 2(XY + XZ + YZ)$$

Assume that earlier statements in a program have given values to X, Y, and Z. Write statements to compute VOLUME and AREA.

6. The volume and surface area of a sphere having a radius of R are given by

$$\text{VOLUME} = 4.189 \ R^3$$
$$\text{AREA} \quad = 12.57 \ R^2$$

Assume that an earlier statement has given a value to R; write statements to compute VOLUME and AREA.

*7. A certain state withholding tax is computed as 12% of the difference between GROSS and 12.00 times the number of dependents claimed. If the number of dependents claimed is DEPEND and if previous statements have given values to GROSS and DEPEND, write a statement to compute TAX. (Assume that GROSS is larger than 12.00 times the number of dependents; see Exercise 3 in Chapter Four for a more realistic procedure.)

8. A salesman works on a commission basis that gives him $20 plus 8% of the amount by which SALES exceed BASE. Assume that prior statements have given values to SALES and BASE, and write an assignment statement to compute SALARY. (Assume that the value of SALES is not less than the value of BASE. See Exercise 4 in Chapter Four for a more realistic procedure.)

*9. Assume that previous statements have given values to all of the following variables from a simple balance sheet:

CASH	Cash on hand
ACCREC	Accounts receivable
SUPPLS	Supplies
RENT	Prepaid rent
EQUIP	Equipment
DEPREC	Accumulated depreciation
CURRNT	Current assets
PLANT	Plant assets
TOTASS	Total assets

Current assets consist of the sum of cash on hand, accounts receivable, supplies, and prepaid rent. Plant assets consist of equipment minus depreciation. Total assets consist of current assets plus plant assets. Write statements to compute CURRNT, PLANT, and TOTASS.

10. Following from Exercise 9, assume that previous statements have given values to ACCPAY, the accounts payable, and SALARY, salaries payable; TOTLIB is the sum of these. OWNER has been given a value equal to the capital investment of the owner. TOTLIC is the sum of liabilities and capital; write two assignment statements to compute TOTLIB and TOTLIC.

If you want to run this with representative data for a small business, try

CASH	1,062.00	RENT	400.00	ACCPAY	1,400.00
ACCREC	585.00	EQUIP	6,000.00	SALARY	68.00
SUPPLS	230.00	DEPREC	50.00	OWNER	6,759.00

For a check of your work, be sure that total assets equal the sum of liabilities and capital.

(Adapted from C. Rollin Niswonger and Philip E. Fess, *Accounting Principles*, South-Western Publishing Co., Cincinnati, page 69.)

*11. A well-tempered scale is one in which the ratio of the pitches of any two adjacent half tones is always the same. (J. S. Bach gave definitive support to the concept through his *Well-tempered Clavier*, to the point that he is often credited, incorrectly, with having invented the idea.) Since there are 12 notes in a scale of one octave, and since the ratio of pitches in an octave is 2.0, the ratio of pitches of any two half notes is the twelfth root of 2, which can be found by raising 2 to the one-twelfth power. Write an assignment statement to give the variable RATIO this value, using an expression having only constants in it.

12. It has been estimated that the population of the world was 919 million in 1800, 2,245 million in 1940, 3,632 million in 1970, and that it will be 4,933 million in 1985. On the (questionable) assumption that the growth rate in each of these three intervals was a constant percentage each year, the percentage can be found by raising the ratio of the populations in two years to a power equal to one, and dividing by the number of years. Write three assignment statements to find the rate per year—in percentage points—from 1800 to 1940, from 1940 to 1970, and from 1970 to 1985.

(If you raise the ratio of two numbers to a fractional power, you will get a result in the form of a multiplier. For instance, 1.5 raised to the one-fifth power is 1.0845, which means simply that $1.0845^5 = 1.5$. Said otherwise, this is equivalent to a growth rate of 8.45% per year. Remember that you are asked to get the growth rate in percentage points.)

*13. The correct answer to Exercise 11 is that the pitch ratio between two half notes in a well-tempered scale is 1.059463. Write an assignment to raise this result to the seventh power. The result will be the pitch ratio for the interval of one-fifth in a well-tempered scale. Compare with the "perfect fifth" ratio of 1.5.

14. The answer to Exercise 12 includes the fact that the present projected growth rate of world population, that is, the growth from 1970 to 1985, is about 2.062% per year. Write an assignment statement to divide this percentage by 100 to get a decimal fraction, add that to 1.0, and raise the sum to the 50th power; then multiply that factor by the 1970 population to get an estimate for the population in 2020, assuming continuation of present growth rates. Assign the value to a variable named P2020.

*15. If the lengths of the sides of a triangle are given by the values of the variables A, B, and C, then the area of the triangle can be computed by first calculating the value of an intermediate variable named S from

$$S = \frac{A + B + C}{2}$$

then computing the AREA from

$$\text{AREA} = \sqrt{S(S - A)(S - B)(S - C)}$$

Write a program to read a card that contains values of A, B, and C, computes S and the area, and prints a line giving the input and the output. Assume a data card with a four-digit identification number punched in columns 1-4, and with A in 5-9, B in 10-14, and C in 15-19. The identification number is an integer; the others are real, with one digit after an assumed decimal point. After computing S and AREA, the program should write a line containing the identification number, A, B, C, S, and AREA. The identification number should be printed in four printing positions; A, B, C, and S in ten positions each with one digit after the decimal point; and AREA in 14 positions with one digit after the decimal point.

The program will contain two assignment statements, one for S and a second for AREA, in that order. The second will use the value of S computed by the first. This is quite legal and widely done; since the two are executed in sequence, the value computed by the first will be available to the second by the time the second is reached.

16. You are given a data card that contains a student number in columns 1-5, a value of X in columns 6-12, a value of XM in columns 13-19, and a value of S in columns 20-26. The student number is an integer; X, XM, and S are all real with one digit after an assumed decimal point. Using these values, you are to compute Z and T from the following formulas:

$$Z = \frac{X - XM}{S}$$
$$T = 100Z + 500$$

You are then to write a line containing the following:

Student number	Integer; 5 printing positions
X	Real; 12 positions, with one digit after the decimal point
XM	Real; 12 positions, with one digit after the decimal point
S	Real; 12 positions, with one digit after the decimal point
Z	Real; 12 positions, with three digits after the decimal point
T	Real; 14 positions, with one digit after the decimal point

(Readers who know statistics will recognize that if X is a sample value drawn from a population with a mean of XM and a standard deviation of S, then Z is a converted sample point from a distribution with mean zero and standard deviation 1, and T is from a distribution with mean 500 and standard deviation 100. The latter is the normalized form of the College Entrance Examination Board scores, for instance.)

CHAPTER THREE

INPUT AND OUTPUT

Introduction

In this chapter we take up some additional facts about input and output in Fortran such as the way to provide column headings that makes it easier to understand the output of programs. After doing so we shall be in a stronger position to take up the important programming topics that will concern us in subsequent chapters. The program will be a modest extension of the capabilities of the program of Chapter Two.

The card format

The first matter to be dealt with is a change in the format of the data card, which now looks like the sample shown in Figure 3.1. We see that the experiment number is still in columns 1-3, but columns 4-17 are now blank, and the Centigrade temperature now takes up six columns, 18-23, and contains an actual decimal point. The value shown is seen to be negative; we

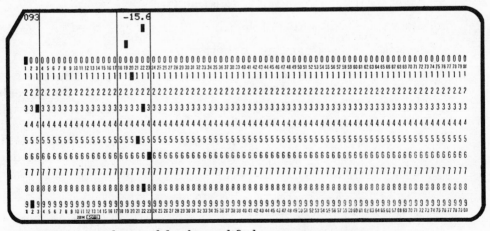

FIGURE 3.1.   A data card for the modified temperature conversion program. The experiment number is in columns 1-3 and the temperature — which may now have an actual decimal point and a sign — is in columns 18-23.

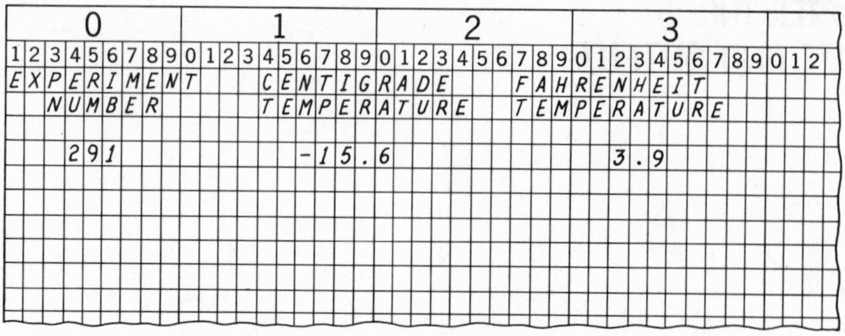

FIGURE 3.2.   A printer spacing chart form for planning the output of the program.

are now allowing the temperature values to be either positive or negative, with negative numbers preceded by a minus sign.

Column headings

The biggest difference between the program of this chapter and that of the preceding is that we are now going to provide column headings on the printed output. In order to see clearly what is required we first write the desired output format on a printer spacing planning chart, like that shown in Figure 3.2. (Printed forms for this purpose are available from the computer manufacturers and elsewhere.) The first requirement is that the first line of the printed output start at the top of a new page. We are not content this time just to let the printer put the line at whatever point it may happen to be on the output form: we wish to force the first line to be at the top of a fresh sheet of paper. Next, we want column headings. These will be printed as two lines—all the printers we are concerned with print one complete line at a time—so that the first line will consist of the words

```
    EXPERIMENT    CENTIGRADE    FAHRENHEIT
```

and the second will consist of the words

```
    NUMBER        TEMPERATURE  TEMPERATURE
```

When the output is read by a human being, the first word of the first line and the first word of the second line will make up the heading for the first column: EXPERIMENT NUMBER, etc. After these two heading lines we wish to have one blank line, then the three numbers, centered under the headings. To do this, it turns out that the experiment number should be printed in six printing positions, and each of the temperatures in 14, with one decimal place as before.

The program; the X field descriptor

Let us examine in some detail how the program of Figure 3.3 meets these requirements.

The READ statement is unchanged. In this program, just as in the previ-

```
C CENTIGRADE TO FAHRENHEIT CONVERSION
C MODIFIED VERSION -- DIFFERENT DATA CARD, COLUMN HEADINGS
C
C VARIABLE NAMES
C     C - DEGREES CENTIGRADE
C     F - DEGREES FAHRENHEIT
C     NUMBER - EXPERIMENT NUMBER
C
      READ (5, 50) NUMBER, C
   50 FORMAT (I3, 14X, F6.0)
      F = (1.8*C) + 32.0
      WRITE (6, 60)
   60 FORMAT ('1','EXPERIMENT    CENTIGRADE    FAHRENHEIT'/' ',' NUMBER',
     1    5X, 'TEMPERATURE    TEMPERATURE'/)
      WRITE (6, 70) NUMBER, C, F
   70 FORMAT (1X, I6, 2F14.1)
      STOP
      END
```

FIGURE 3.3.   A program for the modified temperature conversion application.

ous, we want to read an integer value named NUMBER and a real value named C. The card format this time is rather different, but that is handled through the FORMAT, not the READ. In the FORMAT, the field descriptor for the experiment number is as before, I3, since the number still occupies columns 1-3 and is punched in the same form. Next, however, we have a 14X field descriptor. What the X field descriptor actually does, on input, is simply to skip over the specified number of columns, 14 in this case, *without transmitting anything to the program*. Accordingly, an X field descriptor *does not correspond to any variable name in the associated* READ. Whether or not there is something punched in the columns skipped over is immaterial. Here, they are blank, but other times we might have a situation where we are reading cards prepared for some other purpose and need to skip data that there is no need for. The X field descriptor would be the way to do it.

How the data values may be punched

Finally, we have an F6.0 field descriptor, which goes with the C in the READ list, and describes the Centigrade temperature. What we have specified here is a six-column field in which there are zero digits to the right of an assumed decimal point. This means that if we punch a number without a decimal point in the field, it will be taken as a whole number. For instance, if we punch 000629 in the six columns, it will be taken as 629° C. It is not necessary to punch the leading zeroes, if we choose not to do so: 629 preceded by three blanks would represent the same number. A number that contains fewer digits than there are columns in the field, and which is punched at the *right-hand side* of the field, is said to be *right-justified*. If this were the whole story, we would not be able to punch anything except whole numbers for our temperatures. But in fact we are permitted to punch an *actual* decimal point in a card field that is described by an F field descriptor, and when this is done the actual decimal point completely overrides the assumed decimal point. We could punch

629.71

for instance, and that is the number that would enter the computer. A number like 629 could thus be punched in any of these forms, among others, all of them leading to the same number inside the computer:

```
000629
   629
629.
   629.
629.0
```

About the only thing we cannot do is have embedded blanks in the number, since these are taken to be zeros. If we were to punch

```
62 9.0
```

for instance, the number would be read as if it were

```
6209.0
```

which would hardly be what was intended. Likewise, punching the 629 at the *left* side of the field followed by three blanks, rather than at the right side preceded by three blanks, would result in entering the value 629000.

The assignment statement to compute the Fahrenheit temperature and assign it to F is mathematically the same as before, but parentheses have been placed around the factor 1.8*C to make absolutely certain that the multiplication is done before the addition.

The WRITE statement with no list

Now we have a statement that was not in the earlier version, a WRITE, together with its FORMAT statement. This WRITE is different in an important way from any we have seen so far: it does not have a list of variables. Within the FORMAT we have specified the headings we want, as we shall explore in detail in the next paragraphs, and *all* of the characters will be copied directly from the FORMAT. It is also possible to have a WRITE that does have a list, associated with a FORMAT that supplies identifying information, so that a part of the line comes from variables and part from the FORMAT. We shall show how this might appear later, after completing our study of this program.

Quoted fields in a FORMAT

In the FORMAT statement in question, the one having the statement number 60, we see a variety of things enclosed in quotation marks. Anything so written will be copied directly from the FORMAT to the output, and does not consist of field descriptors at all. Rather than describing the form of other output, this kind of information is *itself* the output.

The carriage control characters

The first quoted field consists of the digit 1, which is the first thing on the line of printed output and is therefore the carriage control character. Previously we have written 1X, which produces a blank that is sent to the printer as the carriage control character to cause single spacing. The character 1 causes a skip to the top of the next page. Other carriage control characters are available, as summarized in this table:

Carriage Control Character	Action
blank	Single space 1H_
zero	Double space 1H∅
1	Skip to top of new page 1H1
+	Suppress spacing 1H+

Double spacing is occasionally useful. The suppression of line spacing is used either to print a line twice and thus get a special heavy-printing effect, or to print underlines. We shall have no occasion to use the suppression of spacing.

Following the carriage control character are the words that are to be printed on the first heading line, all enclosed in another set of quotes. It would have been possible to put both the carriage control character and these words within one set of quotes, but it is better practice to keep the carriage control character separate, as a guard against forgetting it. We shall abide in this book by the policy of beginning *every* line with an explicit carriage control character, since the first character of the line is always interpreted as the carriage control character *and is not printed*. If a character unintentionally so used is a blank, we may not even notice the problem, but if numbers or letters are sent there it may cause erratic and very unacceptable spacing, such as skipping to a new page on every line.

The slash for end-of-line designation

We have now specified everything that is needed on the first heading line. It would be possible at this point to close the FORMAT parentheses and issue another WRITE and another FORMAT. This kind of situation occurs so frequently, however, that the designers of Fortran provided a way to say that we have reached the end of the specifications for one line and want to go on to the specifications for another line. That technique is simply to write a slash, the same character we use in an arithmetic expression for division. Following the slash is the carriage control character for the next line. Since we want single spacing this time we need a blank, here supplied with a quoted blank instead of the 1X, just to demonstrate that either one is permissible.

Continuation cards

Now comes the word NUMBER in quotes . . . and we are out of space in the FORMAT! Not out of space on the line that will be printed; that is a quite different matter. We want to go right on talking about the same line on which the word NUMBER appears, but a Fortran statement may not extend past column 72. This contingency was foreseen by the designers of Fortran, too. What we do in this case is to continue the statement on the next line, which is called a *continuation*. The fact that it is a continuation is specified by

```
C CENTIGRADE TO FAHRENHEIT CONVERSION
C MODIFIED VERSION -- DIFFERENT DATA CARD, COLUMN HEADINGS
C FURTHER MODIFIED TO USE HOLLERITH FIELD DESCRIPTORS
C
C VARIABLE NAMES
C     C - DEGREES CENTIGRADE
C     F - DEGREES FAHRENHEIT
C     NUMBER - EXPERIMENT NUMBER
C
      READ (5, 50) NUMBER, C
   50 FORMAT (I3, 14X, F6.0)
      F = (1.8*C) + 32.0
      WRITE (6, 60)
   60 FORMAT (1H1, 36HEXPERIMENT   CENTIGRADE   FAHRENHEIT/1H ,
     1   37H NUMBER     TEMPERATURE  TEMPERATURE/)
      WRITE (6, 70) NUMBER, C, F
   70 FORMAT (1X, I6, 2F14.1)
      STOP
      END
```

FIGURE 3.4.   A program with the same effect as that of Figure 3.3, but using Hollerith field descriptors to get the column headings instead of quoted literals.

putting any nonzero character in column 6. Column 6 is used for no other purpose. We shall follow the convention in this book of numbering the continuations from one on up, but this is a matter of personal preference only. We shall also indent the contents of the continuation line a few spaces to try to make it more obvious that a continuation is involved.

The X field descriptor on output

Now we are ready to go on with our specifications for the second heading line. What is needed next, looking at the printer spacing chart in Figure 3.2, is five blanks. These can readily enough be provided by starting the next quoted field with five blanks, but it can be done with a 5X field descriptor. This calls for five blanks to be entered into the output line at this point. Thus, whereas an X field descriptor on input simply skips over the specified number of columns, on output blanks are actually placed in the line. Next is the word TEMPERATURE twice within quotes, as desired for the headings. Finally, there is another slash. When a slash appears at the end of a FORMAT, without anything following it—not even a carriage control character—it causes a blank line to appear at that point. This is because we have said to go to a new line but have provided nothing to go in it. Thus we obtain the blank line between the second heading line and the first (and only, in this case) line of numerical output. Several slashes can be used to get several blank lines.

This completes the discussion of getting the heading line printed. Obviously, it took a lot more space to describe it than to do it. You should not be dismayed, however, because with just a little practice it will become clear that the underlying principles are actually quite simple and that the only challenge is to carry out the details correctly.

Finally, we write the line of numerical output; here there is only one new concept, and that is a simple one. The WRITE statement is as before. In the FORMAT we use the 1X to get single spacing, then an I6 for the experiment number. This provides two extra printing positions, to get the experiment number centered under its column heading where we want it. Now we need two field descriptors of F14.1, and instead of writing them twice we write 2F14.1, which has exactly the same effect. A field descriptor may be repeated this way any number of times, as may be required, by changing this *repeat count* in front of the descriptor.

When we run this program with the data card shown earlier, we get this output:

```
EXPERIMENT    CENTIGRADE    FAHRENHEIT
  NUMBER      TEMPERATURE   TEMPERATURE

    93          -15.6          3.9
```

Another way to get headings — the Hollerith field descriptor

The program of Figure 3.3 used quotation marks within the FORMAT to indicate characters to be copied to the output device. This is the way it will be done in the rest of the book, but readers should be aware that there is another way. Indeed, some readers may have to use this other method since a few Fortrans do not provide for the quotation mark technique.

The alternative method is simply to precede the phrase we want to print with a *Hollerith field descriptor,** which consists of a number specifying how many characters there are, plus the letter H followed by a sequence of characters. This is easier to see by an example than from a verbal explanation. See Figure 3.4, which is a modified version of the program. We see, to start with, that the carriage control character in FORMAT 60 is specified with 1H1. This means that one character is to be sent out, and that that character is a 1. The next grouping starts with 36H and consists of the words and spaces that make up the first line of printing. Counting the blanks, there are exactly 36 characters there, which of course is what the 36 in 36H means. After the slash that specifies starting a new line of printing on the output, there is a 1H followed by a blank, the blank signifying single spacing. Now we move to the continuation so that the Hollerith field descriptor for the second line of output can be put entirely on one line in the FORMAT. This is not strictly necessary, but it is easier this way.

There is no need to show the output again because it would be exactly as displayed before.

Most Fortrans permit characters in the FORMAT statement to be specified either with quotes or the way this program has shown, and the choice is largely of personal taste. The use of quotes is subject to the programming mistake of forgetting the closing quote, which messes things up, but miscounting the number of characters in writing a Hollerith field descriptor also usually causes the program not to work correctly. We prefer the use of quotes, but warn the reader that care is required either way.

Identification on the same line with data

Finally, here is a version of the program that puts characters from the FORMAT on the same line with values from variables. This will demonstrate that we are not limited to just printing headings and things of that sort.

---

* Named after Herman Hollerith, who invented punched card calculating equipment that was used in the 1890 United States Census. The company that Hollerith formed to market his equipment became, through mergers, a part of IBM.

```
C CENTIGRADE TO FAHRENHEIT CONVERSION
C MODIFIED VERSION -- DIFFERENT DATA CARDS, THREE-LINE OUTPUT
C
C VARIABLE NAMES
C     C - DEGREES CENTIGRADE
C     F - DEGREES FAHRENHEIT
C     NUMBER - EXPERIMENT NUMBER
C
      READ (5, 50) NUMBER, C
   50 FORMAT (I3, 14X, F6.0)
      F = (1.8*C) + 32.0
      WRITE (6, 70) NUMBER, C, F
   70 FORMAT ('1', 'EXPERIMENT', I12/
     1  1X, 'CENTIGRADE = ', F10.1/
     2  1X, 'FAHRENHEIT = ', F10.1/)
      STOP
      END
```

FIGURE 3.5. A program to convert temperatures, but with a different form of printing.

We assume that the desired form of the output this time is that the first line should begin with the word EXPERIMENT, followed after some spaces by the numerical value of the experiment number, i.e., the value of the program variable named NUMBER. Then on a second line we are to print the word CENTIGRADE, followed by a space, followed by an equal sign, and then the Centigrade temperature. A third and final line consists of the word FAHRENHEIT, a space, an equal sign, and the Fahrenheit temperature. Since this verbal description may not fully convey what is intended, let us reverse the usual sequence and show the output first:

```
EXPERIMENT          93
CENTIGRADE =      -15.6
FAHRENHEIT =        3.9
```

There are no column headings in this version.

It would be possible to call for this output using three WRITE statements and three FORMAT statements but it will be instructive to do it the simpler way with just one WRITE and one FORMAT. The program for this version is shown in Figure 3.5. There is only one WRITE instead of two, since all the identifying information will be contained within the same FORMAT that describes the formats of the numeric output. The WRITE here is the same as the second WRITE in the earlier versions: the difference in printing is entirely a matter of the FORMAT, not the program variables.

Synchronization between READ/WRITE list and FORMAT

The FORMAT starts with the carriage control character for skipping to the top of the next page, as before, this time using quotes. Then the word EXPERI-MENT appears in quotes, and since it is the first thing on the line it will begin printing in the first printing position on the line. Then there is an I12 field descriptor. Since this is the *first* field descriptor that calls for the transmission of a value for a variable to the printer, it is the *first* variable's value that is transmitted. In other words, we are still keeping nicely in step between variables in the WRITE list and field descriptors in the FORMAT; the difference here is just that this synchronization only applies to field descriptors that actually describe program variables (that is, I and F descriptors). We have allowed 12 printing positions for a value that cannot contain more than three, to provide for blank spaces in the line. The exact number of blanks to be allowed is a matter of esthetic preference, or, we might say, the program design specifications.

The same effect could have been achieved by writing 9X, I3 instead of I12. The choice between the two is a matter of personal preference.

Now—continuing to read through the FORMAT statement—we reach a slash, which means to start a new line in the printing. We have also broken the FORMAT here but that is a matter of convenience, not necessity. On the continuation line, which has a 1 in column 6, we begin with a blank for single spacing. Then come the characters

CENTIGRADE =

all enclosed in quotes. These characters will therefore appear at the start of the second line of printing and will then be followed by the Centigrade temperature as described by the F10.1 field descriptor. The third line of printing is similar.

We see, then, that each line contains some information from within the FORMAT statement and some information from a program variable. This kind of mixture can be extended any way we please. For instance, all of the information printed here in three lines could be placed in just one line, with identifications and values alternating.

The Review Questions and Exercises will give you an opportunity to understand these ideas thoroughly and to practice them a little. Once the ideas are understood, which may take a bit of effort now, you will find that applying them is a fairly simple matter. All programs from now on will include appropriate identifications, so you will have plenty of chances to see the ideas worked out in practical applications.

Summary

We have introduced four types of field descriptors, I, F, X, and H.

In symbols, the I field descriptor is of the form Iw, where w designates a number of card columns (on input) or printing positions (on output). An I field descriptor must be associated with an integer variable only. No decimal points are permitted in card field described by an I field descriptor, and no decimal point is printed in output. Blanks in an input field are treated as though they are zero. The value w includes space for a sign, if there is one.

The F field descriptor is of the form $Fw.d$, where w is the total number of card columns or printing positions, and d is the number of digits after an assumed decimal point for input or an actual decimal point for output. If an actual decimal point is punched in the card field it overrides d. Any blanks in an input field are treated as zeros. The value of w includes space for an actual decimal point and/or sign, if any.

With the I and F field descriptors it is possible to specify that the same descriptor applies to several successive fields by writing a *repeat count* in front of the field descriptor.

The X field descriptor is of the form wX. On input, w columns are skipped over. On output w blank spaces are inserted into the line.

The H (for Hollerith) field descriptor is of the form wH, followed by w

characters that are sent to the printer. Alternatively, in most versions of Fortran, the characters may be enclosed in quotation marks, with the same effect.

The first character of the line sent to a printer is not printed, but rather controls line spacing, according to the following table.

Carriage Control Character	Action
blank	single space
zero	double space
1	skip to top of new page
+	suppress spacing

Every READ or WRITE must specify a FORMAT. If a WRITE has no list of variables, the information contained within the FORMAT is the only thing transmitted to the printer. Otherwise, there is a synchronization between the input or output list of variables, and the field descriptors in the FORMAT: the *first* variable in the list goes with the *first* field descriptor, the *second* variable goes with the *second* field descriptor, etc. The only exception to this rule is that X field descriptors do not correspond to variables, but they are still taken in sequence where they occur.

REVIEW QUESTIONS

1. Distinguish between the action of an X field descriptor in input and its action on output.

2. Name two types of field descriptors that actually describe data associated with program variables, and two that do not.

3. State the difference between the slash (in a FORMAT statement), and a continuation card. Could a FORMAT have only the slash, without a continuation? Could it be continued but not contain a slash?

4. The first thing in an output FORMAT provides for carriage control. How about the first thing after a slash?

5. What is the effect of slashes at the end of a FORMAT, just before the closing parenthesis?

6. Identify three different ways that the carriage control character "blank," for single spacing, could be obtained in a FORMAT.

7. When are blanks in a Fortran program significant?

8. Is this FORMAT statement legal, and if so what does it mean?

    ```
    FORMAT (1X, 2I5, 3F12.3)
    ```

9. Do the following two FORMAT statements have the same result?

    ```
    FORMAT (1X, 5X, I5, F10.0)

    FORMAT (6X, I5, F10.0)
    ```

10. Can you guess what this WRITE-FORMAT combination would do?

    ```
        WRITE (5, 500) A
    500 FORMAT (1X, 13HDATA = ,F10.1)
    ```

11. Assume that in a certain program a value of 12345 has been given to a variable named K, and the value −987.654 has been given to a variable named A. State what would be printed by

```
WRITE (6, 100) K, A
```

if statement 100 were the following

a. 100   FORMAT (1X, I5, F10.3)

b. 100   FORMAT (1X, 2X, 'K', 7X, 'F'/1X, I5, F10.3)

c. 100   FORMAT (1X, 'K = ', I5/1X, 'A = ', F10.3)

d. 100   FORMAT (1X, 'K = ', I5, 3X, 'A = ', F10.3)

e. 100   FORMAT (1X, 'K = ', I5, 3X,
      1   'A = ', F10.3)

12. Consider the following statement.

```
A = (B*C) + (D/E) - (F/(G*H))
```

In the following statement, the 1 and the 2 are each in column 6 of their lines.

```
 A =    (B*C)
1    + (D/E)
2    - (F/(G*H))
```

Do the two statements call for the same computation? Can you think of any advantages to the second form?

13. Identify the two errors in this version of the program of this chapter.

```
C CENTIGRADE TO FAHRENHEIT CONVERSION
C MODIFIED VERSION -- DIFFERENT DATA CARD, COLUMN HEADINGS
C
C VARIABLE NAMES
C     C - DEGREES CENTIGRADE
C     F - DEGREES FAHRENHEIT
C     NUMBER - EXPERIMENT NUMBER
C
      READ (5, 50) NUMBER, C
 50   FORMAT (I3, 14X, F6.0)
      F = (1.8*C) + 32.0
      WRITE (6, 60)
 60   FORMAT ('1','EXPERIMENT   CENTIGRADE   FAHRENHEIT'/' ',' NUMBER,
          5X, 'TEMPERATURE  TEMPERATURE'/)
      WRITE (6, 70) NUMBER, C, F
 70   FORMAT (1X, I6, 2F14.1)
      STOP
      END
```

ANSWERS

1. On *input*, the X says to skip over the specified number of card columns, whether they have punches in them or not. On *output*, it says to insert the specified number of blanks into the line being printed.

2. The I field descriptor is associated with the values of integer variables, for input or output; the F field descriptor is associated with the values of real variables, for input or output; the X field descriptor is not associated with any variable, and may be used to skip columns on input or insert blanks on output; quoted characters or the Hollerith field descriptor may be used to insert characters in output.

3. The slash in a FORMAT statement says to start a new line of output when printing; a continuation card simply provides more space for writing a statement. So far we have seen the continuation card used only with FORMAT, but it can be used with any kind of statement. A slash without a continuation is entirely possible, as is a continuation without a slash. The two are separate concepts.

4. The first thing after a slash in an output FORMAT should also always be provision for a carriage control character.

5. Each slash at the end of a FORMAT causes a blank line to be produced after whatever else the FORMAT did. There may be none, one, or many.

6. Three ways:

```
1X,
' ',
1H ,
```

7. A blank in a Fortran program is significant within quotes or in a Hollerith field in a FORMAT, and ignored altogether everywhere else.

8. It is entirely legal. Assuming that it is associated with a WRITE, it calls for single spacing, then two integers, each in five printing positions, then three real numbers, each in 12 positions with three decimal places. If used with a READ it says to skip over the first column, then read two integers and three real numbers.

9. They have exactly the same result. That is, the blank for carriage control *may* be included in the first field descriptor after the carriage control, if we wish. In this book the carriage control character will always be provided for separately, as this habit makes it less likely that the carriage control character will be forgotten; the practice is recommended.

10. The 13H field descriptor would cause these characters to be printed:

```
DATA = ,F10.1
```

In other words, what was presumably intended as a field descriptor for variable A, the F10.1, would be included within the 13 characters of the Hollerith field descriptor. (*Exactly* what the program would do is a slightly advanced topic, which we shall take up later. There is nothing to stop you, however, from putting these two statements in at the end of your next programming exercise, to see for yourself what happens!)

11. a. `12345   -987.654`

    b. `  K       F`
       `12345   -987.654`

    c. `K = 12345`
       `A =    -987.654`

d. K = 12345   A =   -987.654

e. K = 12345   A =   · -987.654

The last two are identical; the only difference in the two FORMATS is that the second one is continued on a second line.

12. They do indeed do the same thing. One possible argument for using the second form, with its two continuation lines, would be to make doubly clear what the hierarchy of operations is in the expression.

13. A closing quote is missing after the word NUMBER on the first line of FORMAT statement 60, and the line following that is not indicated as being a continuation. Since the second line is not a continuation, Fortran would attempt to interpret it as just another statement; not being able to do so, it would reject it as an illegal statement.

EXERCISES

*1. Show how the given values would be printed under control of the field descriptors stated.

```
I5:  0,  1,  10,  -587,  90062,  123456
I4:  -10,  1098,  12347,  -841
F7.2:  0.0,  1.0,  16.87,  -586.21,  0.04,  12.34
F5.0:  0.0,  1.0,  16.87,  -586.21,  0.04,  12.34
```

2. Given that the values of three variables are as follows:

$M = 12$

$X = 407.8$

$Y = 32.9$

Show exactly what would be printed by

WRITE (6, 110) M, X, Y

with each of the following FORMAT statements.

```
110  FORMAT (1H1, 3HM= , I3, 5H  X= , F6.1, 5H  Y= , F6.1/)

110  FORMAT (1H1, 20HEXPERIMENT NUMBER = , I3/
    1      1H0, 11HPRESSURE = , F6.1, 9H  TEMP = , F6.1)

110  FORMAT ('1', 'EXPERIMENT NUMBER = ', I3/
    1      '0', 'PRESSURE = ', F6.1, '  TEMP = ', F6.1/)

110  FORMAT ('1', 'EXPERIMENT NUMBER = ', I3/
    1      '0', 'PRESSURE', 6X, 'TEMPERATURE'/'0', F7.1, 9X, F6.1/)
```

*3. Suppose that previous statements in a program have given these values to the variables named:

A = 67.901
B = -0.38
K = 49

Write a WRITE/FORMAT combination to print these values as shown:

K = 49　　B = -0.38
A = 67.901

a.　49　　67.901　　-0.38

b.　K = 49　　B = -0.38　　A = 67.901

c.　K = 49, B = -0.38, AND A = 67.901

d.　　K　　　B　　　A
　　　49　　-0.38　　67.901

e.　FOR CODE 49, FACTOR 1 = -0.38 AND FACTOR 2 = 67.901

4. Given a WRITE statement

WRITE (6, 10) I, J, R, S

I and J are integer variables and R and S are real. For each of the following sample output formats, write a FORMAT statement that could produce it. Write only one FORMAT for (d).

a.　　　　-16　　92017　　　16.82　　437.89

b.　　　　-16　　92017　　　　17.　　438.

c.　I =　-16　　J = 92017　　R=　16.8　　S= 437.9

d.　I =　　-16
　　J= 92017
　　R=　16.8
　　S= 437.9

*5. Previous statements have given values to the following variables:

TLABOR　17.50
TPARTS　2.40
ACCESS　0.00
OILGRS　0.00

Write statements to compute the sum of these numbers and assign it to SUBTOT, then compute SALTAX as 5% of SUBTOT, and add that to SUBTOT to get TOTAL. Finally, print the values in this form:

```
TOTAL LABOR      17.50
TOTAL PARTS       2.40
ACCESSORIES       0.00
OIL, GREASE       0.00

SUBTOTAL         19.90

SALES TAX         0.99

GRAND TOTAL      20.89
```

6. Assume that previous statements have given values to the following variables:

PRVBAL　786.43
CHARGS　338.55
CREDIT　168.64
TOTDUE　956.34
ACNO1　029
ACNO2　049
ACNO3　916
ACNO4　9

Devise a program segment to print these values in the following format:

```
PREVIOUS BALANCE
     $786.43

NEW CHARGES
        338.55

CREDITS
        168.64

TOTAL DUE
     $956.34

ACCOUNT NUMBER
29   49 916 9
```

*7. Another student has loaned you a data deck that contains information in the following fields:

Columns 1-9	Social Security number
Columns 10-33	Name
Columns 34-35	Age
Columns 36-40	Blank
Columns 41-42	Total years of education
Columns 43-44	Occupation code
Columns 45-80	Blank

For the purposes of your program it is necessary to read only the age (into a variable named NAGE). Write appropriate READ and FORMAT statements to do this.

8. Modify the program of Exercise 7 so that it also reads the three parts of the Social Security number into N1, N2, and N3. The first part consists of the first three digits, the second part consists of the next two digits, and the last part consists of the last four digits. Thus, for 535221583, N1 = 535, N2 = 22, and N3 = 1583. (Don't be trapped into putting the variable names into the READ in the order in which they are described in these exercises. They will have to appear in the READ list in the order in which they appear on the card.)

*9. Modify the program of Figure 3.3 so that the three columns would appear approximately centered on a page with 132 printing positions in a line, which is a typical number. This will require placing 49 blanks at the beginning of each line. (The spacing between the numbers does not change.)

10. Modify the program of Figure 3.3 so that the three columns are spaced an additional five printing positions apart. That is, there should be five more spaces between READING and CENTIGRADE, and five more between CENTIGRADE and FAHRENHEIT, on the first line, and correspondingly on the second line and in the line that contains the numerical values. Each line should still begin at the left margin, as in the text version of the program.

*11. You are given a card with the following format:

Columns	Contents	Sample
1-4	Blank	

5-11	Customer number	1234567
12-18	Sales	3000000
19-25	Expenses	2500000

The financial figures are in dollars and cents, with an assumed decimal point. Write a program that will read such a card and produce the following report, in which net income is computed by subtracting expenses from sales. Choose your own variable names, remembering the integer-real initial letter problem.

```
CUSTOMER 1234567

SALES                     30000.00
EXPENSES        25000.00
NET INCOME                 5000.00

(DEBITS ARE TOWARD THE WINDOW)
```

12. A school board member is concerned about the effect of continued growth in school population on the need for facilities, and has asked you to prepare a program that will perform one part of the calculation. A card is available; along with much other information it contains a current student population figure (POP) in columns 51-55 with no decimal places, and a growth rate in percentage points per year (PC) in columns 16-19 with an actual decimal point punched. Your program is to read such a card, carry out the calculation of the final population (FINAL) after 10 years of growth at the stated rate, according to the formula

$$\text{FINAL} = \text{POP} * \left(1.0 + \frac{\text{PC}}{100}\right)^{10}$$

and print—beginning at the top of a new page—the following:

```
AN INITIAL POPULATION OF     5631.
AFTER 10 YEARS AT    3.0% PER YEAR INCREASE BECOMES    7568.
```

The illustrative data suggests the form in which the numbers should be printed: the percentage with one decimal place, and the population figures with none. Using a field descriptor such as F10.0 will produce a decimal point but no digits after the decimal point.

CHAPTER FOUR
PROGRAM EXECUTION

Introduction

Most realistic computer applications require a program that can be repeated, in whole or in part, during execution. For example, a payroll program would not be written to compute the pay of just one worker; a company that had only one employee could do the calculations faster and less expensively by hand. The first thing we shall investigate in this chapter is how to write a program so that it can be applied to many data cards instead of just one. The example will be the pay calculation from Chapter One.

A problem arises, however: How is the program supposed to know when the job is finished? We shall see how to use the Fortran IF statement in answering the question. This fundamental programming tool will then be used in a further extension of the program, to make possible an overtime pay calculation. The program will be required to make a decision, since the overtime calculation is not applied unless a certain condition is met.

Repeating a section of a program

The task we have set for ourselves is to write a program that will compute a worker's pay, given the hours worked and the pay rate, and to apply this calculation to as many data cards as there are in the data deck that is supplied to the program. Each card will contain a payroll number for the worker. A final card will contain a payroll number of zero to signal the program that the job is done.

This last card is called a sentinel.

Flowcharts

At this point we pause to introduce an important tool from the programmer's toolkit: the *flowchart*. A flowchart is a pictorial representation of what the program is supposed to do, with special attention to all the choices it makes and the possible sequences of execution of the parts of the program. Figure 4.1 is a flowchart of our task.

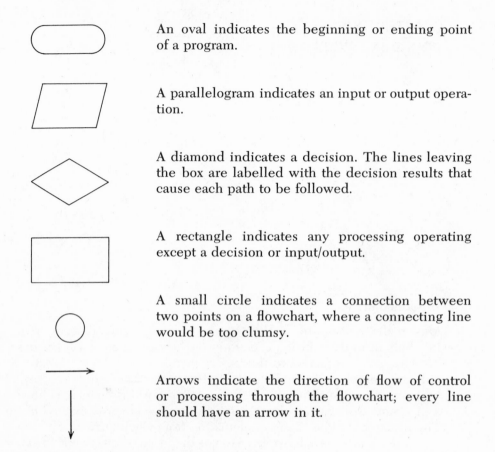

An oval indicates the beginning or ending point of a program.

A parallelogram indicates an input or output operation.

A diamond indicates a decision. The lines leaving the box are labelled with the decision results that cause each path to be followed.

A rectangle indicates any processing operating except a decision or input/output.

A small circle indicates a connection between two points on a flowchart, where a connecting line would be too clumsy.

Arrows indicate the direction of flow of control or processing through the flowchart; every line should have an arrow in it.

The flowchart for the payroll program

Our flowchart is simple enough that it does not need the small circles for connectors, but the other types of boxes are all illustrated. After the start box comes a box that says to write a heading line. Next is a box that calls for reading a card. The same shape of box is used, obviously, both for reading and writing, depending on what is desired in a particular situation. The identification of which one is meant is given by the contents of the box. The card-reading box in this flowchart can be entered two ways: either from the beginning of the program, or by returning to it after the program has been executed. The decision box asks a question: Is the card just read the sentinel? (We shall see in a moment how this is done in the Fortran program.) A decision box always has at least two exits, corresponding to each of the possible outcomes. (Here, the only possible answers are "yes" and "no," so that there are just two exit lines from the box, but there will sometimes be three or more exit lines, such as when a decision box asks whether a number is less than zero, equal to zero, or greater than zero.) If the answer to the question here is "yes, this is the sentinel," we go to a Stop box because there is nothing else for this program to do. If the answer is "no, this is not the sentinel" we go on with the rest of the work of the program. The rest of the program simply computes the pay—just as in Chapter 1—and writes a line containing the data and the result. After doing this it returns to read another card and goes through the process again.

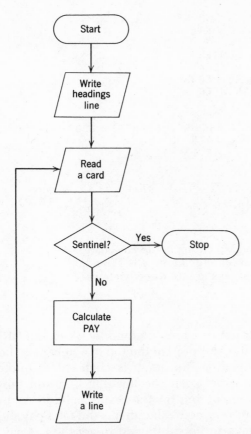

FIGURE 4.1.   A flowchart of a procedure for computing the pay
of a group of workers. An identification number of zero—which
does not correspond to any actual employee—serves as a sentinel
that the end of the deck has been reached.

The data card format involves no new concepts so we shall not display
a sample card this time. The card field layout is:

Columns 1-6   Payroll identification number
Columns 7-9   Hours worked, with one digit after an assumed deci-
                   mal point
Columns 10-13   Pay rate, with two digits after an assumed decimal
                   point

The variable names will be as before, HOURS and RATE, with the addition
of IDNO ("identification number") to stand for payroll number.

The payroll program

The program of Figure 4.2 provides a little review of some of the ideas of
the last chapter, on printing identification of the output, and introduces two
new statements, the GO TO and the IF.

As an example of the possibilities of writing programs for easy understandability, variable names in READ and WRITE statements have been
aligned with the field descriptors that go with them in the associated FOR-
MAT.

```
C PAY CALCULATION WITH HEADINGS AND SENTINEL CARD
C
C VARIABLE NAMES
C     IDNO      IDENTIFICATION NUMBER
C     HOURS     HOURS WORKED FOR WEEK
C     RATE      PAY RATE, DOLLARS PER HOUR
C     PAY       COMPUTED PAY FOR WEEK
C
      WRITE (6, 10)
   10 FORMAT ('1', 'ID NUMBER    HOURS     RATE    GROSS PAY'/)
   20 READ (5, 30) IDNO, HOURS, RATE
   30 FORMAT (     I6,    F3.1,   F4.2)
      IF ( IDNO .EQ. 0 ) STOP
      PAY = HOURS * RATE
      WRITE (6, 40) IDNO, HOURS,        RATE,          PAY
   40 FORMAT (1X,    I7,    F10.1, '    $', F5.2, '    $', F6.2)
      GO TO 20
      END
```

FIGURE 4.2.   A payroll program corresponding to the flowchart
of Figure 4.1. Note the style of writing the list in the WRITE and
the matching FORMAT so that variable names are directly above
their corresponding field descriptors.

The column headings in the first line are obtained by a WRITE-FORMAT
combination. A 1 in quotes specifies skipping to the top of a new page before
printing the heading line; the heading line itself is enclosed in quotes; a
final slash will place a blank line between the heading line and the first
line of the body of the report. The column for the result, called PAY in the
program, is headed GROSS PAY to remind us that this is the total pay, before
various deductions that would have to be subtracted to get the net pay that
goes on the worker's check. Notice that the heading line is printed before
reading the first card. The reason for this sequence is that the heading is
printed only once, whereas the operations that follow will be performed
many times, once for each data card. The only thing unusual about the
READ and FORMAT statements is that the READ has a statement number,
20, the purpose of which will become clear shortly.

The IF statement

The statement that follows, the IF, expresses a conditional command. It says
to carry out a specified action *if* a certain condition is met. The form of the
Fortran IF statement, as we shall use it now, is:

IF (condition) action

In other words, we place the condition within parentheses after the word
IF, and after the closing parenthesis state the action we want carried out if the
condition is met. We shall usually leave a blank on either side of the condition, simply for ease of readability; blanks here are ignored as elsewhere.
The condition within parentheses asks whether a stated relationship
between two values is true. In our case, we ask "Is the value of the variable
named IDNO equal to zero?" "Equal to" is represented by .EQ., which is
one of the six possible *relational operators*:

Meaning	Mathematical Symbol	Fortran Symbol
Equal to	$=$	.EQ.
Not equal to	$\neq$	.NE.
Greater than	$>$	.GT.
Greater than or equal to	$\geqq$ or $\geq$	.GE.
Less than	$<$	.LT.
Less than or equal to	$\leqq$ or $\leq$	.LE.

We shall have occasion to use all of these relational operators in the course of our work. Later in the chapter, for instance, we shall want to determine whether the hours worked are greater than 40.0, so we shall write

```
IF ( HOURS .GT. 40.0 )
```

followed by the desired action.

Actually, the relational operators test for the stated relations between any two *expressions*, so that we can write things like:

```
IF ( A + B .GE. 120.0 ) . . .
IF ( MAX * MIN .LT. N - 3 ) . . .
```

In other words, the general form of the Fortran IF statement, as we are using it, could be written:

IF (expression$_1$ relational-operator expression$_2$) action

(To be precise, this is the Fortran *logical* IF statement. There is also an *arithmetic* IF statement, described in Chapter Ten, that we shall not use in the body of the text.)

In this book we shall generally enclose expressions in an IF statement in parentheses when they involve anything more complex than a single constant or a single variable. Doing so will help to avoid confusion in reading the statement quickly. The two samples just given would be written as follows:

```
IF ( (A + B) .GE. 120.9 ) . . .
IF ( (MAX * MIN) .LT. (N - 3) ) . . .
```

In the present program, the action to be executed when the condition is met is simply to stop the program. Recall that what we are testing for is the end-of-deck sentinel, which is a card that contains a dummy IDNO of zero. The complete statement is thus

```
IF ( IDNO .EQ. 0 ) STOP
```

This statement can be expressed in ordinary English like this:

"If the value of the variable named IDNO is equal to (.EQ.) zero, stop the program. If IDNO is not equal to zero, do not stop."

In an IF statement, if the condition is *not* true the action specified after the parentheses is not carried out. This will do what we want: on the last card, with its dummy IDNO of zero, program execution will be stopped by the IF; on all cards before the last, the IF will have no effect.

Since blanks in a Fortran data field are taken to be zeros, a data card that is completely blank will act as an end-of-deck sentinel. This will be true, naturally, whether the blank card is there intentionally or not. Perhaps that is just as well, since the proper makeup of the data deck is a very important matter that is properly the subject of considerable checking by the program anyway, as we shall see in later illustrative programs. We assume for this program, of course, that there is only one card with a payroll number of zero, and that it is the last card of the deck.

Computation and output

The next three statements of the program contain nothing new. The pay computation is routine, as is the WRITE. The FORMAT contains field descriptors for the four numbers that are printed, together with two quoted fields that insert blanks and dollar signs. Study this FORMAT in conjunction with the printed output shown below, keeping in mind that the four variable names go with the four field descriptors that actually describe data (I7, F10.1, F5.2, and F6.2), and that the field descriptors in the FORMAT are processed in the order in which they appear, from left to right.

The GO TO statement

Now comes the last new feature of this program, the GO TO statement. The GO TO is a command to break out of the usual one-after-the-other pattern of statement execution that we have always taken for granted so far. This says to Fortran: "Don't execute the next statement in normal sequence, but rather execute the one I'm naming in the GO TO." In our case the statement says

```
GO TO 20
```

20 is the statement number of the READ that appeared earlier in the program. In general, the statement named in a GO TO can be any other statement in the program, either before or after the GO TO.

Observe that we have not jumped all the way back to the beginning of the program, which would cause the heading line to be printed again, but rather to the first statement we actually want repeated, the READ that gets another data card.

Statement number conventions

Notice, too, that statement numbers have been assigned by 10's and in ascending sequence. This is not required by Fortran, but is done as a matter of programming style to make programs easier to read and to assist in developing a correct program. Assigning the statement numbers in sequence makes it easier to locate a statement when we come to something like a GO TO. It makes it easier *for us* to locate, that is, in our study of a program; Fortran can find the statements nicely whether they are in ascending sequence or not. We assign them by 10's, usually, in order to permit the insertion of new statement numbers when it is discovered that a numbered statement has to be inserted in a section of a program that had already been written, or when it turns out that an existing statement needs to have a statement number where none had originally been written.

The output of the program, when run with six sample data cards, is:

ID NUMBER	HOURS	RATE	GROSS PAY
103578	38.2	$ 2.93	$111.93
223378	39.1	$10.41	$407.03
223379	32.0	$ 5.00	$160.00
340109	40.0	$ 3.00	$120.00
380012	40.0	$ 3.00	$120.00
452016	37.5	$ 4.32	$162.00

The IF statement in an overtime calculation

The IF statement is a most important part of the Fortran language, and conditional program execution is an important programming concept in any language. You will almost never write a program that does not depend in some way on the idea of doing something or other "only if" some condition is met. Accordingly, let us take another example to get a bit more insight into how the IF statement is used.

The computation required

The application is a simple and realistic extension of the program already shown. We are to read the same card with its payroll number, hours worked, and pay rate, then calculate the pay, but with this difference: hours over 40 — if any — are to be paid at one-and-one-half times the rate otherwise used. Thus, if a person earns $3.00 per hour and works 44 hours, he will be paid $3.00 per hour for the straight-time hours and $4.50 per hour for four overtime hours, $4.50 being one-and-one-half times $3.00. This is a widely used payment system, although the base time is not always 40 hours, and the multiplier is sometimes something other than 1.5.

The flowchart

The flowchart for this modified version of the pay calculation program is shown in Figure 4.3. The only difference between it and the original flowchart, Figure 4.1, is that we have here an additional box to test for the possibility that HOURS is greater than 40. If not, we proceed exactly as before. If more than 40 hours were worked, we recompute PAY using a formula appropriate for the overtime situation. It is important to understand that if the overtime path is taken, the pay as previously computed from

    PAY = HOURS * RATE

will be discarded. This is by no means the only way to arrange this calculation, and you might wonder if it would not be better to test for the overtime situation before doing any calculation. That is indeed possible, but the time saved in the computer is negligible, and this way is easier to understand in a first example.

The program

The program corresponding to this flowchart may be seen in Figure 4.4. It is precisely the same as the program of Figure 4.2, with the addition of a few

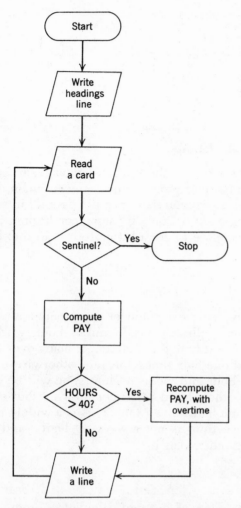

FIGURE 4.3.   A flowchart of a payroll program that computes
pay for hours over 40 at time-and-a-half.

comment lines and the overtime calculation. There is a new comment line
at the start of the program to point out the modification, and there are comment lines within the body of the program to point out how the program
works. Comments within a program are used widely this way, and we shall
do so in most programs for the rest of the book. You are encouraged—nay,
urged!—to do likewise. In the educational situation it will make it much
easier for your instructor or a consultant at the computer center to understand
what you are trying to do, and in a work situation it will help both you and
others understand what the intentions were, when it becomes necessary to
study a program after a lapse of months or years. It is remarkable how difficult it can be to read a program that has no comments, even if you wrote it
yourself, after the passage of time. Virtually all programs from now on will
have comments within them, giving you a chance to see what kinds of comments are helpful. (You are not expected to put a comment before *every*
statement, if the meaning will be obvious a year later without it.)

```
C PAY CALCULATION WITH HEADINGS AND SENTINEL CARD
C MODIFIED TO PAY TIME-AND-A-HALF FOR OVERTIME
C
C VARIABLE NAMES
C     IDNO      IDENTIFICATION NUMBER
C     HOURS     HOURS WORKED FOR WEEK
C     RATE      PAY RATE, DOLLARS PER HOUR
C     PAY       COMPUTED PAY FOR WEEK
C
      WRITE (6, 10)
   10 FORMAT ('1', 'ID NUMBER    HOURS     RATE     GROSS PAY'/)
   20 READ (5, 30) IDNO, HOURS, RATE
   30 FORMAT (    I6,  F3.1,  F4.2)
      IF ( IDNO .EQ. 0 ) STOP
C
C COMPUTE PAY AT STRAIGHT-TIME RATE
C
      PAY = HOURS * RATE
C
C IF MORE THAN 40 HOURS, RECOMPUTE PAY WITH TIME-AND-A-HALF FOR OVERTIME
C
      IF ( HOURS .GT. 40.0 ) PAY = (40.0 + 1.5*(HOURS - 40.0)) * RATE
      WRITE (6, 40) IDNO, HOURS,        RATE,         PAY
   40 FORMAT (1X,   I7,  F10.1, ' $', F5.2, ' $', F6.2)
      GO TO 20
      END
```

FIGURE 4.4. A payroll program corresponding to the flow-chart of Figure 4.3.

The overtime calculation

The heart of the modification to the program of Figure 4.2 is the IF statement that computes the pay according to the overtime formula. First of all, we need to be clear that the recomputation is done *if and only if* the condition within parentheses is true, i.e., if and only if HOURS actually does have a value greater than (.GT.) 40.0. If this is true, then the action specified following the parentheses is carried out. This says to multiply RATE by: 40, plus 1.5 times the number of hours by which HOURS exceeds 40. Saying that again, the worker is paid at the normal rate for the first 40 hours, and 1.5 times the normal rate for all hours beyond 40. In other words, we could have written the expression in the form

```
      PAY = 40.0*RATE + 1.5*(HOURS - 40.0)*RATE
```

This is the formula as it appears in the program, but with the outer parentheses removed by multiplying through by RATE. It makes no important difference in computer time which way we write it; the choice here was made on the thought that the way it is shown in the program might be easier to understand.

It is important to realize that if this computation is done, the result (PAY) destroys and replaces the value of PAY just computed by the previous statement. If the calculation is *not* done, that is, when HOURS is *not* greater than 40.0, the value of PAY computed from

```
      PAY = HOURS * RATE
```

is simply left undisturbed.

Comparing real and integer values

You may wonder whether it makes any difference whether we write 40 or 40.0 in the condition within the parentheses of the IF statement. It turns out that it does, although it is not worth our while to try to delve into the reasons. The best policy on relations in IF statements in this: compare integer values with integer values, and real values with real values. Most Fortrans will *permit* the comparison of integer values with real values, but there are unpleasant surprises in store for those who insist on doing it.

The output

Here is the output when this program was run with a deck that contained the same values as before plus some new ones.

I D NUMBER	HOURS	RATE	GROSS PAY
103578	38.2	$ 2.93	$111.93
223378	39.1	$10.41	$407.03
223379	32.0	$ 5.00	$160.00
340109	40.0	$ 3.00	$120.00
380012	40.0	$ 3.00	$120.00
452016	37.5	$ 4.32	$162.00
504329	30.0	$ 4.00	$120.00
504330	40.0	$ 4.00	$160.00
504331	41.0	$ 4.00	$166.00
504332	42.0	$ 4.00	$172.00
504333	50.0	$ 4.00	$220.00
504334	80.0	$ 4.00	$400.00

We see that worker 504331, for instance, worked 41.0 hours at $4.00 per hour, and earned $166.00. At straight time he would have earned 41.0 × $4.00 = $164.00, but according to the overtime formula he was paid 1.5 times the normal rate for the 1.0 hour by which his HOURS exceeded 40.0. The other cases provide further examples of how the formula works for various other times at the same rate.

The Review Questions that follow, besides helping you nail down the fundamentals, hint at some other typical ways the IF statement is commonly applied.

Summary

This chapter has introduced two new Fortran language elements, the IF statement and the GO TO statement, and has shown some typical ways in which they are used.

The GO TO statement is used to break out of the normal sequence of statement execution, which is simply that statements are executed in the order in which they appear in the program. When proper use is made of the IF statement to execute a program action conditionally, and good use is made of the DO statement considered in Chapter Six, there will not be a great many occasions to use the GO TO. This is good, because a program with a tangled mass of GO TOs is hard to understand and therefore much more likely to have errors in it.

The IF statement is of the form

IF **(condition) action**

The **action** is performed if and only if the **condition** is "satisfied," that is, if the question it asks is true for the values used. The **condition**, as we have so far studied it, is always of the form

expression₁ relational-operator expression₂

The two expressions may be any legal Fortran expressions; it is recommended that they both be integer or that they both be real. Doing otherwise is not actually illegal but frequently leads to problems. There are six relational operators: .EQ. (equal), .NE. (not equal), .GT. (greater than), .GE. (greater than or equal to), .LT. (less than), and .LE. (less than or equal to).

Many other programming languages extend the concept of the IF statement to include an "ELSE action" that is to be performed if the IF condition is *not* true; the form is:

IF (**condition**) THEN **action**₁ ELSE **action**₂

Fortran regrettably does not have this feature, but in many situations its effects can be achieved by a two-statement structure like this:

action₂
IF (**condition**) action₁

In other words, **action₂** is carried out first, unconditionally, then **action₁** is carried out conditionally. This cannot be utilized with the complete generality of the IF-THEN-ELSE construction (not, for instance, if **action₂** destroys· values needed by **action₁**), but it often serves.

It is an excellent idea to begin thinking of programs in terms of a few standard patterns or structures. Here are two that occur frequently presented as flowcharts.

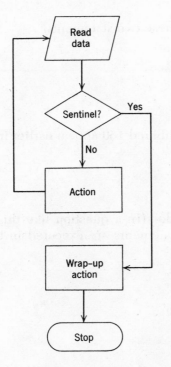

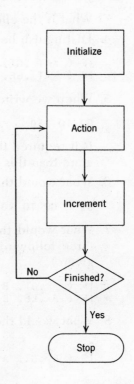

A very high percentage of all programs, even programs very much more complex and extensive than anything we have seen here, can be built around just these two structures and the Fortran version of the IF-THEN-ELSE noted above. Develop the habit of approaching a new programming assignment by asking yourself if the task fits these structures. In Chapter 6 we shall learn how the DO statement provides a streamlined way to write the second structure above.

REVIEW QUESTIONS

1. Write the general form of the IF statement, and explain what each part does.

2. Suppose we have this statement in a program:

```
IF ( LMN .EQ. 21 ) CAT = 34.9
```

   If at the time this statement is executed the value of variable named LMN is equal to 21, what will be the value of the variable named CAT after the statement is executed? What will its value be if LMN is not equal to 21? What is the value of LMN after the statement is executed?

3. Suppose this statement appears in a program:

```
IF ( X .LT. 0.0 ) GO TO 80
```

   What is the effect of the statement?

4. Distinguish between the action of these two statements:

```
IF ( KAT .GT. 0 ) DOG = 49.0
IF ( KAT .GE. 0 ) DOG = 49.0
```

5. When we write a statement such as

```
GO TO 150
```

   is it required that the statement numbered 150 appear earlier in the program than this GO TO?

6. What would this statement do?

```
80    GO TO 80
```

7. What would these two statements do? (In a question like this and the three following, assume that the statements are executed in the order given.)

```
IF ( A .GT. B ) BIG = A
IF ( A .LE. B ) BIG = B
```

8. What would these two statements do?

```
BIG = A
IF ( B .GT. A ) BIG = B
```

9. What would these statements do?

```
      BIG = A
      IF ( A .GT. B ) GO TO 80
      BIG = B
80
```

10. What would these two statements do?

```
      IF ( A .GT. B ) BIG = A
      BIG = B
```

11. Does the flowchart fragment shown represent the same processing action as the Fortran statement that follows it?

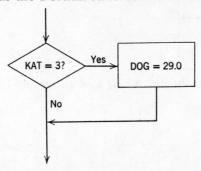

```
      IF ( A .LE. 0.01 ) GO TO 80
50
```

12. Does the flowchart fragment shown represent the same processing action as the Fortran statement that follows it?

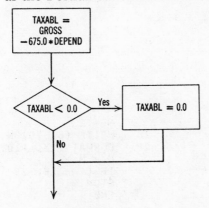

```
      IF ( KAT = 3 ) DOG = 29.0
```

13. Does the flowchart fragment shown represent the same processing action as the Fortran statements that follow it?

```
TAXABL = GROSS - 675.0 * DEPEND
IF ( TAXABL .LT. 0.0 ) TAXABL = 0.0
```

14. State what would be done by the program and corresponding flowchart shown.

```
10      READ (5, 20) N
20      FORMAT (I10)
        IF (N .EQ. 0 ) STOP
        IF ( N .GT. 0 ) WRITE (6, 30) N
30      FORMAT (1X, I10)
        GO TO 10
        END
```

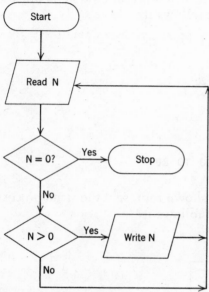

15. State what would be done by the flowchart and program shown.

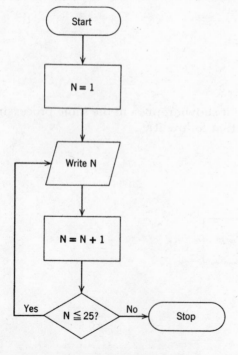

```
        N = 1
10      WRITE (6, 20) N
20      FORMAT (1X, I10)
        N = N + 1
        IF ( N .LE. 25 ) GO TO 10
        STOP
        END
```

JAY PALMER

16. State what would be done by the flowchart and corresponding program shown.

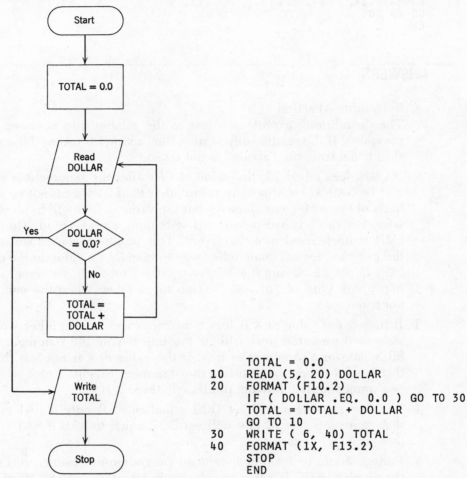

```
      TOTAL = 0.0
10    READ (5, 20) DOLLAR
20    FORMAT (F10.2)
      IF ( DOLLAR .EQ. 0.0 ) GO TO 30
      TOTAL = TOTAL + DOLLAR
      GO TO 10
30    WRITE ( 6, 40) TOTAL
40    FORMAT (1X, F13.2)
      STOP
      END
```

17. Identify two errors in this version of the second program in the chapter.

```
C PAY CALCULATION WITH HEADINGS AND SENTINEL CARD
C
C VARIABLE NAMES
C     IDNO    IDENTIFICATION NUMBER
C     HOURS   HOURS WORKED FOR WEEK
C     RATE    PAY RATE, DOLLARS PER HOUR
C     PAY     COMPUTED PAY FOR WEEK
C
      WRITE (6, 10)
10    FORMAT ('1', 'ID NUMBER    HOURS    RATE    GROSS PAY'/)
20    READ (5, 30) IDNO, HOURS, RATE
30    FORMAT (    I6,   F3.1,   F4.2)
      IF ( IDNO EQ 0 ) STOP
C
C COMPUTE PAY AT STRAIGHT-TIME RATE
C
      PAY = HOURS * RATE
C
C IF MORE THAN 40 HOURS, RECOMPUTE PAY WITH TIME-AND-A-HALF FOR OVERTIME
C
```

```
      IF ( HOURS .GT. 40.0 ) PAY = (40.0 + 1.5*(HOURS - 40.0) * RATE
      WRITE (6, 40) IDNO, HOURS,          RATE,          PAY
 40   FORMAT (1X,    I7,    F10.1, '   $', F5.2, '   $', F6.2)
      GO TO 20
      END
```

ANSWERS

1. IF (condition) action
   The "condition" expresses a test of the relationship between two expressions. If the relationship is true, the "action" is taken; if the relationship is not true, the "action" is not taken.

2. If LMN does equal 21, the value of CAT after the statement is executed will be 34.9. If LMN has any value other than 21 we cannot say—on the basis of this statement alone—what the value of CAT will be; it will have whatever value it had before this statement was executed. The value of LMN is unchanged in either event. This statement makes sense only if the programmer has some other way to give CAT a value in the case that LMN is not 21. Saying it another way, the Fortran IF statement does not imply any kind of "or else" action to be taken when the condition is not true.

3. If in fact the value of X is less than zero (negative, in other words) the statement executed next will be the one having the statement number 80, whatever and wherever it is. If the value of X is not less than zero, that is, if it is zero or positive, the statement executed next will be the one immediately following the IF, whatever it is.

4. The first statement will set DOG equal to 49.0 only if KAT is *greater* than zero; the second one will set DOG equal to 49.0 if KAT is greater than or *equal to* zero.

5. Fortran doesn't care, but it is good programming practice to minimize the number of GO TOs that transfer back. An interwoven tangle of forward and backward pointing GO TOs, referred to by some writers as *spaghetti programming*, rapidly gets beyond easy comprehensibility. The effect, naturally, is that even the programmer who wrote it cannot be sure what it does, and the probability of errors accordingly increases.

6. Many Fortrans would flag this as an error, and the computer would never attempt to execute it. If it were executed it would cause a GO TO to itself, over and over for as long as the program was permitted to run. This is called an *infinite loop* or an *endless loop*. Although this most flagrant version would usually be diagnosed and not executed, there are more subtle ways to get caught in this sort of trap, that Fortran may not be able to catch.

7. The first statement will set BIG equal to A if A is greater than B. The second will set BIG equal to B if A is less than or equal to B. Since the conditions in the two statements are mutually exclusive and exhaust all the possibilities, exactly one of the two actions will be carried out. The net result will be to place the larger of A and B in BIG. (If A and B are equal, B is placed in BIG by the second statement.)

8. The first statement is always executed, since it is not conditional. In other words A always goes into BIG. Then the second statement places B in BIG — but only if A is less than or equal to B. The net result is to place the larger of A and B in BIG — the same thing the program segment in Question 7 did.

9. The first statement places A in BIG. The GO TO in the second statement is executed only if A is greater than B; if this is done, the effect is to skip around the third statement, which places B in BIG. The net result is to place the larger of A and B in BIG — the same thing the program segments in Questions 7 and 8 did. But why do it this way, when it can be done more clearly without GO TOs?

10. The first statement places A in BIG if and only if A is greater than B. The second statement then places B in BIG, *regardless of what happened in the* IF. The net result is to place B in BIG no matter whether A is larger than B or not. This is a mistake beginners frequently make.

11. Close, but not quite: the flowchart decision box says *less than*, but the IF has less than or equal (.LE.).

12. The equal sign is not permitted as a relational operator in Fortran.

13. Yes.

14. A deck of cards is read until encountering one on which the integer punched in columns 1-10 is zero, at which point it stops. Up to that point, all positive numbers read are printed.

15. The program prints the integers from 1 to 25, one to a line.

16. The program reads a deck of cards, adding the amount in columns 1-10 to a total that is set to zero before beginning to read. When a zero amount is encountered, the sum of all the amounts read is printed and the program stops.

17. Periods around the EQ are missing in the first IF, and there is a missing right parenthesis in the assignment statement contained in the second IF.

EXERCISES

1. Draw flowcharts and write program segments to carry out the following actions.

   The parts of this exercise are independent of each other; they do not together form a program. You should also assume that each action is a small part of some larger program that has given values to the variables, etc., so that you do not need to provide READ, WRITE, or END statements, for instance. (If not clear what is wanted, just peek at the answer to the first one!)

   *a. Stop program execution if the value of the variable named DOG is greater than zero.

   b. Stop program execution if the value of the variable named DOG is not equal to the value of the variable named CAT.

*c. If the value of the variable named DAY exceeds 8.0, set EXTRA to the amount by which DAY exceeds 8.0. If DAY does not exceed 8.0, do nothing to EXTRA.

d. If SALES is less than QUOTA, set SHORT equal to amount by which SALES is less than QUOTA. Otherwise do nothing to SHORT.

*e. If SALES is less than QUOTA, set SHORT equal to the amount by which SALES is less than QUOTA. Otherwise set SHORT to zero.

f. If THI is less than or equal to 70, set COMFRT to 1.0; if THI is greater than 70, set COMFRT to 0.0. (Not that it matters, but THI is the abbreviation for "temperature-humidity index.")

*g. If the sum of XNORML and BONUS is greater than QUOTA, execute statement 800 next. Otherwise continue in normal sequence of statement execution.

h. If R plus S is less than 0.00001, execute statement 900 next; otherwise continue in normal statement execution sequence.

*i. Add 1 to NADULT if NAGE is greater than or equal to 18.

j. If HOURS is not equal to 40.0, go to statement 800.

*k. If KSHIFT equals 2, add 10% of GROSS to GROSS.

l. Set CIRCLE to 1.0 if $(X^2 + Y^2)^{0.5}$ is less than 1.0, and do nothing otherwise.

2. In the following exercises you are to draw a flowchart and write a complete program. Use I10 field descriptors for integer values and F10.2 for real values, both input and output.

*a. Read a card containing a value of ANNERN (annual earnings). Compute the TAX as zero if ANNERN is less than or equal to 2000.00, and as 2% of the amount over 2000.00 otherwise. Print ANNERN and TAX, then stop.

b. Read a card containing values for BASE, SALES, and QUOTA. Compute BONUS as zero if SALES do not exceed QUOTA, and as 8% of the amount by which SALES exceed QUOTA otherwise. Compute GROSS = BASE + BONUS. Print BASE, SALES, QUOTA, and GROSS.

*c. Refer to Review Question 15. Draw a flowchart and write a program to print 50 lines consisting of the integers from 1 to 50 in sequence, together with the square and cube of each integer on the same line with it.

d. Refer to Review Question 15. Draw a flowchart and write a program to print the odd integers from 1 to 99 on successive lines. Each line should contain not only an odd integer, but also the third and fifth power of the integer.

*e. Refer to Review Question 16. Draw a flowchart and write a program to carry out the following procedure. You are to read a deck of cards, each card containing an integer KODE and a real DOLLAR. For each card, if KODE = 1 add DOLLAR to TOTAL1 and otherwise to TOTAL2. (TOTAL1 and TOTAL2 should be set to zero before beginning to read cards.) Upon encountering a card for which KODE = 0, print both totals and stop.

f. Refer to Review Question 16. Draw a flowchart and write a program to carry out the following procedure. You are to read a deck of cards, each card containing a real AMOUNT. For each card, if

AMOUNT is less than zero add it to NEGSUM and otherwise to POSSUM. (NEGSUM and POSSUM should be set to zero before beginning to read cards.) Upon encountering a card for which AMOUNT equals zero, print both sums and stop.

*g. You are to draw a flowchart and write a program to produce the following table. There will be two columns. The left column will consist of the values of a variable named X, ranging from 0.1 to 5.0 inclusive. For each value of X, the number in the second column gives the value of Y computed from

$$Y = 1.0 + \sqrt{X^2 + 12.5}$$

You can get the X values by letting an integer variable, call it N, run from 1 to 50. For each N, divide by 10.0 to get X.

h. Building on the concepts in the previous exercises, write a program to prepare a table giving — for all values of X between 0.2 and 10.0 in steps of 0.2 — the value of Y from this rule:

If $X \leqslant 6$, $Y = 2X + 14$
If $X > 6$, $Y = 3X + 8$

For each X, print a line giving X and Y.

*3. Refer to Exercise 7, Chapter 2, page 29. After computing the tax, test to be sure that the tax is not negative, which would indicate that the person did not earn more than his allowance for dependents. If the computed tax is negative, set the tax to zero.

4. Refer to Exercise 8, Chapter 2, page 29. Add a test to set SALARY to $20 if the computed value is less than 20.

*5. The Traphagen School of Fashion in New York has the following refund policy. If a student requests a cancellation more than 3 days after signing an agreement, but before the starting date of the course, the cancellation charge is 15% of the tuition and registration fees or $100, whichever is less. Write a statement that assigns a value to CHARGE, given a value for TUITN. (TUITN is the sum of tuition and registration fees.) Assume that the other conditions are met.

6. A student committee was organized to handle arrangements for a concert of Beethoven's Tenth, a rock group. The value of ORCH gives the number of orchestra tickets sold in advance at $4.75, and the value of BALC gives the number of advance sale balcony tickets at $2.25. Variables named FEE and EXP give the group's fee and the fixed expenses, respectively. DOOR contains a dollar estimate for sales at the door. Write a program that will compute the dollar value of the total estimated sales, compare it with the sum of FEE and EXP, and print either

WE PREDICT A LOSS OF xxxx.xx DOLLARS

or

WE PREDICT A PROFIT OF xxxx.xx DOLLARS

as the case may be.

*7. You are given a deck of cards, each of which contains a golfer's identification in columns 1-3, his actual score in columns 4-6, and his handicap in columns 7-9. An identification of zero serves as an end-of-deck sentinel. Write a program that will read the deck and, for each golfer, print his identification, score, handicap, and net score. (The net score is his actual score minus his handicap.) Print appropriate column headings.

8. Extend the program of Exercise 7 so that it finds lowest net score, using the following procedure. Before going into the card reading loop, set LOW to some large number, say 999. Then compare every net score with the current contents of LOW, and place the net score in LOW anytime it is less than the current contents of LOW. When the sentinel is detected, do not stop immediately, but transfer to a section of the program where the low net is printed, and then stop.

*9. Suppose that the dimensions of a rectangular box are A, B, and C. Write a program segment that first determines which of the three is smallest; call that D. Then compute the volume of the largest sphere that can be contained within the box, which is given by:

0.5236 D^3

10. Given three lengths, A, B, and C, they may or may not form the sides of a triangle. If A and B are both 1.5, for instance, and C is 22, there is no corresponding triangle. Write a program segment that will read three numbers from a card and print THESE VALUES DO NOT CORRESPOND TO A TRIANGLE if that is the case. The test is made by determining whether any two sides have a sum that is less than or equal to the third side; all possible combinations must be tested.

*11. You are given a card containing either a 1 or a 2 in column 1, and a value in inches in columns 10-14. Write a program that will carry out the following procedure.

    If the number in column 1 is 1, the length is the side of a cube, and you are to print the length and the volume of the cube, which is just the length raised to the third power. If the number in column 1 is a 2, the length is the diameter of a sphere, and you are to print the volume of the sphere, which is 0.5236 times the length raised to the third power. If the number in column 1 is neither 1 nor 2, print "TILT."

12. You are given two times, expressed as hours and minutes since midnight. For instance, 0800 is 8:00 AM, 1430 is 2:30 PM, etc. You are guaranteed that the first time is earlier than the second and that the times are less than 24 hours apart. You are not guaranteed that they are in the same day, however. For example 2350 is 20 minutes earlier than 0010 of the next day, midnight falling between the two.

    Outline a procedure for finding the difference in times between the two, in minutes.

CHAPTER FIVE

PROGRAM DEVELOPMENT AND CHECKOUT

The programs that have been shown so far have been presented to you already completed, and all have been correct. If you are like most people you have been saying to yourself, "Yes, but how would *I* go about writing a program to do something that *I'm* interested in?" And if you have run some programs, you most likely have already discovered that programs often do not operate correctly when first tried. An incorrect program is obviously useless, and an important part of the total programming job is making programs correct.

In this chapter we take up another rather simple processing task—the creation of a miles-to-kilometers conversion table, concentrating on how one could go about developing an algorithm for it; we then consider another version of the program that has a number of typical errors in it to see how one might go about finding and eliminating them.

The first miles-to-kilometers conversion program

An American student planning a bicycle trip in Europe wishes to prepare a short table showing the metric equivalents, in kilometers, of various mileage figures. The formula for this conversion is

$$\text{Kilometers} = 1.6093 \times \text{Miles}$$

In the first version of his program he has decided that he wants the miles to run from 1 to 10 in steps of 1. The mileage figures are to be printed in a column headed MILES and the metric equivalents in a column headed KILOMETERS.

Thinking through a flowchart

We begin our thinking about how to do this job with the drawing of a flowchart, and this time we shall draw it one box at a time, in the order in which a person might think through the process.

The job has to do with converting miles to kilometers, so we draw an appropriate box, not worrying much about things like variable names and Fortran assignment statements:

```
Convert from
miles to
kilometers
```

We know that for each mileage figure and its equivalent kilometers figure we are going to want to write a line, so we add that box, getting this combination:

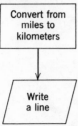

Now we have to think some about how the miles figure is going to take on all the whole-number values from 1 to 10 inclusive. A reasonable starting place, in this thinking, would seem to be getting the very first mileage value. We certainly can't assume anything about what value a variable will have if we don't assign it a value. So we add a box at the top:

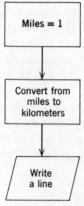

Now we add a box at the bottom, to increase the mileage by 1. This will take care of getting the successive values, having started the variable at 1:

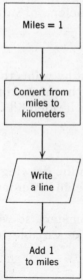

Now—a careless programmer might leap to conclude—we can draw a line going back to the conversion box. But how are we going to stop this process after 10? So we add a decision box that tests whether the mileage is less than or equal to 10 and go back only if so, otherwise stopping:

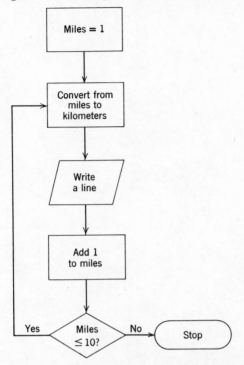

Now we can finish off the job by putting a box at the top to write the heading line and adding a start box. The final result is our flowchart, shown in Figure 5.1.

Observe that we have here an example of a complete program with no input; all values are generated within the program itself.

The precise sequence in which a programmer thinks about the functions to be performed in a program and the order in which he therefore writes them in a flowchart is, naturally, an individual matter. Not everyone would do it in exactly the sequence stated above. There is no need to apologize for individual differences. And there is certainly no need to apologize for not starting at the top with a box marked Start. There is nothing whatever wrong with a thinking process that begins in the middle and works in stages toward top and bottom. There is nothing that says the human brain has to work the same way the computer program will. Each person should go about the drawing of the first version of the flowchart in whatever way seems most natural to him and most likely to produce a correct result.

Back to programming

Notice that in the development of an algorithm for our present example we have not yet worried about printer spacing, variable names, real vs. integer variables, and all such specific programming matters. Now is the time to do that; maybe you will wait to draw your final flowcharts until after some of these decisions have been made, so that you can prepare a flowchart that is easier to compare with the program.

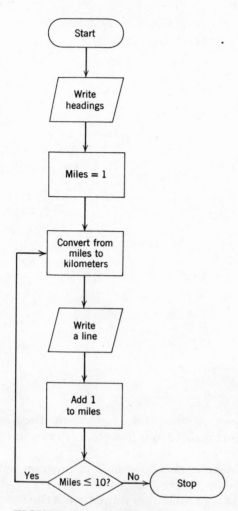

FIGURE 5.1. Flowchart of a procedure for producing a miles-to-kilometers conversion table. Note that no data values are read.

One decision that has to be made fairly early, since it affects almost everything in the program, is the form in which the two distance figures are to be printed. Since all the mileage values are to be whole numbers, it would seem reasonable to use an integer variable for the mileage. What could be more reasonable as a name than MILES? With MILES being an integer variable, we will use an I field descriptor in the FORMAT so no decimal point will be printed.

Since the conversion formula guarantees that the kilometers figure will contain noninteger values, we will have to use a real variable for it. Let's call it XKILOS, the X being added to make a legal real variable name. The question of how many decimal places to print is up to the person requesting the results, and depends on how much accuracy he will need for the intended uses. Let us assume that our student wants the kilometer values printed with one decimal place.

Next we think about the spacing of the results. Suppose we put two blanks between the words MILES and KILOMETERS, like this:

MILES   KILOMETERS

Using a printer spacing chart and knowing the sizes of the numbers to be printed, we can sketch possible spacing to approximately center each column under its heading, using X's to stand for the values.

MILES   KILOMETERS

XX   XX.X

Now we count the number of printing positions required in each field for the numbers, and find that it is four positions for MILES and ten for XKILOS. The necessary field descriptors are therefore I4 and F10.1.

Figure 5.2 shows the flowchart redrawn to use the variable names that have been decided upon, and putting things in terms that are a little closer to Fortran, whereas Figure 5.1 was a little closer to English. This question— whether flowcharts should use programming notation or ordinary English— is a matter of mild controversy in the programming field. We will not take a

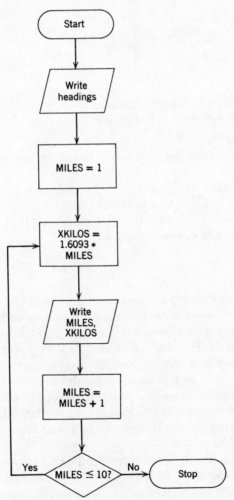

FIGURE 5.2. A flowchart closely related to that of Figure 5.1, but in a form closer to the style of the program.

```
C A MILES TO KILOMETERS CONVERSION TABLE
C
C      WRITE HEADINGS
C
       WRITE (6, 10)
  10   FORMAT ('1', 'MILES   KILOMETERS'/)
C
C      GIVE A STARTING VALUE TO THE MILES VARIABLE
C
       MILES = 1
C
C      CONVERT TO KILOMETERS; PROGRAM REPEATS FROM HERE
C
  20   XKILOS = 1.6093 * MILES
C
C      WRITE RESULTS
C
       WRITE (6, 30) MILES, XKILOS
  30   FORMAT (1X, I4, F10.1)
C
C      INCREMENT THE VALUE OF MILES
C
       MILES = MILES + 1
C
C      TEST TO SEE IF WE ARE DONE; BRANCH BACK IF NOT
C
       IF ( MILES .LE. 10 ) GO TO 20
       STOP
       END
```

FIGURE 5.3. A program for producing a miles-to-kilometers conversion table, corresponding to the flowchart of Figure 5.2.

dogmatic stance, but merely note that the present trend is a slow movement toward something closer to English.

With all of these matters settled, writing down the program is fairly simple. It is admittedly misleading to present a finished program and simply analyze how it works; that conceals all the effort of the decisions that went into devising it. That is why this chapter is in the book.

Writing comments

Figure 5.3 is a program corresponding to the flowchart of Figure 5.2. The first thing you will notice is that comments have been used much more heavily than in the past in an attempt to make absolutely clear what each part of the program does. "Blank comment cards," lines with only a C in position 1, have been used to attempt to improve readability. Not all programmers agree that using so many comments is good, and practicing programmers almost never write this many. It is done here to show one possibility, and to emphasize once again the importance of writing programs that are understandable to other people — and to the original programmer six months or a year later when he comes back to make a modification.

The statement that does the actual conversion from miles to kilometers has a statement number so that we can refer to it in a GO TO statement later in the program. Readers who do not use mixed mode will need to modify this statement appropriately.

An important statement

The statement that adds 1 to the mileage will startle those who may have been told that Fortran is "just like mathematics":

```
MILES = MILES + 1
```

is pretty obviously not an equation, but it is a perfectly legal Fortran statement and is illustrative of something that is frequently done. Returning to the language of an earlier chapter, we can say that this statement means: "Add 1 to the value of a variable named MILES, and make the result the new value of a variable named MILES." The fact that MILES appears on both sides of the equal sign poses no problems. The net result is to add 1 to MILES, wiping out the old value in the process.

In other contexts this kind of variable is often called a *counter*, since it can be used to keep track of the number of times something has happened in a program. Adding a constant to a counter is called *incrementing* it.

The IF statement

The IF statement this time is used to determine whether to repeat program execution or to stop it. The fact that the relational operator is .LE. and not .LT. is important; it is a question of whether the last values of MILES is going to be 9 or 10. Since we have added 1 to MILES *after* printing, when MILES equals 10 at the point of execution of the IF statement we will not yet have printed a line in which MILES is 10. Therefore we do want to say less than *or equal to* here. This kind of question (when to do incrementing and/or testing) is a frequent source of programming errors and should always be considered carefully.

We have here our first example of a program in which the statement that is conditionally executed in the IF is a GO TO. If the test is satisfied, that is, if MILES really is less than or equal to 10, the GO TO will be executed, taking us back to the conversion statement. If MILES is greater than 10, the GO TO is not executed, and we reach the STOP that terminates program execution.

The output of the program is shown in Figure 5.4. Everything seems to have worked as intended.

```
MILES   KILOMETERS

    1        1.6
    2        3.2
    3        4.8
    4        6.4
    5        8.0
    6        9.7
    7       11.3
    8       12.9
    9       14.5
   10       16.1
```

FIGURE 5.4. The output of the program of 5.3.

A modified program—which contains deliberate errors

Let us now attempt to modify the program to prepare a somewhat more useful table, and take this task as an opportunity to study the question of locating various kinds of errors that a program may contain.

Our travelling student has looked at his table and realized that he wants a greater range of mileage values, but that he doesn't want them printed at an interval of one mile all the way. To be specific: he wants the table just as it now exists, but with added entries from 15 to 100 steps of 5 miles. (If this isn't clear, glance at Figure 5.12 to see what is meant.)

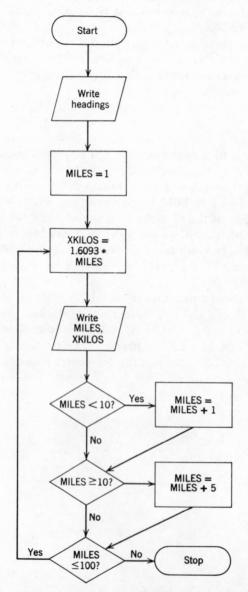

FIGURE 5.5.   A flowchart of a procedure for extending the range of the miles-to-kilometers conversion program. *This flowchart contains an error in logic.*

The new—and wrong—logic

Let us pretend to follow the thinking of our student as he considers how to modify the program.

"Only two boxes have to be changed. The 10 in the decision box has to be changed to 100 to extend the table. And the incrementing of MILES has to be changed so that after 10 the increment is 5 instead of 1. I'll replace the incrementing box with two decision boxes, corresponding to these two IF statements:

```
IF ( MILES .LT. 10 ) MILES = MILES + 1
IF ( MILES .GE. 10 ) MILES = MILES + 5
```

MILES must be either less than 10, or greater than or equal to 10; it can't be both at any one time. Therefore only one of the incrementing statements will be executed."

If you see a problem in this logic, congratulations! You are right; there is one. If you don't see a problem, read on. It will turn up in due course. It's a bit subtle, and typical of the kind of thing that can happen. The modified flowchart is shown in Figure 5.5.

The program shown in Figure 5.6 has been modified to take these changes into account, and several deliberate errors have been introduced.

```
C A MILES TO KILOMETERS CONVERSION TABLE
C MODIFIED VERSION -- GOES BY 5'S AFTER 10
C THIS PROGRAM CONTAINS DELIBERATE ERRORS
C ---- ------- -------- ---------- ------
C
C      ... WRITE HEADINGS
C
       WRITE (6, 10)
  10   FORMAT ('1', 'MILES   KILOMETERS/)
C
C      ... GIVE A STARTING VALUE TO THE MILES VARIABLE
C
       MILES = 1
C
C      ... CONVERT TO KILOMETERS; PROGRAM REPEATS FROM HERE
C
  20   XKILOS = 1.6093 MILES
C
C      ... WRITE RESULTS
C
       WRITE (6, 30) MILES, KILOS
  30   FORMAT (1X, I4, F10.1)
C
C      ... INCREMENT THE VALUE OF MILES
C
       IF ( MILES .LT. 10 ) MILES = MILES + 1
       IF ( MILES .GE. 10 ) MILES = MILES + 5
C
C      ... TEST TO SEE IF WE ARE DONE; BRANCH BACK IF NOT
C
       IF ( MILES .LE. 100 ) GO TO 20
       STOP
       END
```

FIGURE 5.6. A program for the miles-to-kilometers problem. *This program contains deliberate errors.*

Try to find these errors, for practice, before going on. If you don't find all of them, that may be educational, too. Notice the slightly different style of writing comments, to make reading the program easier.

All Fortrans include some degree of checking for errors in programs. As we shall see, Fortran cannot catch all types of errors, but when something is clearly illegal Fortran can often detect the problem and point it out.

In order to talk more sensibly about this subject it is necessary to dig a little more deeply into what is meant by saying "Fortran does" something or other. A few definitions are needed.

The compilation process

The Fortran program that we write is more precisely called the *source program*. Now, no computer can actually carry out a Fortran source program di-

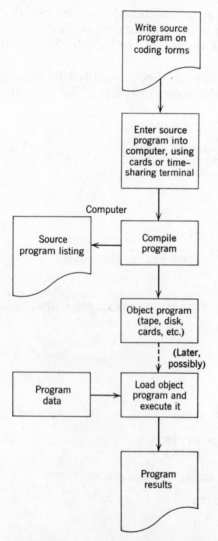

FIGURE 5.7.   Schematic diagram of the compilation procedure, showing the relation between source program, object program, and source program listing.

rectly. First, the source program must be translated into the much more elementary language of the computer itself, which is called *machine language.* The result of the translation of the source program into machine language is called an *object program.* The translation is also called, more commonly, *compilation,* and we speak of a Fortran *compiler.*

The complete process can be summarized with the help of a schematic diagram, Figure 5.7. We write a Fortran source program on a coding sheet and, most commonly these days, punch a deck of cards from it. (Sometimes it is possible to enter the program directly into the computer using a time-sharing terminal, a device like a typewriter that is connected to the computer by telephone wires.) We tell the computing system to compile our program. (The compiler is itself a large computer program, always available within the machine, and usually supplied by the computer manufacturer.) The compilation process produces both an object program and a *source program listing,* the latter being a printed copy of our source program, with indications of any errors the compiler found. If there are disabling errors, that is the end of the story until we correct the errors and resubmit the deck. If the object program is runnable, and assuming we told the system to try to run it, it is next executed, during which time it calls for cards to be read, calculations performed, lines printed, and whatever else the Fortran program said to do.

An example of an object program

For an extremely simple example of what an object program is like, suppose this is our source program:

```
        READ ( 5, 10) A
   10   FORMAT (F10.0)
        B = 12.0 + A/9.0
        WRITE (6, 20) A, B
   20   FORMAT (1X, 2F12.4)
        STOP
        END
```

The compiler would produce machine instructions corresponding to each of the actions here. Reading and writing are surprisingly complex processes, each requiring many hundreds of instructions, so we look only at the instructions compiled from the assignment statement. Here are the instructions for an IBM 360 or 370 produced by one of the Fortran compilers available for it:

```
   LE    0,100(0,13)
   DE    0,184(0,13)
   AE    0,188(0,13)
   STE   0,104(0,13)
```

The first instruction says to load an arithmetic register with the value of A. The instruction contains not A itself, but the address of a storage location where the READ has placed A. Then follows a divide, an add, and a store (STE).

Different computers follow different types of instructions and have different arrangements of the registers in which arithmetic is done, so that the object program produced for another machine—from the same source program—might be quite different. But in every case the source program must be translated into a set of the elementary instructions that the particular machine is able to follow.

It may now be seen that we have been using shorthand up to now. When we have said, for example, "the READ calls for reading data from a card," that was shorthand for "the object program instructions compiled from the READ call for reading data from a card." The distinction is often not important, and the reader has not been misled by the simplified phrasing that has been used so far. We have needed to introduce the true facts now so that we can talk about how and when the compiler detects errors, and where the source program listing comes from.

The source program listing and error messages

The source program listing for our program is shown in Figure 5.8. We see that everything in the original program is there, plus some numbers on the left and some error indications. The numbers on the left are called *internal sequence numbers* (ISNs), and have no relation to the statement number in our program. The ISNs are there simply for identification in certain situations where the errors are listed separately. The error indications here are

```
        C A MILES TO KILOMETERS CONVERSION TABLE
        C MODIFIED VERSION -- GOES BY 5'S AFTER 10
        C THIS PROGRAM CONTAINS DELIBERATE ERRORS
        C ---- ------- -------- ---------- ------
        C
        C      ... WRITE HEADINGS
        C
0001           WRITE (6, 10)
0002    10     FORMAT ('1', 'MILES   KILOMETERS/)
                                                                    $
    01) IEY0131 SYNTAX
        C
        C      ... GIVE A STARTING VALUE TO THE MILES VARIABLE
        C
0003           MILES = 1
        C
        C      ... CONVERT TO KILOMETERS; PROGRAM REPEATS FROM HERE
        C
0004    20     XKILOS = 1.6093 MILES
                                 $
    01) IEY0131 SYNTAX
        C
        C      ... WRITE RESULTS
        C
0005           WRITE (6, 30) MILES, KILOS
0006    30     FORMAT (1X, I4, F10.1)
        C
        C      ... INCREMENT THE VALUE OF MILES
        C
0007           IF ( MILES .LT. 10 ) MILES = MILES + 1
0008           IF ( MILES .GE. 10 ) MILES = MILES + 5
        C
        C      ... TEST TO SEE IF WE ARE DONE; BRANCH BACK IF NOT
        C
0009           IF ( MILES .LE. 100 ) GO TO 20
0010           STOP
0011           END
```

FIGURE 5.8.   The source program listing corresponding to the program of Figure 5.6. Note the diagnostic indications of two errors in syntax, using the dollar sign as a pointer.

printed under the statements to which they apply, with a dollar sign used as pointer to the possible location of the error. The first error is identified as having to do with syntax, and there is a dollar sign at the end of the line. "Syntax" is a term borrowed from grammar, and has to do with the rules for forming a correct Fortran statement. Study shows a missing quote in the FORMAT. The compiler kept looking for the closing quote, and when it came to the end of the statement without finding it, marked the statement as being in error. The second error is also a syntax error, quite explicitly marked: an operator is missing between the constant and the variable.

Sometimes error indications are less helpful. For a simple example, suppose the assignment statement had been

```
CAT = DOGGY 527
```

where an operator is missing between DOGGY and 527. This time the error indication would be "variable name too long." The blank means nothing in Fortran, and the compiler has no way to know what our intention was. Something like

```
CAT = DOGGY 5
```

would be completely legal, with DOGGY 5 taken as DOGGY5 and therefore a quite legitimate variable name. All this is simply to say that detective work is sometimes necessary when error indications are less explicit then we might wish.

Other types of errors

Both of the errors found by the compiler here were syntactic errors, which made the statements illegal in all cases. There are other types of errors, and indeed this program contains such, that the compiler cannot catch. One of them is that in the second WRITE statement we have KILOS where is should be XKILOS. Now, taking this one statement by itself, that is not an error. A variable named KILOS has never been given a value anywhere in the program, but that fact cannot be known by looking at this one statement. If this statement is compared with its associated FORMAT we see that an integer variable is associated with a real field descriptor, but our compiler did not catch that fact. There are lots of Fortran compilers—at least one for every type of computer that can run Fortran—and often several for one machine. Another compiler available to the author on the same computer used for this example did catch this error.

Uninitialized variables

If we correct the two syntactic errors that our compiler caught and then recompile, there are no error diagnostics, and the compiled object program is run. The output is shown in Figure 5.9. The first things that hits the eye is the repeated value of 0.3 for kilometers. This is the value produced, in this Fortran system on this run, for the undefined variable named KILOS. Actually, since no value was ever given to this variable, whatever was lying around in that storage location in the computer was printed. Running the program again, we may well find something else in that location and get something

```
MILES   KILOMETERS

   1       0.3
   2       0.3
   3       0.3
   4       0.3
   5       0.3
   6       0.3
   7       0.3
   8       0.3
   9       0.3
  15       0.3
  20       0.3
  25       0.3
  30       0.3
  35       0.3
  40       0.3
  45       0.3
  50       0.3
  55       0.3
  60       0.3
  65       0.3
  70       0.3
  75       0.3
  80       0.3
  85       0.3
  90       0.3
  95       0.3
 100       0.3
```

FIGURE 5.9.   The output of a program like that of Figure 5.6,
but with the two syntactic errors removed. Note the repeated
erroneous value for kilometers and the absence of an entry for
10 miles.

else printed. What we would really like would be for the system to tell us
that we tried to use an undefined variable. Some compilers and associated
operating systems will do just that. The Fortran variation called WATFIV,
developed at the University of Waterloo, Canada, and named for *WATerloo
Fortran IV*, would print a field full of U's here, pointing out immediately
that an undefined variable was used.

This turns out to be a fairly common type of error, and one that in some
circumstances can be terribly difficult to locate. Worst is the fact that it may
not show any symptoms whatever during testing. If an uninitialized variable
should have been set to zero, and what happens by chance to be in its storage
location is a zero, there is no problem. The program in fact is operating correctly. (One is tempted at first to say, "by good luck," but actually it is bad
luck: the programmer would much prefer to have had the program disabled
by the error, so that he could detect and correct it.) Then perhaps a year later,
something other than zero will happen to be in the location for this unitial-
ized variable, and the program "blows up." (Then is heard the plaintive cry
of the wounded programmer, "But it's been running correctly for a year—
there couldn't be any errors in it!")

An error in logic

The next error is more subtle and is not in any way detectable by Fortran.
What we told it to do was legal—it just wasn't what we really meant. That

is the problem that leads to the omission of a line for 10 miles from the table. Didn't we say that at the incrementing step MILES would always be either less than 10, or greater than or equal to 10? That is indeed true, but what happens when MILES comes to these two successive IF statements having a value of 9? Then the first IF, finding MILES to be less than 10, adds 1. The second IF immediately tests MILES—the *new* value, of course—and finds that it is greater than or equal to 10, and adds 5! Net result: no line is ever printed for MILES exactly equal to 10.

This is called a *logical error*. It is an error *we* made in analyzing the procedure. There is no way in the world Fortran can catch this kind of error for us.

A simple solution, in this case, is to reverse the order of the two IF statements. Study what happens when MILES is equal to 8, 9, and 10, to satisfy yourself that this does work. If you don't believe it, turn to Figure 5.10, the final correct version of the program, and a corresponding flowchart in Figure 5.11; the final, correct, output is shown in Figure 5.12.

A checklist on program checkout

The best ways to go about finding errors in programs and assuring that the program is really correct can be the subject of an entire book. We may close this chapter with at least a few suggestions for how to go about it.

```
C A MILES TO KILOMETERS CONVERSION TABLE
C MODIFIED VERSION -- GOES BY 5'S AFTER 10
C FINAL MODIFIED VERSION -- ALL ERRORS REMOVED
C
C          WRITE HEADINGS
C
      WRITE (6, 10)
  10  FORMAT ('1', 'MILES   KILOMETERS'/)
C
C          GIVE A STARTING VALUE TO THE MILES VARIABLE
C
      MILES = 1
C
C          CONVERT TO KILOMETERS; PROGRAM REPEATS FROM HERE
C
  20  XKILOS = 1.6093 * MILES
C
C          WRITE RESULTS
C
      WRITE (6, 30) MILES, XKILOS
  30  FORMAT (1X, I4, F10.1)
C
C          INCREMENT THE VALUE OF MILES
C
      IF ( MILES .GE. 10 ) MILES = MILES + 5
      IF ( MILES .LT. 10 ) MILES = MILES + 1
C
C          TEST TO SEE IF WE ARE DONE; BRANCH BACK IF NOT
C
      IF ( MILES .LE. 100 ) GO TO 20
      STOP
      END
```

FIGURE 5.10. A final, correct version of the program for producing a miles-to-kilometers conversion table.

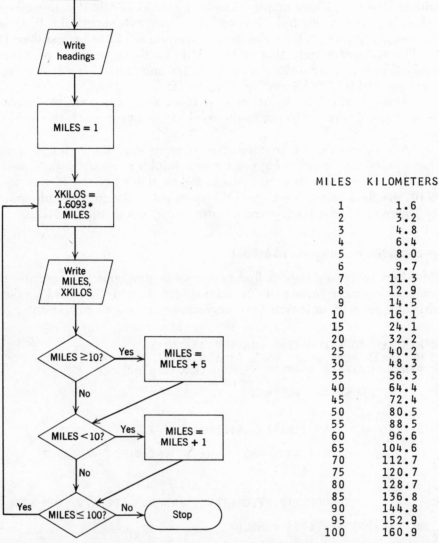

MILES   KILOMETERS

MILES	KILOMETERS
1	1.6
2	3.2
3	4.8
4	6.4
5	8.0
6	9.7
7	11.3
8	12.9
9	14.5
10	16.1
15	24.1
20	32.2
25	40.2
30	48.3
35	56.3
40	64.4
45	72.4
50	80.5
55	88.5
60	96.6
65	104.6
70	112.7
75	120.7
80	128.7
85	136.8
90	144.8
95	152.9
100	160.9

FIGURE 5.11. A corrected version of the flowchart of Figure 5.5.

FIGURE 5.12. The output of the program of Figure 5.10.

1. Time spent in *desk-checking* the program, that is, simply sitting at your desk and studying the program, will usually shorten the total time you have to spend getting the program running and will almost certainly save machine time. Proofread every line of your program, and all sample data cards. Be especially certain that the arithmetic assignment statements really do represent what you meant to write.

An excellent practice is to "play computer" with your program: using simple but representative data, go through the program carrying out with pencil and paper the actions the program specifies.

2. Accomplish as much as you can with each computer run. Resist the almost overwhelming temptation to rush back to the machine after finding one error. Ask yourself, "Does this error explain *all* the symptoms that I see in this run?" For small student jobs, you ought to be getting your programs running in no more than three runs on the computer. If you are averaging five or ten, you are doing a poor job of programming and checkout, besides wasting a lot of your time and computer time.

3. Never assume that a program is correct just because the compiler diagnoses no errors.

4. If the answers do not come out the way you expected, there is no point in running the program again — unchanged — to see if it was the machine's fault. It wasn't.

5. When in doubt about exactly how to write a statement, *look it up.*

6. The final test of the correctness of a program is comparison with hand-calculated test cases. In choosing test values, try to select values that bring all parts of the program into operation.

(Aside to computer center consultants: Sooner or later someone is going to say to you, "But I ran this just yesterday and I haven't changed anything." Your answer should be, "If you haven't changed anything, why are you running it again?" The response will of course be, "Well, I made one little change, but *that* couldn't have caused *this* trouble." Ah, but it could, and probably did.)

REVIEW QUESTIONS

1. Distinguish between a source program and an object program. What does the Fortran compiler do?

2. Rewrite this statement in a way which would more precisely indicate what happens: "An assignment statement is an order to Fortran to evaluate the expression on the right and assign that value to the variable on the left."

3. Identify any errors in the following that a Fortran compiler might always be expected to catch, any that it might or might not catch, and any that it could not possibly catch. The programmer's intention was to read ten cards, do the indicated arithmetic, and write a line for each card.

```
C PROGRAM FOR REVIEW QUESTION 3
C
 10    READ (5, 10) A, B
 20    FORMAT (2F10.2)
       C = A * -12.3/B
       WRITE (6, 30) A, B, C
 30    FORMAT (3F15.2)
       KOUNT = KOUNT + 1
       IF ( KOUNT .LT. 10 ) GO TO 10
       END
```

4. A beginning programmer wrote the following program.

```
C PROGRAM FOR REVIEW QUESTION 4
C
        READ (5, 200) A, B  C
 200    FORMAT F10.0)
        D = A - B
        E = A - C
        B + C = F
        WRITE (6, 210) A, B, C, D, E
 210    FORMAT (5F6.2)
        STOP
```

Here is the source listing he got back.

```
              C PROGRAM FOR REVIEW QUESTION 4
              C
0001                  READ (5, 200) A, B  C
0002              200 FORMAT F10.0)
                         $        $
       01)  IEY003I NAME LENGTH            02)  IEY013I SYNTAX
0003                  D = A - B
0004                  E = A - C
0005                  B + C = F
                            $
       01)  IEY013I SYNTAX
0006                  WRITE (6, 210) A, B, C, D, E
0007              210 FORMAT (5F6.2)
0008                  STOP
                         $
       01)  IEY015I NO END CARD
```

Why did the missing left parenthesis in the FORMAT statement generate the "NAME LENGTH" error message? Exactly what was the "SYN-
TAX" error below? Do you think the compiler caught all the errors?

5. A student wrote the following program.

```
C PROGRAM FOR REVIEW QUESTION 5
C
        READ (5, 300) X, Y, Z
 300    FORMAT (3F10.0)
 310    N = 1
        Q = X + Y + Z
        WRITE (6, 300) X, Y, Z, Q
        N =N + 1
        IF ( N .GT. 5 ) STOP
        GO TO 310
        END
```

What do you think the output was? Is it an error for the READ and the
WRITE both to refer to the same FORMAT?

6. Here is another student program.

```
C PROGRAM FOR REVIEW QUESTION 6
C
        J = 1
 10     READ (5, 20) M, N
 20     FORMAT (2I6)
        K = M/N
        WRITE (6, 30) J, M, N, K
 30     FORMAT (1X, 4I6)
        J = J + 2
        IF ( J .EQ. 20 ) STOP
        GO TO 10
        END
```

What do you think the program produced?

7. A pharmacy student wanted to prepare a table showing 20 weights in grains, from 1 to 20, and for each its equivalent in milligrams (mg). Here is the program as he first wrote it:

```
C PROGRAM FOR REVIEW QUESTION 7
C PREPARES A GRAINS-TO-MILLIGRAMS TABLE
C
      WRITE (6, 10)
   10 FORMAT ('1', '       GRAINS        MG'/)
   20 GRAIN = 1.0
      MG = 64.8 * GRAIN
      WRITE (6, 30) GRAIN, MG
   30 FORMAT (1X, F10.0, I10)
      GRAINS = GRAIN + 1.0
      IF ( GRAIN .LE. 20.0 ) GO TO 20
      STOP
      END
```

When he ran the program no errors were diagnosed, but after the heading the output consisted of the same line printed over and over, the one for one grain. (Fortran execution was stopped by the computer operating system after printing the maximum number of lines permitted for student jobs, 2000 lines, or over 30 pages!) Upon inspection the student realized that the statement number 20 should have been on the statement following the one on which it actually appears. He made this change and resubmitted the program. The output was exactly as before. What is the problem?

ANSWERS

1. We write a source program, consisting of Fortran statements; this is translated (or, compiled) into an object program of machine instructions by the Fortran compiler. It is the machine language object program that is executed by the computer.

2. "An assignment statement is an order that is translated by the Fortran compiler into machine instructions that result in evaluating the expression on the right and assigning the value to the variable named on the left."

3. Hopefully, the compiler would always catch the fact that the statement number within parentheses in the READ is not the statement number of a FORMAT statement; that statement number 20 is never referred to; and that there are two arithmetic operators in succession in the assignment statement. The compiler would not detect that KOUNT is never given an initial value, but some compilers would produce an object program that would point it out. No compiler would catch the fact that the IF statement will result in reading only nine cards instead of ten; the compiler cannot know what we *meant* to write if what we *did* write is completely legal. Likewise the absence of a carriage control character in the FORMAT would never be diagnosed. Unless the value of A were very large, the first character of the field sent to the printer would probably be a blank anyway and there would be no problem.

There is no STOP in the program, but most compilers would supply one upon detecting the END statement.

4. There are no *reserved words* in Fortran, that is, there are no words that have a special meaning in Fortran and which may not therefore be used in any other way. "FORMAT" is a legal data name, although it would be foolish practice to use it as such. The compiler, ignoring blanks, took FORMATF10 as a variable name, and, as such, rejected it as too long. The syntax error below was writing the assignment statement backwards, i.e., instead of

F = B + C

It happens that no legal Fortran statement can ever begin with a variable name followed by a plus sign, and that is what the compiler rejected.

It certainly did not catch all the errors. The comma missing between B and C in the READ is not by itself an error: BC is a legal name. However, this leads to using values for B and C that have never been defined. The absence of a carriage control character is not an error to Fortran, although it is surely bad programming.

5. The data values read determine the exact form of the output, but what is produced is those three values and the value of D, over and over indefinitely. The problem is the GO TO 310, which takes the program back to the initialization of N. The program would run until some limit was exceeded in the computer center's normal mode of operation for student jobs. This is an example of an endless loop. (Presumably, the 310 should have been on the following statement.)

It is not an error for the READ and WRITE statements to refer to the same FORMAT, although it is perhaps uncommon. Since there are fewer field descriptors in the FORMAT than there are variables in the WRITE, however, the results will be printed on two lines: X, Y, and F on one line and Q on the next. This matter is taken up in Chapter Eight.

6. Here is the output, where ten lines of results show some representative examples of integer division. After the last one comes an indication of an error, the exact nature of which would vary for different systems. At any rate, the problem is the test for exact equality between the loop counter (J) and 20; as written the program can never give J the value 20. This is another endless loop, in other words.

```
EXECUTION:
     1        1        2        0
     3        2        1        2
     5        2        3        0
     7        5        2        2
     9        7        2        3
    11       99      100        0
    13       34       12        2
    15       12       34        0
    17       80        9        8
    19        9       80        0

IHC217I FIOCS - END OF DATA SET ON UNIT      5
```

The beginning of an error message after the last line of data is an indication that the program ran out of data.

7. The statement

GRAINS = GRAIN + 1

is in error, since the variable on the left appears nowhere else in the program. The correct variable, GRAIN, is never incremented and the IF statement therefore always tests a GRAIN value of 1. With this error corrected, the output was:

GRAINS	MG
1.	64
2.	129
3.	194
4.	259
5.	323
6.	388
7.	453
8.	518
9.	583
10.	647
11.	712
12.	777
13.	842
14.	907
15.	971
16.	1036
17.	1101
18.	1166
19.	1231
20.	1295

EXERCISES

Note. By this point in your studies it is quite possible that you are doing programming assignments from your other studies or from your work. This is the best way to make use of a programming course, and these exercises are presented mostly for those readers who may not have real life applications to program.

*1. You are given a deck of cards with the following format

Columns	Content
1-4	Stock number
5-8	Amount on hand
9-12	Reorder point

Write a program to read the deck and print a line for any stock item in which the amount on hand is less than the reorder point. You need make no provision for sensing the end of the deck, if you wish; attempting to read a nonexistent record after the end of valid data will stop program execution.

2. Extend the program of Exercise 1 so that it takes into account the following additional information. Columns 13-16 contain an amount on order. You are to write a line for an item only if the amount on hand *plus the amount on order* is less than the reorder point. Furthermore, columns 17-20 contain a quantity for reorder that should be printed along with the other information. Proper column headings should of course be provided.

*3. You are given a deck of cards, each of which has a three-digit identification number punched in columns 72-74, along with much other information on the card. An identification number of zero signals the end of the deck. Write a program that will print "OK" if the cards are in ascending sequence on the identification number, and "NO GOOD" otherwise.

4. Extend the program of Exercise 3 so that it allows for duplicate identification numbers but prints a line to identify the fact that duplicates did occur. Include the duplicated identification number in the line printed.

*5. A deck of cards each has five fields named F1, F2, F3, F4, and F5 in successive ten-column fields beginning in column 1. Prepare a program that will read such a deck of cards; make no provision for ending it— running out of cards will stop the program automatically. For each card, perform these *validity checks*: F1 must be positive, F2 + F3 must be greater than F4, and F5 must *not* be zero. Any card record that "passes" should be printed, in a format of your choosing. Any card that "fails" should have only F1 printed, together with the words "DID NOT PASS VALIDITY TESTS."

6. A certain company pays its salesmen according to the following formulas, where each salesman works under one of the formulas as given by this code:

Code	Formula
1	0.15 ★ PRICE
2	0.40 ★ (PRICE − BASE)
3	$10.00 + 0.05★BASE
4	$110.00

You are to write a program that will read a deck of cards containing one card for each of a number of salesmen. Each card contains the salesman's number in columns 1-3, the code in column 14, the PRICE in 20-27 with a decimal point, and—if appropriate—a BASE in 28-36. A salesman's number of zero will serve as an end-of-deck sentinel. The program should print one line for each salesman, the format to be of your design, giving all the input data and his PAY, as computed from the formula.

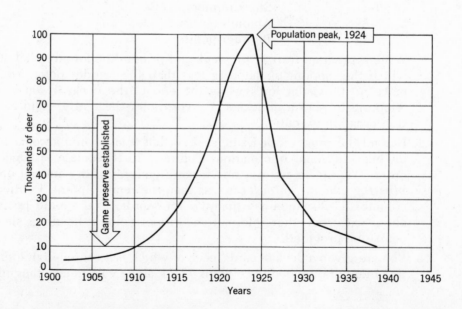

*7. The accompanying figure[1] shows the population of Kaibab deer in the Kaibab National Forest in northern Arizona over a period of years. You are given a deck of cards, each card containing a year in columns 1-4 and the deer population for that year (in thousands) in columns 5-7. Write a program to read the deck and determine which year had the highest deer population.

8. The table on pages 92 and 93 is from a widely used economics text.[2] We shall turn to it again in later chapters. Suppose for this exercise that you are given a deck of cards containing a year in 1-4 (zero serving as sentinel), and the Gross National Product (1958 prices, in billions of dollars) in columns 5-9 with a decimal point punched. You are to determine the year in which the Gross National Product was the least.

*9. A deck of cards contains the scores of a class on a midterm examination, a negative score serving as a sentinel. Prepare a program that will read the scores and sum them, and at the same time determine the number of cards. When the sentinel is detected, the average grade (the total of the scores divided by the number of scores) should be printed.

10. You are given a deck of cards, each of which contains either a 1 in column 1, signifying a debit, or a 2 in column 1 signifying a credit. The dollar amount in question is punched in columns 12-17, with a decimal point. Write a program that will read such a deck, looking for a code of zero in column 1 as a sentinel. Each value should be printed, with debits in a left-hand column and credits in a right-hand column. Furthermore, arrange to total the debits and credits separately; at the end, print both totals under their columns and finally the net, which is equal to the credits less the debits.

Note. the following four exercises are for the mathematically inclined.

*11. Write a program to do the following. Read a card containing values of variables named A, B, and C. If the quantity $B^2 - 4AC$ is negative, write a line that says "ROOTS IMAGINARY," and do nothing else. If $B^2 - 4AC$ is zero or positive, compute the roots from

$$X1 = \frac{-B + \sqrt{B^2 - 4AC}}{2A}$$

$$X2 = \frac{-B - \sqrt{B^2 - 4AC}}{2A}$$

and print them. The square root of a quantity can be found by raising it to the 0.5 power.

12. An integer is said to be *prime* if it is exactly divisible only by one and itself. Write a program that will read an odd integer greater than 3 from a card and then divide it by every odd integer from 3 up to one-half of the given number. Print the number and write either "PRIME" or "COMPOSITE," as the case may be. If the number is composite, print the smallest integer by which it is divisible.

[1] Raymond F. Dasmann, *Environmental Conservation*, third edition, New York, Wiley, 1972, page 281.
[2] Paul A. Samuelson, *Economics*, ninth edition, New York, McGraw-Hill, 1973, page 203.

PRINCIPAL ECONOMIC AGGREGATES (all income data in billions of current dollars)

Year	Gross National Product (current prices)	Net National Product	Gross National Product (1958 prices)	Disposable Income	Net Personal Saving as Percentage of Disposable Income
1929	103.1	95.2	203.6	83.3	5.0
1931	75.8	68.0	169.3	64.0	4.1
1933	55.6	48.6	141.5	45.5	−2.0
1935	72.7	65.4	169.5	58.5	3.7
1937	90.4	83.3	203.2	71.2	5.3
1938	84.7	77.4	192.9	65.5	1.1
1939	90.5	83.2	209.4	70.3	3.7
1940	99.7	92.2	227.2	75.7	5.1
1941	124.5	116.3	263.7	92.7	11.8
1942	157.9	148.1	297.8	116.9	23.6
1944	210.1	199.1	361.3	146.3	25.5
1945	212.0	200.7	355.2	150.2	19.7
1946	208.5	198.6	312.6	160.0	9.5
1948	257.6	243.0	323.7	189.1	7.1
1949	256.5	239.9	324.1	188.6	5.0
1950	284.8	266.4	355.3	206.9	6.3
1951	328.4	307.2	383.4	226.6	7.6
1952	345.5	322.3	395.1	238.3	7.6
1953	364.6	338.9	412.8	252.6	7.2
1954	364.8	336.8	407.0	257.4	6.4
1955	398.0	366.5	438.0	275.3	5.7
1956	419.2	385.2	446.1	293.2	7.0
1957	441.1	404.0	452.5	308.5	6.7
1958	447.3	408.4	447.3	318.8	7.0
1959	483.7	442.3	475.9	337.3	5.6
1960	503.8	460.3	487.7	350.0	4.9
1961	520.1	474.9	497.2	364.4	5.8
1962	560.3	510.4	529.8	385.3	5.6
1963	590.5	537.9	551.0	404.6	4.9
1964	632.4	576.3	581.1	438.1	6.0
1965	684.9	625.1	617.8	473.2	6.0
1966	749.9	685.9	658.1	511.9	6.3
1967	793.9	725.0	675.2	546.5	7.4
1968	864.2	789.7	706.6	591.0	6.5
1969	930.3	848.7	725.6	634.4	6.0
1970	976.4	890.1	722.1	689.5	8.0
1971	1,050.4	956.6	741.7	744.4	8.2

Government Expenditure on Goods and Services as Percentage of GNP	Federal Reserve Board Index of Industrial Production (1967 = 100)	Civilian Labor Force (thousands)	Unemployment as Percentage of Civilian Labor Force
8.2	21.6	49,180	3.2
12.2	14.9	50,420	15.9
14.5	13.7	51,590	24.9
13.9	17.3	52,870	20.1
13.1	22.3	54,000	14.3
15.3	17.6	54,610	19.0
14.7	21.7	55,230	17.2
14.1	25.4	55,640	14.6
19.8	31.6	55,910	9.9
37.8	36.3	56,410	4.7
45.8	47.4	54,630	1.2
38.5	40.6	53,860	1.9
12.9	35.0	57,520	3.9
12.2	41.0	60,621	3.8
14.7	38.8	61,286	5.9
13.3	44.9	62,208	5.3
17.9	48.7	62,017	3.3
21.6	50.6	62,138	3.0
22.4	54.8	63,015	2.9
20.4	51.9	63,643	5.5
18.7	58.5	65,023	4.4
18.7	61.1	66,552	4.1
19.5	61.9	66,929	4.3
21.1	57.9	67,639	6.8
22.1	64.8	68,639	5.5
19.8	66.2	69,628	5.5
20.7	66.7	70,459	6.7
20.9	72.2	70,614	5.5
20.7	76.5	71,833	5.7
20.4	81.7	73,091	5.2
20.0	89.2	74,455	4.5
20.9	97.9	75,770	3.8
22.7	100.0	77,347	3.8
23.1	105.7	78,737	3.6
22.6	110.7	80,734	3.5
22.4	106.7	82,715	4.9
22.2	106.8	84,113	5.9

*13. The value of e, the base of the natural logarithms, may be found by evaluating the series

$$e = 1 + \frac{1}{1!} + \frac{1}{2!} + \frac{1}{3!} + \ldots$$

Write a program to evaluate the series out through ten terms, using a loop to get the individual terms. Compare your results with the correct value of approximately 2.7182818.

14. Revise the program of the previous exercise to reduce the amount of arithmetic required in the program, by rewriting the formula this way:

$$e = 1 + \frac{1}{1}(1 + \frac{1}{2}(1 + \frac{1}{3}(1 + \ldots \frac{1}{10})))$$

CHAPTER SIX
THE DO STATEMENT

Introduction

Almost all computer applications require repeated execution of parts of programs. We have seen how this may be done using the IF statement, but in many situations the DO statement offers a much more powerful technique that is at the same time simpler to use, leading to more rapid production of programs that are easier to understand and test and therefore more likely to be correct. Some of the most important applications of the DO statement involve the use of subscripted variables, discussed in the next chapter, but there are many other uses. We shall explore the form and usefulness of the DO in several illustrative applications.

The first example is a rewrite of the program of Figure 5.3, in which we produced a short table of the equivalents, in kilometers, of mileages from 1 to 10 in steps of 1.

Basics

Let us begin by examining the general form of the DO statement, which may be written in either of these ways:

$$\text{DO } n \; i = m_1, m_2 \qquad \text{for example:} \quad \text{DO 120 K = 1, 10}$$

or

$$\text{DO } n \; i = m_1, m_2, m_3 \qquad \text{for example:} \quad \text{DO 55 L = 1, N, 2}$$

In these statements n must be a statement number, i must be an integer variable, written without a sign, and m_1, m_2, and m_3, much each be either an unsigned integer constant or an unsigned integer variable. If m_3 is not stated, as in the first form of the statement, it is taken to be 1.

The way we shall use the DO statement, the statement number n will always refer to a CONTINUE statement that appears at some point in the program after the DO. CONTINUE is a dummy statement, which causes no processing action; its sole function is to act as the end of the range of a DO. Strictly speaking, things don't have to be done exactly this way, but this way is simpler to explain and use, and has no important disadvantages.

The action of the DO statement is as follows. The statements between

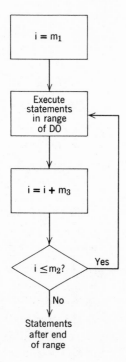

FIGURE 6.1.   Schematic representation of the actions of the
DO statement.

the DO and the CONTINUE, which are called the *range* of the DO, are executed
repeatedly. They are executed first with the *index*, i, equal to m_1. Before each
successive repetition the index is increased by m_3. Repeated execution continues until the range has been executed for the largest value of the index
that does not exceed m_2.

A flowchart representation of the DO

A flowchart of this logic may help to make clearer what this definition means.
See Figure 6.1. It is important to note that the range is executed once regardless of the values of m_1 and m_2. If for some reason, intentional or not, m_2 is
less than m_1, one might think that the logical thing would be for the range
not to be executed at all—but it doesn't work that way.

The miles-to-kilometers table again

Let us now see how the program to produce the miles-to-kilometers conversion table could be written to use the DO effectively, as shown in Figure 6.2.
After writing the column headings in the ordinary way, we come to the statement

```
DO 30 MILES = 1, 10
```

This says to do all the statements from here down to the CONTINUE, which
has the statement number 30, for all values of the integer variable MILES from

```
C A MILES TO KILOMETERS CONVERSION TABLE USING THE DO STATEMENT
C COMPARE WITH FIGURE 5.3
C
C WRITE HEADINGS
C
      WRITE (6, 10)
   10 FORMAT ('1', 'MILES   KILOMETERS'/)
C
C THE FOLLOWING DO GENERATES THE MILES VALUES, FROM 1 TO 10
C
      DO 30 MILES = 1, 10
         XKILOS = 1.6093 * MILES
         WRITE (6, 20) MILES, XKILOS
   20    FORMAT (1X, I4, F10.1)
   30 CONTINUE
      STOP
      END
```

FIGURE 6.2.   A program to convert from miles to kilometers, using the DO statement.

1 to 10, inclusive, in steps of 1. The "in steps of 1" part is implicit in the fact that there is not a third number after the equal sign. The effect is thus just as if we had written

```
DO 30 MILES = 1, 10, 1
```

There are three statements between the DO and the CONTINUE, counting the FORMAT. Notice that these three statements are each indented five spaces. This is done to display the structure of the program more clearly, showing in a graphic way which statements make up the range that is controlled by the DO. This is not required by the rules of Fortran, but is strongly recommended and will always be done in this text.

The first time the range is executed, the value of MILES is 1. This is converted to kilometers and both numbers are printed. Then 1 is added to MILES and a check is made to see if the new value is greater than 10. Since it is not, the range is executed again, causing the printing of 2 MILES and the corresponding value in kilometers. This process is repeated until the range has been executed with MILES equal to 10; now, when 1 is added to MILES, the result is greater than 10 and program execution passes on to the statement following the CONTINUE.

It is instructive to realize that the sequence of operations here, including the incrementing and testing of the MILES variable, is precisely the same as in Figure 5.3. The DO statement takes over the functions of the statement

```
MILES = 1
```

that initializes the loop variable, the statement

```
MILES = MILES + 1
```

that increments it, and the statement

```
IF ( MILES .LE. 10 ) GO TO 20
```

that tests it.

The output of this program is identical with that of Figure 5.4.

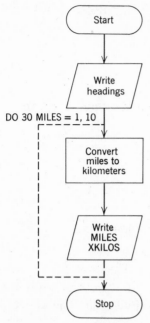

FIGURE 6.3.   A possible flowchart of the actions of the DO
statement in the miles-to-kilometers conversion program.

Flowcharts

There is no suggested symbol for the DO statement actions in the flowcharting standard, so we are left to represent it however seems convenient. In
fact, there is sometimes less occasion to use a flowchart at all, since the purpose and functioning of the program are in some cases quite clear without
using any flowchart. Figure 6.3 shows one way we might indicate the actions of the program just discussed. We see a dotted line used to indicate the
range of the DO, with the DO itself written near the line. A dotted line is also
used between the box at the end of the range and the next box after it, to
indicate that this flow depends on the action of the DO.

To see how the increment (m_3) might need to be something other than
1, let us modify this program so that it carries out the actions of the program of
Figure 5.10, which produces the table shown in Figure 5.12. All that is required is another DO, this time looking like this:

```
DO 40 MILES = 15, 100, 5
```

where 40 is the statement number of another CONTINUE. See Figure 6.4.
Observe that the range of the DO this time includes the assignment statement
that converts from MILES to XKILOS, and a WRITE—but no FORMAT. The
FORMAT referred to by this WRITE is the same one as before. This illustrates that a FORMAT statement need not immediately follow the READ or
WRITE that refers to it, and that more than one READ or WRITE can refer to
the same FORMAT.

Once again, the output of this program is identical to that of the one of
which it represents a simplified version.

```
C A MILES TO KILOMETERS CONVERSION TABLE USING THE DO STATEMENT
C COMPARE WITH FIGURE 5.10
C
C WRITE HEADINGS
C
      WRITE (6, 10)
 10   FORMAT ('1', 'MILES  KILOMETERS'/)
C
C THE FOLLOWING DO GENERATES THE MILES VALUES, FROM 1 TO 10
C
      DO 30 MILES = 1, 10
         XKILOS = 1.6093 * MILES
         WRITE (6, 20) MILES, XKILOS
 20      FORMAT (      I4,      F10.1 )
 30   CONTINUE
C
C THIS DO GENERATES THE MILES VALUES FROM 15 TO 100 IN STEPS OF 5
C
      DO 40 MILES = 15, 100, 5
         XKILOS = 1.6093 * MILES
         WRITE (6, 20) MILES, XKILOS
 40   CONTINUE
      STOP
      END
```

FIGURE 6.4.   A miles-to-kilometers conversion program, using
two DO statements to generate the miles figures in two ranges.

The index of a DO

The index of a DO is strictly limited to an integer variable. Much as we might
often like to be able to do so, it is not possible to write a statement such as

```
DO 100 X = 0.5, 10.0, 0.5
```

Furthermore, the indexing parameters must be either integer constants or
integer variables. We cannot write something like

```
DO 200 J = 1, N+1
```

The latter restriction is fairly readily bypassed by computing the desired
expression in advance:

```
NPLUS1 = N + 1
DO 200 J = 1, NPLUS1
```

The restriction to an integer variable for the index is not so simple to get
around in all situations, but sometimes stratagems can be worked out. Suppose, for example, that we wanted to compute the miles-to-kilometers table
for values from 0.5 to 10.0 in steps of 0.5. This one is easy: let the index run
from 5 to 100 in steps of 5, then before the assignment statement that converts
from miles to kilometers divide the index by 10.0. The complete program, with this modification, is shown in Figure 6.5. It produces the output
in Figure 6.6.

It would have been just as good to write

```
DO 30 INDEX = 1, 20
```

followed by

```
XMILES = INDEX / 2.0
```

which would also generate the values from 0.5 to 10.0 in steps of 0.5.

```
C A MILES TO KILOMETERS CONVERSION TABLE USING THE DO STATEMENT
C MODIFIED VERSION -- GOES FROM 0.5 TO 10.0 IN STEPS OF 0.5
C COMPARE WITH FIGURE 5.3
C
C WRITE HEADINGS
C
      WRITE (6, 10)
  10    FORMAT ('1', 'MILES  KILOMETERS'/)
C
C THIS DO GENERATES AN INDEX FROM 5 TO 100 IN STEPS OF 5
C
      DO 30 INDEX = 5, 100, 5
C
C CONVERT TO MILES, AS A REAL VARIABLE
C
          XMILES = INDEX / 10.0
          XKILOS = 1.6093 * XMILES
          WRITE (6, 20) XMILES, XKILOS
  20        FORMAT (1X,   F4.1,   F10.1 )
  30    CONTINUE
      STOP
      END
```

FIGURE 6.5.   A program illustrating how the DO statement can be used to generate non-integer values.

MILES	KILOMETERS
0.5	0.8
1.0	1.6
1.5	2.4
2.0	3.2
2.5	4.0
3.0	4.8
3.5	5.6
4.0	6.4
4.5	7.2
5.0	8.0
5.5	8.9
6.0	9.7
6.5	10.5
7.0	11.3
7.5	12.1
8.0	12.9
8.5	13.7
9.0	14.5
9.5	15.3
10.0	16.1

FIGURE 6.6   The output of the program of Figure 6.5.

A Compound Interest Calculation

These last programs have involved computations not requiring the reading of data. Let us turn to a realistic application from banking, where a modest amount of data can be used with a DO to produce a fair amount of output.

One card is to be read, containing the following information:

Variable	Variable Name	Columns and Format
Starting deposit	START	1-10, F10.2
Interest rate, in percentage points	PERCNT	11-14, F4.2
Number of years starting deposit is left on deposit	NYEARS	15-16, I2
Number of times per year interest is compounded	NTIMES	17-18, I2

The situation is this. A bank customer places START dollars in a savings account, at PERCNT percent per year, compounded NTIMES per year. We are to compute and print the balance in his account at the end of each year until it has been printed for NYEARS years.

First of all, what is the computation, mathematically? To begin with, PERCNT is stated in percentage points: 6% would be entered as 6.0, for instance. To convert such a number to a decimal fraction it is necessary to divide by 100, getting, for this example, 0.06. If this is added to one, we get a multiplier such as 1.06. The balance at the end of a year at 6% simple interest (compounded once at the end of the year) is then given by multiplying the starting balance by 1.06. Mathematically, this is exactly the same thing as computing 6% of the starting balance and adding it to the starting balance. (Try it on an example, if you're not sure.)

Now suppose that the interest rate is still 6% per year, but compounded semiannually. This means that at the end of *half* the year we add on the interest computed at *half* the rate for the full year, then do the same computation at the end of the year—except that the starting principal for the second computation includes the interest from the first half-year. This is the essence of compound interest, that the depositor earns interest on his interest.

In terms of our example, the balance after computing the interest the first time is just 1.03 times that starting balance (0.03 being half of 0.06), and the balance at the end of the year is just 1.03 times *that*, or 1.03 times 1.03 times the starting deposit. In terms of our problem, where the starting deposit is START and the annual interest is PERCNT, the balance after one year at semiannual compounding would be given by

START $*$ (1.0 + PERCNT/(100.0$*$2.0))$**$2

Let us use this formula as an opportunity to review the meaning of parentheses in arithmetic expressions. The rules say that innermost parentheses dictate what is to be done first. The innermost parentheses here are those enclosing 100.0$*$2.0, which means that we are going to force both items to be in the denominator of a fraction. What we are doing here is to divide the stated interest rate in percentage points, 6% in the example, by 100 to get it in the form of a decimal, i.e., 0.06. But we also want to divide by 2, the number of compoundings per year, to get 0.03 in this case. It is necessary to use parentheses to force both of these numbers (100.0 and 2.0) to be in the denominator when we divide PERCNT by them.

The next set of parentheses, working from the inside out, as always, say that the quotient that results from the division should be added to 1.0, to get 1.03 in our numerical example. What is left is a multiplication (by START) and an exponentiation. Another rule says that exponentiations are done first, so, in the example, 1.03 is raised to the second power, giving 1.0609. Finally, this is multiplied by the starting balance START to get the amount of money after one year, with interest compounded semiannually. Perhaps you can convince yourself, with hand computation if necessary, that the general expression, for NTIMES compoundings per year, is just

```
START * (1.0 + PERCNT/(100.0*NTIMES))**NTIMES
```

What we have here is a formula for finding the balance at the end of a year, given NTIMES compoundings at PERCNT interest. This applies for *any* year. Suppose, for instance, that a depositor places $1000 dollars in a savings account that pays 6% compounded four times a year. Then at the end of the first year he has

$$\$1000 * (1.0 + 6.0/(100.0*4.0))**4 = 1061.36$$

If he simply leaves this amount on deposit, what will he have at the end of rhe second year? Answer:

$$\$1061.36 * (1.0 + 6.0/(100.0*4))**4 = \$1126.49$$

At the end of the third year he would have

$$\$1126.49 * (1.0 + 6.0/(100.0*4.0))**4 = \$1195.62$$

The common factor in all of these expressions is the multiplier

$$(1.0 + PERCNT/(100.0*NTIMES))**NTIMES$$

Taking any starting balance at all, at the end of any year the new balance is to be found by multiplying the starting balance by this multiplier.

A program

All of this is readily embodied in a Fortran program, as shown in Figure 6.7. We read the data and stop on finding a sentinel consisting of a zero interest rate. Then the data values are printed on two lines, using a long FORMAT that provides identifications within the lines. Take a look at the output on the next page to see what this produces. After these routine preliminaries we compute the yearly multiplier, called FACTOR in the program, following the formula developed above. BALNCE will keep the running balance at the end of each year. To start the process, we assign it the value of the starting deposit, START. Now a simple DO loop, running from 1 to NYEARS in steps of 1, controls repetition of the process of multiplying each year's starting balance by the yearly factor to get the balance at the end of the year. Each new balance is printed as it is computed. Note that the DO index is printed along with the balance. Thus we see that the index can be used within the range of the DO for any purpose permitted for an integer variable. This is subject to the important qualification, however, that we must never assign

```
C COMPUTING THE BALANCE IN A SAVINGS ACCOUNT AT COMPOUND INTEREST
C
5       READ (5, 10) START, PERCNT, NYEARS, NTIMES
10      FORMAT (      F10.2, F4.2,    I2,      I2     )
        IF ( PERCNT .EQ. 0.0 ) STOP
        WRITE (6, 20) START, PERCNT, NYEARS, NTIMES
20      FORMAT ('1', F10.2, '  WAS PLACED ON DEPOSIT AT    ', F5.2,
       1  '  PER CENT PER YEAR'/1X, 'FOR', I4, '  YEARS, COMPOUNDED', I4,
       2  '  TIMES PER YEAR.'///)
        FACTOR = (1.0 + PERCNT/(100.0*NTIMES))**NTIMES
        BALNCE = START
        DO 40 I = 1, NYEARS
            BALNCE = FACTOR * BALNCE
            WRITE (6, 30) I, BALNCE
30          FORMAT (1X, 'BALANCE AT END OF YEAR ', I2, ' = ', F10.2)
40      CONTINUE
        GO TO 5
        END
```

FIGURE 6.7. A program using a DO statement to compute compound interest.

a new value to the DO index, which would destroy the function of the DO in controlling loop repetition.

Here are a few representative runs with this program. Observe the testing with a case involving one year and one compounding, the latter reducing to simple interest. It is always a good idea to see if programs containing loops work correctly in extreme cases such as precisely one execution of the range. The grammar here is admittedly not the best ("1.00 per cent per year for 1 years . . .") but presumably this is an uncommon enough situation not to be worth setting up a test and a separate FORMAT to handle it, although that could certainly be done.

Observe in the last example that the results differ by a few pennies from the illustrative values cited earlier. This is the unfortunate consequence of the fact that the Fortran system used does not provide for the rounding of arithmetic results, so that fractions of pennies are simply dropped during the computations. (There are good reasons for designing Fortran this way, but they are too complicated to go into here.) Results are rounded for printing, but this does not change the values retained for further computation. If rounding is essential, it can be programmed.

```
    12345.67  WAS PLACED ON DEPOSIT AT    1.00   PER CENT PER YEAR
    FOR   1  YEARS, COMPOUNDED   1  TIMES PER YEAR.

    BALANCE AT END OF YEAR   1   =     12469.11

     1000.00  WAS PLACED ON DEPOSIT AT    6.00   PER CENT PER YEAR
    FOR  10  YEARS, COMPOUNDED   1  TIMES PER YEAR.

    BALANCE AT END OF YEAR   1   =      1060.00
    BALANCE AT END OF YEAR   2   =      1123.60
    BALANCE AT END OF YEAR   3   =      1191.01
    BALANCE AT END OF YEAR   4   =      1262.47
    BALANCE AT END OF YEAR   5   =      1338.22
    BALANCE AT END OF YEAR   6   =      1418.51
    BALANCE AT END OF YEAR   7   =      1503.62
    BALANCE AT END OF YEAR   8   =      1593.84
    BALANCE AT END OF YEAR   9   =      1689.47
    BALANCE AT END OF YEAR  10   =      1790.84
```

```
    1000.00  WAS  PLACED  ON  DEPOSIT  AT      6.00   PER  CENT  PER  YEAR
 FOR  10   YEARS,  COMPOUNDED    4   TIMES  PER  YEAR.
 BALANCE  AT  END  OF  YEAR    1  =       1061.36
 BALANCE  AT  END  OF  YEAR    2  =       1126.48
 BALANCE  AT  END  OF  YEAR    3  =       1195.60
 BALANCE  AT  END  OF  YEAR    4  =       1268.96
 BALANCE  AT  END  OF  YEAR    5  =       1346.82
 BALANCE  AT  END  OF  YEAR    6  =       1429.46
 BALANCE  AT  END  OF  YEAR    7  =       1517.17
 BALANCE  AT  END  OF  YEAR    8  =       1610.26
 BALANCE  AT  END  OF  YEAR    9  =       1709.06
 BALANCE  AT  END  OF  YEAR   10  =       1813.93
```

Finding the Range of Grades and the Average Grade for an Examination

Here is a realistic example of the use of the DO statement that will let us investigate how one might want the repetition of execution of the range of the DO never to be completed normally.

The situation is this. An instructor has given midterm exams, and when she returns the papers she wants to announce the lowest grade, the highest grade, and the average. She is interested in setting up a general-purpose computer program to do this chore. One of the features it should have is a limit on the number of cards it reads, to guard against mistakes in setting up the deck; it has been decided that for the classes involved a reasonable limit would be 100. To be precise, the program is to process grade cards until finding one having a negative grade, which serves as sentinel; if the program reaches the 101st card and it is not a sentinel, it is to write an error comment and stop. Further, there is to be a check that the first card is not a sentinel, which could also indicate some kind of data preparation or deck make-up error.

The procedure for doing all this is presented in flowchart form in Figure 6.8. Let us attempt to analyze it somewhat as we might think it through in planning.

We know to begin with that we are going to have to take special action for the first data card, to assure ourselves that it is not a sentinel, so the reading of it is not going to be within the DO loop anyway. There will accordingly have to be two READs, one at the very beginning of the program and one within the DO. After the first one it is necessary to test immediately to see if it is a sentinel and if so write an error message and stop. If it is not, we place the grade from that card into the three variables that will be used in getting the lowest, average, and highest grades, namely, SMALL, SUM, and BIG, respectively. What this means is that after reading one card containing one GRADE, the smallest grade we have seen so far is GRADE, the sum of all the grades we have seen so far is GRADE, and the largest grade we have seen so far is also GRADE. If by any chance there is only one data card in the deck prior to the sentinel, the program had better give correct results for such a case. One card doesn't make much sense in this application, but one of the easiest things to do wrong in writing looping programs is to overlook such special cases, and we want to develop good habits.

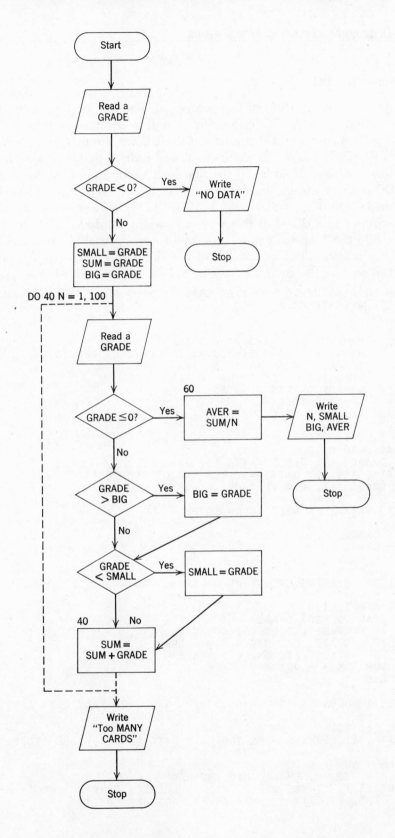

FIGURE 6.8. Flowchart of a procedure for finding statistics about examination grades.

Using the index of a DO

Now we enter the loop portion of the procedure. The DO loop has been indicated by a dotted line. The DO loop index, N, will be used to count the number of data cards. As we enter the range of the DO for the first time, before executing its READ, N has just been set to 1, and indeed that is exactly how many grades we have read so far. If the first card encountered by the READ within the DO is the sentinel, we will immediately get out of the DO loop by the IF, and the value of N at that point will still be 1. We are expressly permitted to jump out of a DO loop this way, and when we do the DO index is available outside the loop for use as a normal integer variable. This can be very useful. Here, we shall use the value of the index in computing the average and in writing the final message as to how many grades there were.

```
C A PROGRAM TO READ UP TO 100 EXAM GRADES, FIND SMALLEST AND LARGEST,
C AND COMPUTE AVERAGE GRADE
C
C VARIABLES
C      GRADE     NAME OF EACH INDIVIDUAL GRADE AS READ
C                NEGATIVE GRADE SERVES AS END-OF-DECK SENTINEL
C      BIG       LARGEST GRADE FOUND SO FAR
C      SMALL     SMALLEST GRADE FOUND SO FAR
C      SUM       SUM OF GRADES READ SO FAR
C      N         DO LOOP INDEX
C      AVERAG    AVERAGE GRADE FOR EXAM
C
       READ (5, 20) GRADE
   20  FORMAT (F10.0)
       IF ( GRADE .LT. 0.0 ) WRITE (6, 30)
   30  FORMAT ('1', 'NO DATA PROVIDED -- JOB STOPPED')
       IF ( GRADE .LT. 0.0 ) STOP
C
C INITIALIZE VARIABLES USED IN DO LOOP
C
       SUM = GRADE
       BIG = GRADE
       SMALL = GRADE
C
C GO INTO LOOP, READING CARDS AND UPDATING VARIABLES
C
       DO 40 N = 1, 100
           READ (5, 20) GRADE
           IF ( GRADE .LT. 0.0 ) GO TO 60
           IF ( GRADE .GT. BIG ) BIG = GRADE
           IF ( GRADE .LT. SMALL ) SMALL = GRADE
           SUM = SUM + GRADE
   40  CONTINUE
C
C IF WE FALL THROUGH END OF RANGE, THERE WERE TOO MANY DATA CARDS
C
       WRITE (6, 50)
   50  FORMAT ('1', 'THERE WERE TOO MANY DATA CARDS -- JOB STOPPED')
       STOP
   60  AVERAG = SUM / N
       WRITE (6, 70) N, SMALL, BIG, AVERAG
   70  FORMAT ('1', 'THERE WERE', I5, ' GRADES, RANGING FROM', F7.1,
      1 ' TO', F7.1/1X ' WITH AN AVERAGE OF', F8.1)
       STOP
       END
```

FIGURE 6.9. A program corresponding to the flowchart of Figure 6.8. Note the listing of variable names and their meanings.

When the DO loop is exited in the normal way, by completing the number of range executions specified in the DO, the index is *not* available, in most compilers. In practice this is no serious limitation, because in such a case we know already from the indexing parameters what the final value of the index must be. In our case we are setting up the DO to be executed exactly 100 times. Remembering that we have already read one card, if the READ within the DO should ever be executed 100 times without detecting a sentinel, then there must have been more than 100 data cards, and something is amiss. The "normal" exit, in this case, will actually be taken only in an error condition. The DO statement with a "normal" error exit is often used this way.

Within the DO, we next make a test for the sentinel. If the data value is negative we use a GO TO to jump completely out of the range of the DO (which stops the action of the DO in the repeating of the range), compute the average, print the results, and stop. If the card is not a sentinel, we need first to see if the grade from it is bigger than BIG. If so, the new grade is larger than any previously encountered, and we want to put it in BIG. This will be easy to do with an IF. Ditto for the smallest so far and SMALL. Next we will need to add this grade to SUM, in preparation for computing the average by dividing the sum of all grades by N, the number of grades. This completes the actions that are carried out repeatedly within the range of the DO.

The actions to be done outside the range of the DO, whether by the "normal" (error) exit, or by transferring out on encountering the sentinel, have already been discussed.

The program

The program is shown in Figure 6.9. Observe the listing of the variable names at the beginning of the program, a documentation practice that has much to recommend it. About the only thing that is not a direct translation of the flowchart is the repetition of the IF that checks whether the first data card is erroneously a sentinel.

Here is a sampling of program output when run with various cases that test all the possible outcomes of the various tests.

```
NO DATA PROVIDED -- JOB STOPPED


THERE WERE    1  GRADES, RANGING FROM  100.0  TO  100.0
   WITH AN AVERAGE OF    100.0


THERE WERE    2  GRADES, RANGING FROM   0.0  TO  100.0
   WITH AN AVERAGE OF     50.0


THERE WERE  100  GRADES, RANGING FROM   0.0  TO   90.0
   WITH AN AVERAGE OF     45.0


THERE WERE TOO MANY DATA CARDS -- JOB STOPPED
```

A Summary of the DO Statement

The DO is so important a feature of the Fortran language, and so widely used in practical applications, that it will be a good idea to summarize its features and the rules governing its use.

The DO statement takes either of these forms:

DO n $i = m_1, m_2$

or

DO n $i = m_1, m_2, m_3$

As we are using it, n must always be the statement number of a CONTINUE. The statements between the DO and the CONTINUE constitute the *range* of the DO. The integer variable i is called the *index* of the DO and m_1, m_2, m_3 are called the *indexing parameters*. If m_3 is not stated, as in the first form of the statement, it is taken as 1. All indexing parameters must be either unsigned integer constants or unsigned integer variables.

The action of the DO is this: the statements in the range are always executed at least once, with i initially set equal to m_1. At the end of each execution of the range m_3 is added to i and the sum compared to m_2; if the newly incremented value of i is less than or equal to m_2 the range i is executed again.

There are two ways by which control can get outside the range of the DO. The *normal exit* occurs when the DO is *satisfied*, that is, at the completion of the number of executions of the range as specified by the indexing parameters. When this happens, control passes to the statement following the CONTINUE, and the value of the index variable is undefined. The other way control can get outside the range is by the execution of a GO TO that transfers completely outside the range of the DO. When this is done, the value of the index variable is defined and may be used however one wishes.

Nothing within the range of a DO is permitted to alter the index variable or any of the indexing parameters.

It is not permissible to transfer from outside the range of a DO to inside the range, without first executing the DO statement itself, with one exception. We are permitted to execute a GO TO that transfers completely outside the range of a DO, perform any desired operations that do not alter the index or the indexing parameters, then transfer back into the range of the DO. We shall have no occasion to use this feature, and its use is to be discouraged.

REVIEW QUESTIONS

1. How many times would the range of the DO be executed in each of the following cases?

   a. DO 50 K = 1, 9

   b. DO 50 K = 1, 9, 2

   c. DO 50 K = 1, 1

d. DO 50 K = 10, 20, 2

e. DO 50 K = 1, 1, 2

f. DO 50 K = 2, 1

2. What will this program fragment do?

```
      NSUM = 0
      DO 100 J = 1, 15
          NSUM = NSUM + J
100   CONTINUE
```

3. What will this program fragment do?

```
      NSUM = 0
      DO 110 N = 1, 21, 2
          NSUM = NSUM + N**2
110   CONTINUE
```

4. What will this program fragment do?

```
      NUMBER = 157
      DO 40 N = 3, 77, 2
          IF ( NUMBER .EQ. N*(NUMBER/N) ) GO TO 60
40    CONTINUE
      WRITE (6, 50)
50    FORMAT (1X, 'NUMBER IS PRIME')
      STOP
60    WRITE (6, 70)
70    FORMAT (1X, 'NUMBER IS NOT PRIME')
```

5. What will this DO do?

```
      SUM = 0.0
      DO 10 K = 1, 20
          READ (5, 5) X
5         FORMAT (F10.0)
          SUM = SUM + X
10    CONTINUE
      WRITE (6, 20) SUM
20    FORMAT (1X, F12.4)
      STOP
      END
```

6. In the program of Figure 6.5, suppose integer arithmetic had been used, in the statement

XMILES = INDEX / 10

What would the output have been?

7. Identify an error in each of the following DO statements.

DO 20 X = 1.0, 10.0, 0.5

DO 20 K = -10, +10, 2

DO 20 K = 10, 1, -1

DO 20 K = 1, 2*N+1

DO 20 N = 1, 100 WHILE (GRADE .GE. 0.0)

8. Show how to do all the things in Question 7 that we wish we could do, but are not possible directly in Fortran. In other words, find an indirect way in each case.

9. The program that follows is intended to read a number N and compute its factorial. (The factorial of a number N, written $N!$, is the product of all numbers from 1 up to and including the number. (Thus, $1! = 1 \cdot 1 = 1, 2! = 1 \cdot 2 = 2, 3! = 1 \cdot 2 \cdot 3 = 6, 4! = 1 \cdot 2 \cdot 3 \cdot 4 = 24$, etc.) The program is set up using a DO loop containing the entire program, with an index that allows up to 500 numbers to be entered, checking each for a value less than 1 as a sentinel. This makes it possible to write the program without a GO TO, so that the entire program can be read straight through from top to bottom without ever having to trace through any flow of control that goes backwards through the program. This latter is one aspect of what is called *structured programming*, which holds great promise of converting programming from a hit-or-miss craft into an engineering science. Unfortunately, structured programming is difficult in Fortran for lack of certain language features, but steps in the right direction should be taken when possible.

Does the program do what it is claimed to do? Do you see any limitations to it? Zero factorial is defined to be 1; could you modify the program so that it would handle this case?

```
C PROGRAM FOR REVIEW QUESTION 9
C
      DO 40 NDUMMY = 1, 500
         READ (5, 10) N
10       FORMAT (I2)
         IF ( N .LT. 1 ) STOP
         NFACT = 1
         DO 20 K = 1, N
            NFACT = NFACT * K
20       CONTINUE
         WRITE (6, 30) N, NFACT
30       FORMAT (1X, I4, I14)
40    CONTINUE
      END
```

10. It is shown in economics texts[1] that if banks are permitted to loan out 80% of the money they have on deposit, in an endless chain of one bank lending to another indefinitely, then an initial deposit of $1000 in one bank becomes a theoretical total of $5000 of deposits through the entire banking system. The formula is

$$\$1000 + \$800 + \$640 + \ldots = \$1000 \, (1 + 4/5 + (4/5)^2 + (4/5)^3 + \ldots)$$

$$= \$1000 \left(\frac{1}{1 - 4/5}\right) = \$1000 \times 5 = \$5000$$

An economics student decided to write a program using a DO loop to satisfy his curiosity whether a reasonably large number of terms of the infinite series in parentheses do add up to something close to 5. His first program worked by starting a variable named SUM at 1.0, then adding to it repeatedly the fraction 0.8, raised to a power provided by the index of a DO that runs from 1 to 30. Here is the program:

```
C THE CREATION OF DEPOSITS IN BANKING
C A NUMERICAL CHECK OF THE EQUILIBRIUM FORMULA
C
      SUM = 1.0
      DO 10 K = 1, 30
         SUM = SUM + 0.8**K
```

[1] See, for example, Paul A. Samuelson, *Economics*, ninth edition, New York, McGraw-Hill, 1973, page 305.

```
10      CONTINUE
        WRITE (6, 20) SUM
20      FORMAT (1X, F10.5)
        STOP
        END
```

When he ran it, the output was 4.99503, which is convincingly close to 5.

Now our ambitious student started thinking. "This program is pretty wasteful. Consider that when I have just computed 0.8 raised to the 23rd power, say, I could get 0.8 raised to the 24th power simply by multiplying by the previous result 0.8, thus saving a lot of computing in raising 0.8 to all the large powers. Why not start a variable named TERM at 0.8, add it to SUM repeatedly, and each time through the loop simply multiply TERM by 0.8?" Here is the program he wrote on this logic:

```
C THE CREATION OF DEPOSITS IN BANKING
C A NUMERICAL CHECK OF THE EQUILIBRIUM FORMULA
C AN 'IMPROVED' VERSION THAT HAS AN ERROR
C
        SUM = 1.0
        TERM = 0.8
        DO 10 K = 1, 30
             TERM = 0.8 * TERM
             SUM = SUM + TERM
10      CONTINUE
        WRITE (6, 20) SUM
20      FORMAT (1X, F10.5)
        STOP
        END
```

Unfortunately, the output was 4.19602. What happened?

11. A student needed to write a program that would run a variable named X through all values from 0.01 to 1.00 in steps of 0.01. He had in mind to use these values in a computation that we shall not show. Here in his first version, minus the usage to which the value of X would have been put within the range of the DO:

```
C A PROGRAM FOR REVIEW QUESTION 11
C ADDING 0.01 TO A COUNTER 100 TIMES
C
        X = 0.0
        DO 10 L = 1, 100
             X = X + 0.01
10      CONTINUE
        WRITE (6, 20) X
20      FORMAT (1X, F10.6)
        STOP
        END
```

The output printed was 0.999999.

We seem to have the very strange result that adding 0.01 to itself 100 times does not give 1.0. Is not 100.0*0.01 = 1.00? Can you explain this behavior? Can you suggest a solution?

ANSWERS

1. a. 9, with K equal to 1, 2, 3, 4, 5, 6, 7, 8, and 9.
   b. 5, with K equal to 1, 3, 5, 7, and 9.

    c. Once, with K equal to 1.

    d. 6, with K equal to 10, 12, 14, 16, 18, and 20.

    e. Once, with K equal to 1.

    f. Once, with K equal to 2. We might prefer a diagnostic error indication here, but most Fortran systems will not give one.

2. The program forms in NSUM the sum of the integers from 1 to 15.

3. The program forms in NSUM the sum of the squares of the odd integers from 1 to 21.

4. The program establishes whether or not 157 is a prime number, a prime number being one that has no divisors except 1 and itself. It depends for its operation on the fact that integer division in Fortran does not round, so that the quantity

```
N * (NUMBER/N)
```

will be equal to NUMBER only if N is an exact divisor of NUMBER.

5. The program reads 20 cards and adds the values in columns 1-10 from all of them, then prints the sum.

6. Integer division would have been used, since there would be no real quantities to force the arithmetic to be real. Remembering that integer division does not round, the successive values of XMILES would have been 0, 1, 1, 2, 2, 3, 3, etc., up to 9, 9, 10. To avoid this erroneous result it is necessary either to use mixed-mode arithmetic or, and probably better, convert the DO index to real form before using it:

```
RINDEX = INDEX
XMILES = RINDEX / 10.0
```

7. All of these errors involve things we could wish to be able to do, that have to be obtained in other ways in Fortran.

    a. The index of a DO must be an integer variable.

    b. The indexing parameters must be written without signs, and if they are variables their values must be greater than zero.

    c. Ditto.

    d. Generalized expressions are not permitted in place of the indexing parameters.

    e. Oops! This is not Fortran at all, but PL/I, where it would call for a Fortran-type indexing through values of N from 1 to 100, but with the variable GRADE tested before every execution of the range. *Very* useful.

8. a.
```
  DO 20 K = 10, 100, 5
        X = K/10.0
        ...
20    CONTINUE
```

  b.
```
  DO 20 K = 2, 22, 2
        KK = K - 12
        ...
20    CONTINUE
```

  c.
```
  DO 20 KK = 1, 10
        K = 11 - KK
        ...
20    CONTINUE
```

```
  d. LIMIT = 2*N+1
     DO 20 K = 1, LIMIT
        ...
20   CONTINUE

  e. DO 20 N = 1, 100
        IF ( GRADE .LT. 0.0 ) GO TO 30
        ...
20   CONTINUE
30   ...
```

9. The program performs as advertised until it runs out of space in the storage for an integer variable value when we try to compute a factorial for any number larger than 12. This limit depends strongly on the computer used; some machines allow larger integers than this and some smaller. The output from one computer for all the integers from 1 to 20 looked like this:

```
 1              1
 2              2
 3              6
 4             24
 5            120
 6            720
 7           5040
 8          40320
 9         362880
10        3628800
11       39916800
12      479001600
13     1932053504
14     1278945280
15     2004310016
16     2004189184
17     -288522240
18     -898433024
19      109641728
20    -2102132736
```

It is worth pondering that no warning was given when we exceeded the size permitted for the value of an integer variable in the computer used (an IBM System/360); this is something to think about, for if the erroneous values were concealed as intermediate variables we might never realize that anything had gone amiss. The precise point at which the program breaks down depends heavily, of course, on the maximum size permitted of an integer variable in the computer used. Other machines have different limits.

10. The modified program computes the new TERM before adding its initial value to SUM. The term for 0.8 is therefore never added in, and indeed, the result is low by about that amount. (The reason it isn't *exactly* 0.8 less is a matter of rounding and the approximation of fractions.)

   The solution, in this case, is to reverse the order of the assignment statements for TERM and SUM.

11. The computer does not represent real numbers in decimal form, but in hexadecimal (base 16). All computers in the IBM System/360 and System/370 are of this type, as are some others. In hexadecimal there is no exact representation of decimal 0.01, which is one-hundredth, just as in decimal there is no exact representation of the fraction one-third. The constant 0.01 used in the program therefore contains a small error, which accumulates when it is added to X 100 times.

The solution, in this case, is to use the index of the DO and convert it to the desired form, as in this program:

```
C ANSWER PROGRAM FOR REVIEW QUESTION 11
C RUNNING A VARIABLE FROM 0.01 TO 1.00 WITHOUT ROUNDOFF ERRORS
C
      DO 10 I = 1, 100
          X = I / 100.0
   10    CONTINUE
         WRITE (6, 20) X
   20    FORMAT (1X, F10.6)
         STOP
         END
```

Naturally, if you do not use mixed mode, it would be necessary to replace the statement

```
      X = I / 100.0
```

with the two statements

```
      AI = I
      X = AI/100.0
```

(or whatever other intermediate variable name you like) but that is always true. The output this time was 1.000000. This is not to say that the result of the division will always be exact. *But this error does not accumulate,* and therefore remains small.

EXERCISES

*1. Write a program that will print the integers from 1 to 40, one to a line. There will be no input.

2. Write a program that will read an integer from a card (columns 1-3). If the number is greater than 200, stop program execution. Otherwise print all the integers from 1 up to and including the number read.

*3. Write a program fragment, consisting of a DO and any other statements that may be required, to do the following.
   a. A DO range is to be executed $N+3$ times, where N has already been computed by the program.
   b. A DO range is to be executed N^2 times, N given.
   c. A program fragment is to be executed 12 times, with a variable running from 0 to 11.
   d. A program fragment is to be executed for all values of Y from 0.1 to 10.0 in steps of 0.1.

4. Write a program fragment, consisting of a DO and any other statements that may be required, to do the following.
   a. A DO range is to be executed $N - 3$ times, N given. If $N - 3$ is not greater than zero, stop program execution.
   b. A DO range is to be executed $N^2 + N$ times, N given. If $N^2 + N$ is greater than 100, stop program execution.

c. A program fragment is to be executed 31 times, with an integer variable running from 33 down through 3.

d. A program fragment is to be executed for all values of Y from 5.0 to 50.0 in steps of 5.0.

*5. Write a program that will produce a conversion table from temperatures in Centigrade degrees to Fahrenheit, according to the formula from Chapter 1:

$$F = 1.8 \ C + 32.0$$

for all Centigrade temperatures from 0 to 100 in steps of 1 degree. There will be no input to the program.

6. Write a program that reads a card giving two integer values in columns 1-3 and 4-6. These are to be the beginning and ending temperatures for a conversion table like that of the previous exercise. Make a test that the first number is actually less than the second before proceeding, and determine that the difference between the two is not greater than 200; stop program execution if the data fails either test.

*7. Write a program to print 20 lines, each line giving one of the numbers from 1 to 20, together with its square root.

8. Write a program to print 20 lines, each line giving one of the integers from 50 to 69, together with its square and square root.

*9. Write a program to read a deck of cards, each card containing a real quantity in columns 1-8. Print a line giving the quantity for all cards in which the number read is greater than 100.

10. Extend the program of Exercise 9 so that it prints a total of the amounts printed. (This means not to include in the total the data values of 100 or less.)

*11. Modify the program of Figure 6.9 so that it ignores any grades under 40 or over 100, and counts the number of such erroneous data points. The program should not, of course, include these error values in computing the average.

12. Modify the program of Figure 6.4 so that the table is extended to include all mileages from 110 to 300 in steps of 10 miles.

*13. Write a program that will read exactly 21 cards, taking the number in columns 1-5 as an integer. Print each of the 21 numbers, one number per line.

14. Modify the program of Exercise 13 so that the program expects the 21st card to be a sentinel consisting of a negative integer on the card. If there are not exactly 21 cards, counting the sentinel, write an error message.

*15. Modify the program of Exercise 14 so that it prints the total of all the numbers at the end of the listing of the individual numbers.

16. Modify the program of Exercise 15 so that it will deal correctly with any number of cards followed by a sentinel.

*17. Modify the program of Exercise 16 so that along with each number as read from a card it prints the item number, which you can get from the index of a DO.

18. Modify the program of Exercise 17 so that along with the item numbers,

the integers as read, and the total of all the numbers, it prints the average of all the numbers. Convert the total and the number of lines to real form before doing the division, to avoid the problems of integer division.

*19. Write a program that will print two columns of numbers. The item in the left column is to be a line count, obtained from the DO index, and the item in the right column should be the square of the line number. There is no input to be read.

20. Following the outline of Exercise 7, have the program print $N^2 + N$ in the right column, where N is the line number.

*21. A deck of cards is punched with a real number in columns 1-8, with a decimal point. The numbers should be all positive except for a zero sentinel, but it is thought that there may be quite a few error cards with negative numbers on them. Write a program that will read such a deck and print all the positive numbers together with the card numbers from which they came. Upon detecting the sentinel, print a count of the number of error cards.

22. Modify the program of Exercise 21 as follows. The number from every card (except the sentinel) is to be printed: every line should have a line number, with the negative numbers printed in a middle column and the positive ones in a right-hand column.

*23. Write a program that will read a card containing an integer in the range of 2 to 20; call the number N. Then use a DO loop to produce the sum of the squares of the integers from 1 to N. Also compute the quantity $(N^2 + N)/2$ and print it. The complete output of the program is to be these two numbers, which ought to be equal. Use integer arithmetic throughout.

24. Modify the program of Exercise 23 so that for each integer K, from 1 to N, the program prints the quantity $(K^2 + K)/2$ on a line, preceded by K. (Each line will then give the sum of the squares of the integers from 1 to K.)

*25. Write a program that will read a deck of cards, getting from each a real number in columns 2-9, punched with a decimal point. Print one line giving the value of the largest element in the deck, together with its sequence number.

26. Write a program that will read a card containing a starting balance in a savings account, START, together with a number NTIMES that says how many times a year the interest is compounded. The program should compute and print the balance at the end of one year, for all interest rates from 4.0 to 8.0 in steps of 0.1.

CHAPTER SEVEN
SUBSCRIPTED VARIABLES

We have now learned a good deal about how to make effective use of a computer in solving practical problems. But there is another whole class of problems that we need new tools for, and that class consists of applications where many data values need to be referred to by one general name rather than giving each one a distinct name. The major example in this chapter, for instance, will be an extension of the program of the previous chapter for computing summary statistics on an examination, except that this time we shall be adding a feature that requires having the complete list of up to 100 grades in the computer at once, each individually accessible. What are we to do? Give them 100 different names, like GR1, GR2, etc? This would be not only time-consuming, boring, and error-prone but it would make the processing we shall want to do extremely cumbersome.

Subscripted variables help solve this problem, as well as being of great importance in many computer applications. Using a subscripted variable it is possible to give one name to the whole collection of data; there is a subscripted variable called GRADE in the example that follows. Then, to indicate to Fortran which one of the various grades we want in a particular case, we follow the name with parentheses enclosing a subscript expression. For example, suppose that 100 grades have already been assigned as the 100 values of the subscripted variable GRADE. Then if we want the first of them assigned to the variable named START we can write:

```
START = GRADE(1)
```

Or if N has been given any value between 1 and 100, the corresponding grade can be added to the current value of SUM and the total placed back in SUM by

```
SUM = SUM + GRADE(N)
```

Or if we wanted to replace the second grade by the average of the first, second, and third:

```
GRADE(2) = ( GRADE(1) + GRADE(2) + GRADE(3) ) / 3.0
```

The DIMENSION statement

Fortran has to be told, somehow, that when we write "GRADE" in this kind of situation, we don't mean just one number as heretofore, but rather a whole collection of numbers. Furthermore, Fortran has to be told *how many* different values are involved. The answer to these needs is the DIMENSION statement, in which we list each subscripted variable name together with the number of elements that it has, like this:

```
DIMENSION GRADE (101)
```

If there are several subscripted variables, they may all be listed in one DIMENSION, or there may be several DIMENSION statements, as one may wish. It makes no difference to Fortran whether one writes

```
DIMENSION CAT(10), DOG(12), SAM(500)
```

or

```
DIMENSION CAT(10)
DIMENSION SAM(500), DOG(12)
```

or however else the programmer wishes.

A Few Simple Rules

Before moving on to some examples of complete programs utilizing subscripted variables, let us pause to assemble the facts we need.

1. Every subscripted variable must appear in a DIMENSION statement, and the DIMENSION statement(s) must appear before the first executable statement of the program. (The DIMENSION, FORMAT, and certain other statements are said to be *nonexecutable* because they provide information about the program or data, rather than themselves calling for processing actions as the executable statements do.)

The DIMENSION statement informs the Fortran compiler that the variables named in it are subscripted and, for each, gives the maximum size of the subscript.

2. Subscripts must be integer-valued expressions. Most Fortran systems permit integer expressions of any type, including other subscripted variables. The American National Standard, however, specifies that variables appearing in a subscript expression must not themselves be subscripted, and furthermore limits the expressions to the following forms:

General Form	Example
Constant	12
Variable	KODE
Variable ± constant	N+1
Constant * variable	2*LIMIT
Constant * variable ± constant	3*M - 2

If one is working with a Fortran system that does not permit the extended forms of subscript expression, or if one is concerned that programs be "portable" (usable on other systems), then the rules above must of course be followed. Situations that would otherwise violate these rules can always be handled by computing the desired subscript expression in a separate assignment statement before using it, like this:

```
K = M*N(3) + 2*L
SAM = 2.0 * VALUE(K)
```

3. The value of a subscript expression must never be less than 1, nor greater than the size specified for that subscript in the DIMENSION statement. That is, if the DIMENSION statement said that X was a one-dimensional subscripted variable with 100 elements, we must never write a statement containing X(101), or X(N) where N has a value less than 1 or greater than 100. Some Fortran systems, notably WATFIV, will diagnose such errors, but many Fortrans will not, and the trouble caused can be exquisite.

4. A subscripted variable may be either real or integer, but all elements must be of the same type. The initial-letter naming rule applies to subscripted variables just as to nonsubscripted variables.

5. Any one name may be used either for a subscripted or a nonsubscripted variable, but not both within the same program.

The Exam Grades Again

Recall the major example of the previous chapter, where an instructor wanted to find the lowest, average, and highest out of a set of examination grades. As our major example in this chapter we shall add a new requirement for that program, namely, it is also to produce the *median* grade. The median of a set of numbers is the value that divides the set into two parts, half of which are smaller and half of which are larger. Putting it another way, if the individual grades are arranged into increasing sequence, the median is the value of the middle grade if N is odd and lies midway between the two middle grades if N is even.

Once the exam grades are in ascending sequence and once we know how many of them there are, it is not too much trouble to find the median. The first problem in modifying the program is that the grades as they appear in the input deck are not in sequence, and the second is that we do not know how many of them there are. This means that it is impossible to get the median until all the grades have been read and arranged into sequence, which in turn means that the grades must all be stored within the computer. The only feasible way to do this is with a subscripted variable, since the alternative of assigning up to 100 distinct names to the (potentially) 100 grades would be impossibly cumbersome.

The first chore we will need to do in the program will be to read the exam grades and to determine how many of them there are, as before, checking to be sure there are not more than 100 grades. Recall that at the end of the grade cards there is a sentinel card containing a negative score. Since we are going to read the grades directly into the array that will hold them for later processing, we shall have to allow space for the sentinel. This means that the array for the grades will have 101 elements even though the maximum legitimate number of grades is 100. (This is by no means the only way to do the job, of course, but it is a reasonably simple way that works.) The first thing in our program will accordingly be a statement

```
DIMENSION GRADE(101)
```

Now consider that we must still compute the average, which requires adding up all the individual scores. This can be done as the cards are read or at some later time; it is a trifle easier to do it as they are being read, which saves setting up a separate DO loop for the adding. Therefore, before going into the reading loop, it will be necessary to initialize the variable SUM where the total of all grades will be accumulated:

```
SUM = 0.0
```

A DO statement gets right into the working of reading the cards, with the DO being used this time both to check for too many cards and to produce the subscript that controls assignment of the grades to the successive elements of the array GRADE:

```
DO 20 INDEX = 1, 101
```

The integer variable INDEX can now be used to control assignment of the exam grades to the successive elements of the array GRADE, starting with 1 and running up through 101 if there are that many:

```
      READ (5, 10) GRADE(INDEX)
10    FORMAT (F10.0)
```

As each grade is read, it can be checked to see if it is a negative value signifying a sentinel, which means that the previous card held the last valid grade:

```
IF ( GRADE(INDEX) .LT. 0.0 ) GO TO 40
```

Finally, for the last action within the reading loop, the grade can be added to the total of all grades:

```
SUM = SUM + GRADE(INDEX)
```

The first part of the program, putting it all in one place, now looks like this:

```
      DIMENSION GRADE (101)
      SUM = 0.0
      DO 20 INDEX = 1, 101
          READ (5, 10) GRADE(INDEX)
10        FORMAT (F10.0)
          IF ( GRADE(INDEX) .LT. 0.0 ) GO TO 40
          SUM = SUM + GRADE(INDEX)
20    CONTINUE
```

As in the program of Figure 6.9 the normal exit from the DO is an error exit, requiring the writing of an error message. This will be shown in the final program.

With all the grades read into the array named GRADE, where are we? Since the last card read must have been a sentinel, that negative value is in place in the GRADE array, at element number INDEX; INDEX has a value equal to the number of cards, including the sentinel. We have no interest in the sentinel itself, certainly, and so we need to subtract 1 from the value of INDEX and give this value to a variable named N. After doing that it is necessary to establish that there were at least two grades, or else the actions that are to be carried out next make no sense at all.

The grades are now all in GRADE, and the value of N tells how many of them there are. The next task is to get them into ascending sequence, an operation that occurs frequently in data processing, and which generally goes by the name of *sorting*. There are many ways to do the job, as there has been a great deal of research into methods that are faster or use less storage or take advantage of special characteristics of the data sorted. Here we shall use about the simplest way known which, unfortunately, is also among the least efficient.

The process begins with the notion that what we want to do first is to get the smallest grade in the whole array into the first position. This can be done by systematically comparing the value in GRADE (1) to see if it is larger than the one with which it is being compared. Consider this DO loop:

```
DO 50 J = 2, N
      IF ( GRADE(1) .LE. GRADE(J) ) GO TO 50
          TEMP = GRADE(1)
          GRADE(1) = GRADE(J)
          GRADE(J) = TEMP
  50    CONTINUE
```

The DO statement makes the integer variable J run through all the values from 2 to N in steps of 1, where N is the number of grades in GRADE. (Elements in GRADE beyond element N are of no interest to us.) For each value of J, the IF statement makes a comparison between element 1 and element J: if element 1 is less than or equal to element J, that is, if those two are already relatively in correct position in the array, a jump is made to the CONTINUE, around the intervening three statements. These three statements, if they are executed, result in interchanging elements 1 and J. The first statement moves the first element to a temporary storage location (TEMP), the second moves the Jth element to the first element, and the third statement moves the former first element (now in TEMP) to the location previously occupied by element J. (Study the action of these three statements with examples to make sure you understand them.)

When the range of this DO is first executed, it compares elements 1 and 2 and interchanges them if necessary. The second time the range is executed it compares the first and third elements and interchanges them if necessary. Naturally, if there was an interchange on the first execution of the range, what is now in the first position may be what was initially in the second position—but the program cares not. Likewise for the first and fourth, first and fifth, . . . , up to the first and Nth (last). In sum: the occupant of the first position—which may change from time to time—is compared with every other element in the array, interchanging whenever it is found that the first element is not smaller. Net result of the entire loop: at the end, the first position, that is, GRADE(1), *must* contain the smallest element in the entire array.

Good. What next? Well, it would seem reasonable now to make sure that the second element in the array contains the smallest of all the elements other than the first. This could be done in a very straightforward way by a separate DO loop just like the previous one, with the index running from 3 up through N, which would compare the second element with all following, interchanging as necessary. Then we would need another DO loop, with its index running from 4 up through N, to get the next larger element in the third position, etc., but this isn't the way to do things! The pattern here is so regular that we should recognize the opportunity to use a DO loop to generate it.

What we seem to need is an outer loop to contain the one just studied.

The index of this new outer loop would need to run from 1 up through $N-1$; this index points to the element that is currently being compared with all the elements below it in the list. Now, the index of the inner loop needs to start at one more than the index of the outer loop, and run up through N.

Remembering that the indexing parameters of a DO can only be single integer constants or variables, it will be necessary to compute the expressions $I+1$ and $N-1$ in separate assignment statements prior to the DO statements. The complete sorting routine looks like this:

```
      NM1 = N - 1
      DO 60 I = 1, NM1
         IPLUS1 = I + 1
         DO 50 J = IPLUS1, N
            IF ( GRADE(I) .LE. GRADE(J) ) GO TO 50
               TEMP = GRADE(I)
               GRADE(I) = GRADE(J)
               GRADE(J) = TEMP
50       CONTINUE
60    CONTINUE
```

Comparing this segment with what we had before, we see that the constant subscript 1 before has become the variable subscript I, and that the inner loop runs from $I+1$ to N where the earlier loop ran from 2 to N.

Let us take a small example and see how this sorting method works out. Suppose there are five grades, initially in this order:

70 80 60 90 50

The 70 and the 80 are compared, and do not have to be interchanged. The 70 and 60 are compared and are interchanged:

60 80 70 90 50

60 and 90 do not have to be interchanged, but 60 and 50 do:

50 80 70 90 60

The smallest grade is now in the first element position. 80 and 70 are now compared and interchanged:

50 70 80 90 60

70 and 90 are alright, but 70 and 60 have to be interchanged:

50 60 80 90 70

The second smallest grade is now in the second position. Now 80 and 90 are compared and left alone, then 80 and 70 move:

50 60 70 90 80

Finally, the 90 and 80 are compared and interchanged:

50 60 70 80 90

Observe that there was considerable moving of items, sometimes wastefully. The 70, for instance, was in its correct final location after one interchange, but got moved three more times before the process was done.

This method, which is called *interchange sorting*, for fairly obvious reasons, is by no means the most efficient method known, but it is one of the simplest to program. For small files this programming simplicity can be more

---

Read cards, looking for sentinel;
   sum grades

If more than 101 cards, write
   error message and stop

On sentinel: Sort grades

Compute average = sum / N

Find median = average of
   2 middle grades

If N odd, recompute median
   = middle grade

FIGURE 7.1.   A flowchart of a procedure for finding statistics
about examination grades, including the median grade.

important than the amount of comparison and data movement required. (A
complete treatment of computer sorting methods fills a large book.[1])

This whole procedure is based on the assumption that there are at least
two elements in the array, which is an entirely reasonable assumption for
the task. It would be a good idea to insert a test in the program to be sure
that at least two grades are read.

With the grades sorted into ascending sequence it is a reasonably simple
matter to get the mean and median. The mean is just the sum of the grades
divided by N, as always. The median is a little more complicated, because
we have to distinguish between the cases for N odd and N even. If N is odd,
the median is just the middle grade; the middle grade is the one having the
number N/2 + 1, remembering that integer division truncates. For example:
7 divided by 2, using integer division, is 3; the remainder of 1 is simply
dropped. If N is even, then the median is the average of the two middle
elements, which are those having element numbers of N/2 and N/2 + 1.
Finally, how can the program tell whether N is odd or even? There are a
number of ways to accomplish this. One easy way is to compare N with two
times the integer quotient N/2. If N is even, N/2 is exactly half of N since
there was no remainder to be dropped in the integer division. But if N is
odd the integer quotient N/2 is *not* half of N.

From a programming standpoint the simplest procedure is to assume
that N is even, compute the median accordingly, then recompute it if a test
shows that in fact N is odd.

Now that we have developed the logic of the algorithm that will be
used, essentially in the form of program segments that can be put together
into a complete program, there is not much need for a flowchart, unless it
is felt necessary for documentation and communication. The latter is enough
of a reason, of course, but this time let us display a rather different form of
flowchart, as shown in Figure 7.1. Observe that the notation is a mixture of
ordinary English combined with any fragments of Fortran notation that are
convenient. Furthermore, any processing actions that we understand without
charting in detail are described at a broader level. The phrase "sort grades"

[1] The standard reference is Donald E. Knuth, *The Art of Computer Programming*, Volume 3:
Sorting and Searching. Reading, Massachusetts, Addison-Wesley, 1973.

```
C A PROGRAM TO READ UP TO 100 EXAM GRADES AND FIND SMALLEST, LARGEST,
C MEAN (AVERAGE), AND MEDIAN (THE GRADE THAT DIVIDES THE CLASS
C INTO TWO GROUPS, HALF WITH HIGHER GRADES AND HALF WITH LOWER)
C
C USES SUBSCRIPTING AND THE DO STATEMENT IN A SORTING ROUTINE
C
C VARIABLES
C     GRADE     AN ARRAY OF 101 ELEMENTS TO HOLD GRADES AND SENTINEL
C     SUM       SUM OF GRADES READ SO FAR
C     INDEX     READING LOOP INDEX
C     N         NUMBER OF GRADES, = 1 LESS THAN NUMBER OF CARDS READ
C     I         OUTER SORTING LOOP INDEX
C     NM1       N - 1: OUTER LOOP INDEXING PARAMETER
C     J         INNER LOOP INDEX
C     IPLUS1    I + 1: INNER LOOP INDEXING PARAMETER
C     TEMP      TEMPORARY STORAGE DURING SORTING
C     AVERAG    AVERAGE (MEAN)
C     NMED      ELEMENT NUMBER OF MEDIAN
C               HANDLED DIFFERENTLY FOR ODD AND EVEN N; SEE TEXT
C
      DIMENSION GRADE(101)
      SUM = 0.0
      DO 20 INDEX = 1, 101
          READ (5, 10) GRADE(INDEX)
   10     FORMAT (F10.0)
          IF ( GRADE(INDEX) .LT. 0.0 ) GO TO 40
          SUM = SUM + GRADE(INDEX)
   20 CONTINUE
C
C IF WE FALL THROUGH END OF RANGE, THERE WERE TOO MANY DATA CARDS
C
      WRITE (6, 30)
   30 FORMAT ('1', 'THERE WERE TOO MANY DATA CARDS -- JOB STOPPED')
      STOP
C
C SORT THE GRADES INTO ASCENDING SEQUENCE
C FIRST SUBTRACT 1 FROM DO INDEX, SINCE IT COUNTED THE SENTINEL
C
   40 N = INDEX - 1
C
C BE SURE THERE WERE AT LEAST TWO GRADES, OR SORT ROUTINE FAILS
C
      IF ( N .LT. 2 ) WRITE (6, 45)
   45 FORMAT ('1', 'NOT ENOUGH DATA -- JOB STOPPED')
      IF ( N .LT. 2 ) STOP
      NM1 = N - 1
      DO 60 I = 1, NM1
          IPLUS1 = I + 1
          DO 50 J = IPLUS1, N
              IF ( GRADE(I) .LE. GRADE(J) ) GO TO 50
                  TEMP = GRADE(I)
                  GRADE(I) = GRADE(J)
                  GRADE(J) = TEMP
   50     CONTINUE
   60 CONTINUE
C
C GET MEAN AND MEDIAN
C
      AVERAG = SUM / N
      NMED = N/2
      XMED = ( GRADE(NMED) + GRADE(NMED+1) ) / 2.0
C
C REVISE IF N ODD, WHICH WILL BE SHOWN IF 2 TIMES NMED NOT EQUAL TO N
C
      IF ( 2*NMED .NE. N ) XMED = GRADE(NMED+1)
      WRITE (6, 70) N, GRADE(1), GRADE(N), AVERAG, XMED
   70 FORMAT ('1', 'THERE WERE', I5, '  GRADES, RANGING FROM', F7.1,
     1    '   TO', F7.1/1X, 'WITH A MEAN OF', F7.1,
     2    '   AND A MEDIAN OF', F7.1)
      STOP
      END
```

FIGURE 7.2. A program corresponding to the flowchart of
Figure 7.1, for finding statistics about examination grades.

corresponds to ten statements in the final program, but at the level of detail desired to show the overall flow of the processing, this description is perfectly adequate. If, on the other hand, one needed to emphasize the method by which the sorting is to be done, a more detailed flowchart of the sorting could of course be developed.

There is considerable debate in the programming field about how flowcharts can best be drawn to be most useful, and whether in fact they are needed at all if programs are written properly. It is very important to realize that this "looser" flowcharting style is feasible only if the algorithm logic avoids almost all situations that in a program would require the GO TO statement. Otherwise the tangle of flow lines going in all directions pretty much requires the use of boxes and a more rigid style.

The complete program is shown in Figure 7.2.

Observe that each data value from a card is read directly into the array named GRADE, using the DO index as a subscript. Since a legitimate deck could contain 100 grades and a sentinel, we do have to provide one extra element in the GRADE array for the sentinel in this extreme case. If we were to forget this situation and set up the DIMENSION statement with GRADE(100) there would be no problem on any deck smaller than 100 grades; but in that one case, the sentinel would go into element 101, which would not exist. Some Fortran compilers would catch the error, but many would simply place the sentinel into the next computer storage location after GRADE(100). Assuming that something else had already been assigned to that location, the program could be badly messed up, without any explicit indication of the nature of the problem. This is, unfortunately, a rather common error, which is a good argument for using a Fortran system that checks subscripts during object program execution to see that they are within range of the limits given in the DIMENSION.

Most of the rest of the program has already been discussed. Before we leave it, however, note that the final WRITE, near the end of the program, has subscripted variables in its list, a common occurrence. With the grades sorted into ascending sequence, GRADE(1) must be the smallest and GRADE(N) the largest. This made it unnecessary to set up the variables SMALL and BIG as before.

Here are some representative lines of output from this program. The four grades in the third run were 10, 40, 50, and 60; the five grades in the fourth run were 10, 40, 50, 60, and 70.

```
NOT ENOUGH DATA -- JOB STOPPED

THERE WERE      2    GRADES, RANGING FROM    0.0  TO    10.0
WITH A MEAN OF     5.0   AND A MEDIAN OF     5.0

THERE WERE      4    GRADES, RANGING FROM   10.0  TO    60.0

WITH A MEAN OF    40.0   AND A MEDIAN OF    45.0

THERE WERE      5    GRADES, RANGING FROM   10.0  TO    70.0
WITH A MEAN OF    46.0   AND A MEDIAN OF    50.0

THERE WERE    100    GRADES, RANGING FROM   10.0  TO   100.0
WITH A MEAN OF    55.8   AND A MEDIAN OF    57.0

THERE WERE TOO MANY DATA CARDS -- JOB STOPPED
```

An Income Tax Calculation

For a second example, which it will be possible to cover rather more briefly now that the basics have been illustrated, consider a portion of the computation of the United States federal income tax. This is a "progressive" tax, which means that the tax rate is higher for higher incomes. Here is the tax table for single taxpayers for the 1973 tax year:

1973 Tax Rate Schedules

SCHEDULE X — Single Taxpayers not Qualifying for Rates in Schedule Y or Z

If the amount on line 3, Estimated Tax Worksheet, is:	Enter on line 4, Estimated Tax Worksheet:

Not over $500 . . . 14% of the amount on line 3.

Over—	But not over—		of excess over—
$500	$1,000	$70 + 15%	$500
$1,000	$1,500	$145 + 16%	$1,000
$1,500	$2,000	$225 + 17%	$1,500
$2,000	$4,000	$310 + 19%	$2,000
$4,000	$6,000	$690 + 21%	$4,000
$6,000	$8,000	$1,110 + 24%	$6,000
$8,000	$10,000	$1,590 + 25%	$8,000
$10,000	$12,000	$2,090 + 27%	$10,000
$12,000	$14,000	$2,630 + 29%	$12,000
$14,000	$16,000	$3,210 + 31%	$14,000
$16,000	$18,000	$3,830 + 34%	$16,000
$18,000	$20,000	$4,510 + 36%	$18,000
$20,000	$22,000	$5,230 + 38%	$20,000
$22,000	$26,000	$5,990 + 40%	$22,000
$26,000	$32,000	$7,590 + 45%	$26,000
$32,000	$38,000	$10,290 + 50%	$32,000
$38,000	$44,000	$13,290 + 55%	$38,000
$44,000	$50,000	$16,590 + 60%	$44,000
$50,000	$60,000	$20,190 + 62%	$50,000
$60,000	$70,000	$26,390 + 64%	$60,000
$70,000	$80,000	$32,790 + 66%	$70,000
$80,000	$90,000	$39,390 + 68%	$80,000
$90,000	$100,000	$46,190 + 69%	$90,000
$100,000	————	$53,090 + 70%	$100,000

We do not concern ourselves here with the question of exemptions and deductions, but assume that the taxable income ("the amount on line 3") has already been determined; it will be the value of a variable named TAXABL. The computational problem then is to find what tax bracket the individual is in and to compute the tax. For instance, if TAXABL is $6200, we must somehow establish that the taxpayer is in the "over $6,000 but not over $8,000" bracket, and that his tax is accordingly $1,110 plus 24% of the amount over $6,000.

Computationally this will require three arrays, which will be called BRACKT, BASE, and TAXRAT. BRACKT will contain all the values in the first column of the table on the preceding page ($500, $1,000, $1,500, . . . , $100,000). This one column actually contains all the information in the first two columns of the table: each entry in the second column is the same as the entry one position down in the first column. We need two additional entries, however. First, an entry of zero at the beginning will make it possible to fit the computation of *all* taxes into one algorithm. The line at the top of the table, which says "Not over $500 . . . 14% of the amount on line 3," can be handled as though there were a new first line stating that if the taxable amount is over $0.00 but not over $500, the tax is $0.00 plus 14% of the excess over $0.00. The Internal Revenue Service wisely did not express it this way, which would confuse most people, but the effect is precisely the same, in which case we prefer to do it this way because the program need not be set up to handle an "exception" that is not actually an exception at all. Secondly, we need a dummy line at the end with a very large taxable amount in it, to provide a test that the taxable amount is reasonable. We add a line for $500,000 for this purpose. This line is never used in any other way, so the corresponding entries in BASE and TAXRAT are unimportant; zeros will be placed in them.

The program is to be set up to read cards containing a taxpayer identification and a taxable amount, looking for a negative taxable amount as a sentinel. The main body of the program will be set up as a DO loop with a maximum of 1000 executions of the range, to provide a limit on the number of cards read. (In practical application this limit might need to be larger, or some other kind of test used.) Besides computing and printing the tax for each individual, the program is to accumulate the total tax of all individuals.

A narrative-style flowchart appears in Figure 7.3. After writing appro-

---

 Write headings

 Read tables

 Initialize total tax to zero

DO 70 N = 1, 1000 (sets maximum deck size)

        Read taxable amount, looking for sentinel

        Find tax bracket, identify it by DO subscript K.
           If no find, write error comment
           and proceed to next card

DO

        Compute and write tax

        Add to total tax

If fall through DO: Write 'MORE THAN 1000 DATA CARDS—JOB STOPPED'

        Stop

On sentinel: N = N − 1 (to allow for counting sentinel)

        Write N and total tax

        Stop

FIGURE 7.3. A narrative-style flowchart of a procedure for computing income taxes.

```
C AN INCOME TAX CALCULATION
C GETS TAX FOR EACH EMPLOYEE, AND TOTAL TAX FOR ALL EMPLOYEES
C
C       VARIABLES
C       BRACKT   ARRAY OF 26 STARTING LEVELS FOR TAX BRACKETS
C       BASE     ARRAY OF 26 BASE TAXES FOR CORRESPONDING BRACKETS
C       TAXRAT   ARRAY OF 26 TAX RATES FOR CORRESPONDING BRACKETS
C       TOTTAX   TOTAL TAX FOR ALL EMPLOYEES
C       N        "PROGRAM LOOP" INDEX; COUNTS NUMBER OF DATA CARDS
C       IDENT    EMPLOYEE IDENTIFICATION
C       TAXABL   TAXABLE AMOUNT FOR YEAR FOR EMPLOYEE
C       K        SEARCH LOOP INDEX
C       TAX      TAX FOR CURRENT EMPLOYEE
C
        DIMENSION BRACKT(26), BASE(26), TAXRAT(26)
C       ... WRITE HEADINGS
        WRITE (6, 5)
    5   FORMAT ('1', '     IDENT       TAXABLE       TAX'//)
C
C       ... READ TABLES; NOTE LACK OF INDEXING, TO READ ENTIRE ARRAY
C
        READ (5, 10) BRACKT
   10   FORMAT (10F8.0)
        READ (5, 10) BASE
        READ (5, 10) TAXRAT
C
C       ... INITIALIZE SUM LOCATION FOR TOTAL TAX
C
        TOTTAX = 0.0
C
C       ... THIS DO IS THE "PROGRAM LOOP" THAT COUNTS EMPLOYEE CARDS
C       ... AND SETS LIMIT ON SIZE OF DECK
C
        DO 70 N = 1, 1000
            READ (5, 20) IDENT, TAXABL
   20       FORMAT (I10, F10.0)
            IF ( TAXABL .LT. 0.0 ) GO TO 90
C
C           ... SEARCH FOR THE BRACKET FOR THIS TAXABLE AMOUNT
C
            DO 30 K = 1, 25
                IF (        (TAXABL .GE. BRACKT(K)    )
   1                 .AND. (TAXABL .LT. BRACKT(K+1) ) ) GO TO 50
   30       CONTINUE
C
C           ... IF WE FALL THROUGH THE DO THE TAXABLE AMOUNT WAS INVALID
C
            WRITE (6, 40) IDENT
   40       FORMAT ('0', 'TAXABLE FOR  ', I12, '   INVALID'/)
            GO TO 70
C
C           ... COMPUTE TAX
C
   50       TAX = BASE(K) + TAXRAT(K) * ( TAXABL - BRACKT(K) )
            WRITE (6, 60) IDENT, TAXABL, TAX
            TOTTAX = TOTTAX + TAX
   60       FORMAT (1X, I12, 2F12.2)
   70   CONTINUE
C
C       ... IF WE FALL THROUGH DO LOOP, THERE WERE MORE THAN 1000 CARDS
C
        WRITE (6, 80)
   80   FORMAT ('1', 'THERE WERE MORE THAN 1000 CARDS --- JOB STOPPED')
        STOP
C
C       ... WRAPUP; SUBTRACT 1 FROM N TO ALLOW FOR HAVING COUNTED SENTINEL
C
   90   N = N - 1
        WRITE (6, 100) N, TOTTAX
  100   FORMAT ('0', 'THERE WERE', I6, '   EMPLOYEES; TOTAL TAX =', F12.2/)
        STOP
        END
```

FIGURE 7.4.   A program for finding income taxes, corresponding
to the flowchart of Figure 7.3.

priate headings we read the three tables into their arrays and set to zero the variable that will accumulate the total tax. Now the major DO takes us into a card-reading and computing loop. After reading each card an inner DO searches the array named BRACKT, looking for the bracket that applies to this taxpayer and jumping out to the tax computation upon finding it. If the DO is ever satisfied, the value of TAXABLE must have been greater than $500,000 which is taken to indicate a card preparation error. (Some people do have higher taxable amounts than that, but there are so few that it is better strategy to handle them separately than to take the chance of letting errors slip through.) The computation of the tax will involve using the index of the inner DO to pick out the proper entries from the three tables, as we shall see. The rest of the flowchart should be reasonably clear, but one point of system design should be mentioned. When the final line is written at the end of the program, what does N actually represent? Is it the number of taxpayers for whom taxes were computed? That is what we would presumably like, but it will be the case only if there were no erroneous TAXABL amounts, since N is not adjusted when a bad card is found. And indeed it *cannot* be adjusted; no changing of the index of a DO is permitted within the range of the DO. Exercise 24 asks you to extend the program to count the number of bad cards an take appropriate corrective action at the end of the program.

The program is shown in Figure 7.4. With full explanation of the variables, adequate but not excessive comments, careful indentation, and only three GO TOs—none of which points backward—the program ought to be clear. Not that it will not take study: it is complex enough, just because it does enough, to require careful reading. But careful reading of the program should reward the student with as much understanding of what is being done as the reading of an explanation would.

One exception to that generalization is the technique used for reading the values into the three arrays. Whenever it is desired to read values for all the elements of an array, in order from one up to the maximum, it is possible to write the name of the array with no subscript. The numerical values must then appear in the input in the same order, and there must be exactly the right number of them.

It turns out that the 26 values for any one of the arrays will not fit on one card. The FORMAT here specifies ten values, which means that ten values will be read from one card, ten from another, and the last six from a third. We shall study the rules that govern this kind of *repeat scanning* of a FORMAT in the next chapter. For now, take it on faith; it is not an important consideration for this illustration.

A simpler and less error-prone way to load these arrays would actually be to use the DATA statement, described in Chapter Ten, with which the table entries can be made essentially a part of the program and thus very carefully checked. This approach also avoids the dangers of mixups in deck makeup.

Another new feature is used in the IF statement in the inner DO loop, the one with statement number 30 as its CONTINUE. Here we have used the *logical operator* AND to connect two relationship tests. The IF here is satisfied only if TAXABL is greater than or equal to the element of BRACKT identified by the subscript K *and* less than the element identified by K+1, which is what the notion of a "bracket" is all about. (Try writing the program without this AND!) The logical operator .AND., including the periods, specifies to Fortran that *both* conditions must be true before the statement following the parentheses is to be carried out.

Observe that we have used a continuation line to permit lining up the two conditions one under the other, and that we have enclosed both conditions in parentheses. Both of these conventions are permitted by Fortran but are not required. This is another convention that is used to try to exhibit the structure of the program more clearly, and it is strongly recommended. (*In this case* it would have been necessary to use a continuation line anyway, but that is not the point.)

Fortran also provides the operator .OR., which combines two or more relational tests and specifies carrying out the statement if any or all of the relations are true. Finally, there is a .NOT. operator that reverses the effect of any other test or combination of tests; we shall have little occasion to use this one. Rather complex combinations of tests can be built up, using several operators, many tests, lot of parentheses to control the range of the effect of each operator, etc. However, about 99% of real life situations can be handled with just the .AND. or just the .OR. combining two relations, so the more complicated cases will not be studied here.

The comments in this program have been indented the same amount as the statement that they precede, and dots have been placed at the beginning of each comment to make it easier to distinguish quickly between comments and statements. This convention is used here as one more illustration of the kinds of things that can be done to make program structure and meaning easier to understand.

Here is the output produced when this program was run with a few sample values.

```
        IDENT          TAXABLE        TAX

     1234567890         200.00        28.00
            123         500.00        70.00
            124         700.00       100.00
            125        1200.00       177.00
            126       23000.00      6390.00
            127       14000.00      3210.00
            128       87420.00     44435.60
 TAXABLE FOR              129    INVALID

            130           1.00         0.14
 THERE WERE      9  EMPLOYEES; TOTAL TAX =      54410.73
```

Finally, just for fun, here is a program segment that could be added at the end of the program to print out the tables for reference or for checking. Rather than printing one table at a time, perhaps without using subscripting, we print one element for each table on a line so that the printed result looks much like the table as printed on the IRS form.

```
        WRITE (6, 110)
110     FORMAT ('1', ' BRACKET       BASE      TAX RATE'//)
        DO 130 K = 1, 26
            NRATE = 100.0 * TAXRAT(K) + 0.5
            WRITE (6, 120) BRACKT(K), BASE(K), NRATE
120         FORMAT (1X, '$', F9.2, '    $', F8.2, I7, '%')
130     CONTINUE
        STOP
        END
```

BRACKET	BASE	TAX RATE
$ 0.0	$ 0.0	14%
$ 500.00	$ 70.00	15%
$ 1000.00	$ 145.00	16%
$ 1500.00	$ 225.00	17%
$ 2000.00	$ 310.00	19%
$ 4000.00	$ 690.00	21%
$ 6000.00	$ 1110.00	24%
$ 8000.00	$ 1590.00	25%
$ 10000.00	$ 2090.00	27%
$ 12000.00	$ 2630.00	29%
$ 14000.00	$ 3210.00	31%
$ 16000.00	$ 3830.00	34%
$ 18000.00	$ 4510.00	36%
$ 20000.00	$ 5230.00	38%
$ 22000.00	$ 5990.00	40%
$ 26000.00	$ 7590.00	45%
$ 32000.00	$10290.00	50%
$ 38000.00	$13290.00	55%
$ 44000.00	$16590.00	60%
$ 50000.00	$20190.00	62%
$ 60000.00	$26390.00	64%
$ 70000.00	$32790.00	66%
$ 80000.00	$39390.00	68%
$ 90000.00	$46190.00	69%
$ 100000.00	$53090.00	70%
$ 500000.00	$ 0.0	0%

The bracket and base figures are printed directly from their arrays, but it was decided to print the tax rate as a percentage rather than as a decimal fraction, the way it appears in the array. Since all the rates are integer values, it was further decided to print them as such, which requires conversion to an integer variable. A complication arises, however: the values in the computer are all a tiny bit lower than the true values, and when the conversion to an integer variable is made any fractional part is dropped: there is no rounding. To get a rounded value it is necessary to explicitly add one-half to the value before the conversion.

Summary of subscripted variables

1. Subscripted variables make it possible to refer to a whole collection of data values by one general name, then pick out a particular one by writing a subscript in parentheses after the variable name.

2. A subscript, in most Fortran versions, can be any expression that produces an integer value. Some Fortrans restrict the expression to the following forms, and even those Fortrans that are not so restrictive will sometimes run faster if these forms are adhered to.

Preferred Expression	Example
Constant	12
Integer variable	K93X
Constant★variable	2★N
Variable ± constant	LIMIT − 2
Constant ★ variable ± another constant	3★M + 13

3. Every subscripted variable must appear in a DIMENSION statement at the beginning of the program. The DIMENSION statement must include the name of the subscripted variable and the number of elements it has.

4. No subscript may be less than 1 or greater than the number of elements stated in the DIMENSION.

5. All the elements in any one array (subscripted variable) must be of the same type, i.e., either all real or all integer.

6. The most useful applications of subscripted variables occur when the subscript is some kind of expression other than a single constant, often with a DO controlling a variable appearing in a subscript expression.

7. Subscripted variables, in full generality, may have more than one dimension. A two-dimensional subscripted variable is like a table; as an example, the rows of the table might give the wage rates for a series of kinds of job, and the columns the pay for each of the different shifts. We shall not use multidimensional arrays in this book.

REVIEW QUESTIONS

1. What does a subscripted variable do that cannot be done with a non-subscripted variable?

2. How does Fortran know that a given variable is subscripted?

3. As used in this text, is there any difference between the terms *subscripted variable* and *array*?

4. Could a subscripted variable have only one element?

5. When we write an arithmetic expression containing a subscripted variable, how does Fortran know that it is a subscripted variable, and how does Fortran know which element we want?

6. What kind of expressions can be used within parentheses in a subscripted variable?

7. Can a variable appearing in a subscripted expression itself be subscripted?

8. What happens if we write a subscript expression that is less than 1 or greater than the maximum stated in the DIMENSION statement?

9. Suppose the program of Figure 7.4 were to be run for a maximum deck size of one box of cards (2000), instead of 1000 as assumed in the program. What would have to be changed in the program?

10. Would the program of Figure 7.4 work correctly if the arrays BASE and TAXRAT were made to contain only 25 elements, dropping the zeros in the 26th positions of each?

11. In the program of Figure 7.2, does it cause any difficulty if there are two or more grades that are the same? In the extreme case, all the grades would be equal — not likely, indeed, but a point to consider in determining whether the program is correct. What would the program do in such a case?

12. Another method of sorting compares the first and second, interchanging if necessary, then the second and third, the third and fourth, etc., until it has compared the next-to-last and last. This process is repeated over and over until it is discovered that in going through the entire list no interchanges were necessary. What would a routine based on this scheme do with a set of identical grades?

13. Identify an error in each of the following statements, which are independent of each other.
    a. DIMENTION X(50)
    b. DIMENSION A(60000)
    c. A(0) = 93
    d. K(K) = NBAD
    e. A(B/6.7) = 12.0

14. A student wanted to write a program that would read 50 data values from 50 cards, and find the average. Here is the program he wrote; find as many errors in it as you can.

```
        DO 20 K = 1, 50
            READ (5, 10) X(K)
10          FORMAT (F10.0)
20      CONTINUE
        DO 30 K = 1, 50
            SUM = SUM + X(K)
30      CONTINUE
        AVER = SUM/50.0
        WRITE (6, 40) AVER
        STOP
        END
```

ANSWERS

1. A subscripted variable refers to a whole collection of data instead of just one variable; a subscript establishes which one of the collection is desired.

2. Every subscripted variable must appear in a DIMENSION statement to inform Fortran that it is a subscripted variable.

3. No.

4. Yes, but only in unusual circumstances would it be useful; no such situation appears in this book.

5. Fortran knows it is a subscripted variable because its name appears in a DIMENSION statement; it knows which one we want by the subscript expression that we write in parentheses following the name of the subscripted variable.

6. If one is following the ANSI standard or is forced to do so by the limitations of the particular compiler, a certain few forms are permitted, as shown on page 131. Otherwise, any expression that yields an integer value is permitted.

7. Again, not under the ANSI standard or in some compilers. Most compilers do permit it, and it is sometimes highly useful.

8. Big trouble. Some compilers will flag the error, which is highly desirable. Others will simply pick up some erroneous value with no warning.

9. Change the DO that appears two statements before statement number 20, to give the limit as 2000 instead of 1000. The comments in statement 80 should be changed also, although the program would work correctly without the change.

10. Yes.

11. Two identical grades would cause no trouble at all. They would not be interchanged, because the IF statement was made to read "less than *or equal to*" with this point in mind. If all grades were identical, the program would go through all its steps except that there would never be any interchanges.

12. The method described, which is sometimes referred to as "bubble sorting" because of the way values move through the array, would discover after one "pass" through the grades that no interchanges were necessary, and would stop. In such an unusual circumstance it would be clearly preferable to the method used in the text.

13. a. DIMENSION is misspelled.
    b. Many computers could not hold an array that large, although some could.
    c. A subscript with a value of zero is illegal in Fortran.
    d. The variable K is being used as subscripted and nonsubscripted at the same time.
    e. A subscript expression must be integer-valued.

14. The variable SUM is never initialized. There is no DIMENSION statement. Although it is not strictly speaking an error, since the corrected program would work, there is no need for the first DO loop: the values can be added as they are read, as in this version of the program.

```
          SUM = 0.0
          DO 20 K = 1, 50
              READ (5, 10) TEMP
    10        FORMAT (F10.0)
              SUM = SUM + TEMP
    20    CONTINUE
          AVER = SUM / 50.0
          WRITE (6, 30) AVER
    30    FORMAT (1X, F12.4)
          STOP
          END
```

EXERCISES

Note. Include an appropriate DIMENSION statement in each program segment for these exercises, realizing, of course, that in a complete program each subscripted variable is dimensioned only once, in a DIMENSION statement at the beginning of the program.

*1. An array named A contains ten elements. Write separate program segments to accomplish the following.

   a. Place the product of the first and second elements in PROD.

   b. Replace the third element by the average of the first, third, and fifth elements.

   c. If the last element is zero or positive, do nothing, but if it is negative reverse its sign.

   d. Replace every element by two times itself, using a DO loop.

2. An array named B contains 20 elements. Write separate program segments to accomplish the following:

   a. Divide the fourth element by the sum of the fifth and sixth elements, and place the result in ABC.

   b. Replace the last four elements by zero, without using a loop.

   c. If the tenth element is greater than TEST, replace the tenth element by the average of the ninth and eleventh elements.

   d. Replace every element in the array by zero, using a DO loop.

*3. Two arrays named SAM and BEN each contain 35 elements. An array named HALL also contains 35 elements. Make each element of HALL equal to the sum of the values of the corresponding elements of SAM and BEN.

4. Two arrays named MARY and JANELL each have 150 elements. Write a program to square each element of MARY, subtract 3 from it, and place the result in the corresponding element position of JANELL.

*5. You are given an array named TOM. Write a program segment to place in RACHEL the sum of the values of the elements of TOM. TOM has five elements. Decide for yourself whether to use a DO loop.

6. Two arrays named A and B each have 15 elements. Form the sum of the products of corresponding elements, take the square root of the result, and assign its value to the proper element of ANORM.

*7. The two arrays named A and B have 15 elements each. If the element from A is greater than the corresponding element from B, for all 15 pairs, write a line that says "OK"; otherwise write a line that says "NO WAY."

8. Two arrays named SAM and GLOTZ contain 22 elements each. For each of the 22 pairs of corresponding values, determine whether the value from SAM is greater than the element from GLOTZ. Write the element number and the values of SAM and GLOTZ for any pairs which fail this test.

*9. Write a program segment that will read 25 values from 25 cards, keeping all of them in a variable named Q.

10. A and B are both subscripted variables having 100 elements. Write a program segment that will make the elements of A equal to the elements of B.

*11. A program has a subscripted variable named NUMBER, containing 400 elements. Read a deck of cards, up to a zero sentinel, that will take a number from columns 1-3, and, if it is in the range of 1 to 400, place a 1 in the corresponding element of NUMBER. All elements of NUMBER should be cleared to zero before beginning to read cards. (This exercise and the five following it may be thought of in terms of a checking account, if one wishes.)

12. Following the logic of Exercise 11, add to the program the capability to read an AMOUNT from columns 4-10 and, if the NUMBER passes its test, place the AMOUNT in the correct element position.

*13. Following the logic of Exercise 11, add a section that, upon detecting the sentinel, will produce a count of how many cards were read before the sentinel. Do this by inspecting the array named NUMBER for entries that contain a 1.

14. In the manner or Exercise 13, produce also a total of the amounts read into AMOUNT.

*15. Continuing with the logic of Exercise 11, write a program that will print element numbers of all the nonzero elements of NUMBER, together with the corresponding elements of AMOUNT. (If viewed as a checking account problem, this lists the checks in order regardless of the way they were entered. It thus performs as a sorting routine.)

16. Modify the logic of Exercise 11 so that it always checks a NUMBER against the element position, to see if there is already a 1 there, indicating a duplicate. Write an error message and stop if there are any duplicates.

> *Note.* The next four exercises are based on the table on pages 92-93, which you may assume is already in storage as a set of ten subscripted variables having names as suggested in the exercises.

*17. Write a program that will have as its output the year (YEAR) in which Government Expenditures on Goods and Services as a percentage of GNP (GOVEXP) was the greatest, and that percentage.

18. Consider the two arrays Federal Reserve Board Index of Industrial Production (FRB) and Civilian Labor Force (LABOR). Write a program that will print out the year in which the ratio of the two, that is, FRB divided by LABOR, was the greatest.

*19. Determine the two years in which the increase in Disposable Income (DISP) from one year to the next was the greatest.

20. Write a program to print out the ratio between Gross National Product (current prices) (GNP) and Gross National Product (1958 prices) (GNP58). This will give an indication of the inflation values compared with 1958 as a base year. (The ratio will be less than 1.00 before 1958, equal to 1.0 in 1958, and greater than 1.0 after 1958.)

*21. Alter the program of Figure 7.2 as follows. Punched in columns 11-13 is a student identification number. Print the numbers of the students having the lowest and highest grades. (To keep it simple, assume no duplicate grades.)

22. Alter the program of Figure 7.2 as follows. Punched in column 14 is a code that identifies the student as undergraduate (1) or graduate (2). Produce separate statistics for the two groups.

*23. Modify the program of Figure 7.4 so that it produces a count of the number of taxpayers in each income bracket. This will require setting up another array to hold the counts; don't forget to initialize this array to zero before starting the computation.

24. Modify the program of Figure 7.4 so that it produces a count of the number of cards for which the taxable amount was invalid. This count should be printed at the end, along with the count of good cards, which will be less than the total unless all cards were valid. Finally, produce an average of the tax amounts from the good cards.

*25. A biology student is working with several hundred experimental insects, which fall into 20 classes numbered from 1 to 20. Part of the experiment requires recording the weight of each insect, and producing a table showing the average weight of each class.

You are given a deck of cards, each card containing a class number in columns 1-2 and a weight in grams in columns 3-8 with a decimal point. Write a program that will read each card, up to a zero sentinel, counting the number in each class and adding up their weights. When the sentinel is detected, compute and print all the average weights, along with identifying class numbers.

26. A psychology student has accumulated some hundreds of test scores, each of which falls into one of 30 groups. He wants to produce a report showing the highest and lowest scores in each group. Make reasonable assumptions about card format and a sentinel, and write a program to produce such a result. The output is to consist of 30 lines, each of which contains a group number, the number of items in that group, and the lowest and highest scores for that group.

CHAPTER EIGHT
MORE ON INPUT AND OUTPUT

Planning for input and output is one of the largest parts of the programmer's job, and one of the most common sources of errors.

In this chapter we shall consolidate the material on input and output that has already been presented in earlier chapters and take up such topics as informing the program what to do when it runs out of data, other types of data storage devices (tapes and disks), reading and writing intermediate results without any FORMAT information, and various features that make it possible to produce output of pleasing appearance that is also easy to use.

The major example for the chapter will be a typical data processing application: reading data from two magnetic disk files and combining information from them to produce a third disk file.

Some of what follows has been presented before, piecemeal, so that this chapter is in part a review of things you already know. This also makes the chapter more suitable for reference use, when it is necessary to look up how something works.

Review of the basics

Reading input data or writing results requires the programmer to provide four categories of information.

1. The selection of an input or output device, which is handled by a combination of the Fortran verb chosen (READ or WRITE) and the unit designation. If in a program we say

```
WRITE (6, 100) X, Y, Z
```

the verb WRITE means that the direction of flow is from the computer to the outside world. What we previously called the unit designation, the 6, is more properly referred to as the *data set reference number*. It specifies which of the various output devices that may be available on the particular computer is to be used. By convention, at most installations, 6 indicates a printer attached to the computer (some other number may be used at your shop—check with your installation staff). Actually, as we shall see, the data set reference numbers can be specified to mean whatever you want them to mean.

2. The second category of information that must be supplied for input or output (I/O) consists of the names of the variables that are to receive new

values on input or have their values sent to an output device. This information is specified by the list of variables in the I/O statement.

3. We must also specify the order in which the values are to be transmitted, which is governed by the order in which the variables are named in the list.

4. Finally, we have to describe the format in which the data appears (input) or is to appear (output). This is the function of the FORMAT statement.

Each of these four areas has been discussed in preceding chapters, and there have been many examples of their use. Each of them is now the subject of further elaboration in the interest either of simplicity of programming or, more commonly, of more powerful techniques directed toward greater usefulness of the total computer system.

The list of an input or output statement

The simplest type of list is one in which all variables are named, in the order in which they are to be transmitted. There are other forms, as we shall see, but in all cases a correspondence carries through: the *first* variable name is associated with the *first* data item, the *second* variable name is associated with the *second* data value, etc.

The first new list feature is a useful one that does not complicate the scanning process: it is permissible to use integer variables in a list as subscripts for arrays elsewhere in the list. This is subject to one reasonable restriction: when used on input, the integer variable must appear *earlier* in the list than its use as a subscript. "Earlier" really means nothing more, in this case, than "to the left of." For an example, we might write

```
      READ (5, 100) K, POWER(K)
100   FORMAT (I2, F10.0)
```

The value of K read from the card would then be used immediately to determine where in the POWER array to place the data value.

Although completely legal from a Fortran syntax standpoint, this technique does carry dangers, and is not recommended for routine use. The problem is that if anything goes wrong in the preparation of the data cards, so that the element number is not valid, the program may not only give incorrect answers, but may be completely aborted. The danger in this instance is that the subscript value may be out of the range of legal subscripts for the array. Some Fortran systems diagnose such errors, but many do not. Going back to the example above, if POWER had been declared to have 25 elements but through mispunching the data card gave K as 90, say, then most computers would store that data value at a position 90 locations after the beginning of the storage for the array named POWER, which could cause destruction of other data.

For this reason we ordinarily read both the element number and the data value into temporary storage locations, not using any subscripting, then make such validity checks as necessary to assure that K is really in the range of the array, and only then do we store the element in the correct position in the array.

Transmitting entire arrays

Another simplification that is sometimes quite useful is the fact that if an entire array is to be transmitted, in standard order, then it is not necessary to use subscripts in the list at all. Consider this example:

```
      DIMENSION X(8)
      ...
      WRITE (6, 110) X
  110 FORMAT (1X, 8F10.4)
```

All elements of X would be transmitted, in standard order: X(1), X(2), etc. This feature is especially handy when dealing with arrays of alphanumeric data, as we shall see a bit later.

The implied DO in a list

When only some of the array elements are to be transferred—such as only the odd-numbered elements or only the first half of the array, it is still sometimes possible to avoid writing out the names of all the elements. The elements and their order can instead be stated within the READ or WRITE statement in a way that closely resembles a DO loop, both in appearance and effect. Suppose, for an example, that we have an array named SUZI that has been declared in a DIMENSION statement to have 40 elements, of which we want to print only the last 20. We could write:

```
      DIMENSION SUZI(40)
      ...
      WRITE (6, 120) (SUZI(K), K = 21, 40)
  120 FORMAT ...
```

or suppose we wanted to print only the odd-numbered elements:

```
      WRITE (6, 130) (SUZI(L), L = 1, 39, 2)
  130 FORMAT ...
```

We see that the indexing information does resemble the DO statement, with the "range" of the DO in this case consisting simply of the array(s) named.

Several arrays may be involved in one READ or WRITE, if one wishes. Consider this example:

```
DIMENSION JOYCE(40), SUZI(40)
```

and suppose we wanted to print all the values, in two columns:

```
      WRITE (6, 140) (JOYCE(M), SUZI(M), M = 1, 40)
  140 FORMAT (1X, I6, F12.7)
```

The "range" of the "DO" in this case consists of both arrays. This two-column effect could *not* be gotten by writing

```
WRITE (6, 150) JOYCE, SUZI
```

with an appropriate FORMAT. This would indeed print all values of the two arrays, but not as desired: it would print all values of JOYCE, then all values of SUZI, instead of alternating the two as specified.

Scanning the list

The scanning of a list can be considerably more complex than it is in a simple list that names each variable explicity. Still, the sequence of transmission of values is completely specified in all cases. The scanning of the list and the scanning of the FORMAT statement entries keep in step: each time another variable is obtained from the list the next field descriptor is obtained from the FORMAT statement. If the closing parenthesis of the FORMAT is reached while more variables still remain in the list, a new card or a new line is called for and FORMAT scanning returns to the start of the FORMAT statement. Thus, if A is an array with 20 elements, the statements

```
        WRITE (6, 160) A
  160   FORMAT (1X, F12.3)
```

would print 20 separate lines with one value on each. On the other hand, these statements

```
        WRITE (6, 170) A
  170   FORMAT (1X, 5F12.3)
```

would print four lines, each having five numbers. Remember that the FOR-MAT statement just given is equivalent to:

```
  170   FORMAT (1X, F12.3, F12.3, F12.3, F12.3, F12.3)
```

The system keeps nicely in step between data items and field descriptors; this permits five numbers to be printed on the first line. But when the field descriptors have all been used once, that is, the FORMAT is exhausted, more values of A remain to be transmitted, so the system starts over again at the beginning of the FORMAT.

We could also write something like this:

```
        WRITE (6, 180) A
  180   FORMAT (1X, F10.1, F10.2, F10.4, F10.3)
```

if we wished. The result would be that *within each line* there would be first a number with one decimal place, the next with two decimal places, etc.

This "repeat scanning," as we might call it, is an important feature of FORMAT statement usage. We shall need to discuss it later as well, on page 146, to see how the effect can be modified by the use of parentheses within the FORMAT statement. It is useful at this point to recall that when the list is exhausted before the FORMAT is, the rest of the FORMAT is simply ignored.

More about field descriptors

The FORMAT statement describes how information is arranged on input or is to be arranged on output. Corresponding to each value transmitted there must be a field descriptor that specifies the kind of information the field contains (in terms of its internal representation) and what it "looks like" externally. Here we shall review the form and function of the five types of field descriptors that have been used in the book to this point. (There are others described in Chapter 10 and Appendix 3.)

In each field descriptor the following must be supplied:

1. A letter (I, F, A, H, or X) to designate the type of information involved and something about how it is to be handled.

2. A number to designate how many card columns or printing positions are being used.

The F field descriptor further requires a designation of the handling of the decimal point.

To avoid repetition, we may note a few matters that apply to both the F and I descriptors.

On input a sign, if any, must be to the left of the first digit of the field. The use of the plus sign is always optional; if no sign appears the number is considered to be positive. Blanks are treated as zeros, and a field that is all blank is treated as zero.

On output, the number will appear at the right of the output field if more positions are specified in the field than there are characters to be printed. If too few character positions are specified, most Fortran systems print a full field of asterisks to signal the problem. Positive numbers are usually printed without signs.

In all types except H and X it is possible to specify that the same field descriptor applies to several fields by writing a repeat count in front of the field descriptor. (The H and X types may also be repeated if they are enclosed in parentheses; see below for this facility.)

The field descriptor I (Integer)

The form of this descriptor is Iw. The I specifies conversion between an internal integer and an external decimal integer. The total number of characters in the field, including any sign and blanks, is w. Decimal points are not permitted.

The field descriptor F (External Fixed point)

The form of this descriptor is $Fw.d$. The F indicates conversion between an internal real number and an external number that is permitted to have a decimal point. The total number of characters in the field, including sign, decimal point, and blanks, is w. The number of digits after the decimal point is d.

On output the use of a decimal point is optional; if one is supplied in the field, it overrides the effect of the d. (The use of an actual decimal point in input in this way is recommended practice.)

On output, the decimal point is printed when the F field descriptor is used; there will be d digits to its right. Both the decimal point and the d digits are included in the total character count, w.

Field descriptor A (Alphanumeric)

In the Aw form of field descriptor the associated variable may be of any kind. The field descriptor causes w characters to be read into, or written from, the associated list element. The alphanumeric characters may be any symbols representable in the particular computer: letters, digits, punctuation, and the "character" blank. The precise action depends on the number of characters held in one storage location in the particular machine, which as a general indication ranges from four to ten. Call this number g.

On input, if w is greater than or equal to g, the right-most g characters will be taken from the external input field; these g characters fill the storage location. If w is less than g, the w characters will appear "left justified" (at the extreme left) in storage, followed by trailing blanks.

On output, if w is greater than g, the external result will consist of $w-g$ blanks followed by the g characters. If w is less than or equal to g, the external result will be the leftmost w characters from storage.

That may sound a lot more complicated than it is, so let us turn immediately to some examples. Suppose first that in the computer being used there is space for four characters in a computer *word*, "word" being simply a term for the amount of information associated with one unsubscripted variable. Then suppose we write

```
        READ (5, 190) GORA
    190 FORMAT (A4)
```

The four characters read from the card will go into the variable named GORA, at which point we can do anything with GORA permitted with alphanumeric values. One obvious thing to do is to print it later:

```
        WRITE (6, 200) GORA
    200 FORMAT (1X, A4)
```

With the same assumption about word size, suppose we wrote

```
        READ (5, 210) JERRY
    210 FORMAT (A1)
```

Then only one character would be read into the variable named JERRY; assuming that that is intentional, there is no problem. In fact, a variation of this "single character read" is about the only use we shall make of alphanumeric fields in this book. As an example, imagine that the first 20 characters on a card contain a person's name, which we want simply to be able to print on output. One technique is to set up enough storage space in an array to hold the 20 characters, one character per array element, then name the array without subscripts in the input or output list. This is done to avoid problems with the varying word sizes in the various computers that readers of this book may be using. The basic field descriptor is therefore A1, but we will need 20 of them, which we can specify with a repeat count. To read a name and immediately print it, then, requires only these statements:

```
        DIMENSION NAME(20)
        ...
        READ (5, 220) NAME
    220 FORMAT (20A1)
        WRITE (6, 230) NAME
    230 FORMAT (1X, 20A1)
```

Now, each character of the person's name, including any blanks or punctuation, will go into one element of an array, from which we may retrieve it at any later time.

The fact that NAME would signify an integer variable if not used for alphanumeric data, is of no significance.

Field descriptor H (Hollerith)

This descriptor takes the form wH. The w characters immediately following the letter H are printed or punched in the position indicated by the position of the Hollerith field descriptor in the FORMAT statement. The Hollerith field descriptor is different from the others so far discussed in that it does not call for the transmission of any values from the list. Instead, it calls for the input or output of the text itself. Any character available in the computer may be used, as it can with the A field descriptor. This, incidentally, is the only case in which a blank in a statement is not ignored by the Fortran compiler.

No indication of the presence of the Hollerith text is required in the list of the input or output statement that refers to the FORMAT statement containing the text. Whenever a Hollerith field descriptor is encountered in the scanning of the FORMAT statement, the text is transmitted without any variable from the list having been transmitted.

Hollerith field descriptors are commonly used to provide headings and other identification on printed reports, as we have seen.

Another very frequent application controls the spacing of lines in printing. The first character of the line printed with a WRITE statement is ordinarily not actually printed, but is used instead to control spacing, according to the following table.

Control Character	Action
Blank	Normal single spacing
0	Double space
1	Skip to top of next page before printing
+	Suppress spacing

Common practice, and strongly recommended, is to start every FORMAT statement for output with a Hollerith field giving the desired vertical spacing. If, by accident, the first data field places a nonblank character into the carriage control position, the character will not be printed and *strange* spacing can result.

As we have seen, many Fortran systems provide what we have called the quoted literal as an alternative to the Hollerith field descriptor. When both are available, the programmer must balance positive and negative factors of the sort discussed on page 39, Chapter 3.

Field descriptor X (blank)

This descriptor has the form wX.

On input, the effect is to skip over w columns regardless of what appears in those columns.

On output, the effect is to insert w blanks into the output record. This is commonly done to space heading information or to spread out results across the line.

Group repeat in the FORMAT statement

Just as it is possible to repeat a field descriptor by writing a repeat count in front of it, it is also possible to repeat a group of field descriptors. The group is enclosed in parentheses and the desired number of repetitions is written before it. For instance, suppose that eight fields on a card are alternately described by I2 and F10.0. We can write

    4(I2, F10.0)

to get the desired action. This is *not* the same as

    4I2, 4F10.0

which describes a card with four I2 fields, then four F10.0 fields, rather than the desired alternation.

Two levels of parentheses, in addition to those required by the FORMAT statement, are permitted.

The slash (/) in the FORMAT statement

When the list of an input or output statement is used to transmit more than one record (card or line) and the different records have different formats, a slash (/) is used to separate the format descriptors for the different lines. For example, suppose that two cards are to be read with a single READ statement; the first card has only a four-digit integer and the second has six real numbers. We could write

FORMAT (I4/6F10.4)

The slash terminates the reading of the first card (skipping over any other punching that it might contain) and, if list variables remain, it initiates the reading of another card, using the field descriptors after the slash.

It is possible to specify a special format for the first (one or more) records and a different format for all subsequent records. This is done by enclosing the last record descriptors in parentheses. For instance, if the first card of a deck has an integer and a real number and all following cards contain two integers and a real number, we could write

    FORMAT (I4, F10.4/(2I4, F10.4))

It is possible to call for the skipping of entire records by writing successive slashes, which is often useful when line spacing is desired and it is not convenient to use a carriage control character in the FORMAT statement for the next line. When $n + 1$ consecutive slashes appear at the end of a FORMAT descriptor, they are treated as follows: for input, $n + 1$ records are skipped; for output, n blank records are written, unless after doing so control reverts for the transmission of additional values, in which case $n + 1$ blank records are written. When $n + 1$ consecutive slashes appear in the middle of the FORMAT statement, n records are skipped or written. Unfortunately, however, different Fortrans are not entirely consistent on the handling of slashes at the end of a FORMAT.

If a FORMAT statement contains nothing but Hollerith and blank field descriptors, there must be no variables listed in the associated input or output statement. This is most commonly done with the WRITE statement to produce page and column headings or to cause line and page spacing. A common FORMAT statement is

```
FORMAT (1H1)
```

Referenced by a WRITE statement with no list, this causes the printer paper to space to the top of the next page.

The READ, WRITE, and PUNCH statements, without unit designations

In the earliest versions of Fortran the only input and output devices were a card reader, a card punch, a line printer, and several magnetic tapes. The concept of the data set reference number was not employed, and we wrote statements like

```
READ 200, A, X, I
PRINT 300, G, K
PUNCH 400, ARRAY
```

The function of the FORMAT statement number was the same, but the information now contained in the data set reference number was provided instead by the I/O verb (READ, PUNCH, or PRINT).

For compatibility with Fortran programs written for earlier systems, many modern Fortrans still accept these statements although they are not part of ANSI Fortran. Their meaning is precisely the same as the following statements, assuming (as is most common) an installation where data set reference numbers 5, 6, and 7 refer by default to a card reader, a printer, and a card punch:

```
READ (5, 200) A, X, I
WRITE (6, 300) G, K
WRITE (7, 400) ARRAY
```

This feature, which is also present in WATFOR and WATFIV, is of benefit to the beginning programmer in simplifying the form of input and output statements.

The BACKSPACE, REWIND, and END FILE statements

When writing a program for a data set that resides on magnetic tape, or other data sets with similar characteristics, it is occasionally useful to be able to change the current position within the data set.

For use with such data sets there are three Fortran statements that find occasional usefulness. They are named BACKSPACE, REWIND, and END FILE, the first two betraying their origin in the early days when they applied only to data sets on magnetic tape.

The statement BACKSPACE n, where n is the data set reference number of a suitable data set, "backs up" one record. (A *record* may be thought of as equivalent to one card or one line of printing. In magnetic tapes or magnetic disks it is a collection of data more or less equivalent to the amount of information on a card.) If we write

```
READ (5, 100) X
BACKSPACE 5
READ (5, 100) X
```

we read the same record twice: the BACKSPACE has moved us back one record in the data set. (Some systems, however, prohibit the use of these operations on data sets 5, 6, and 7.)

If the BACKSPACE statement is executed for a data set where it makes no sense, such as a computer terminal, or if it is executed at a time when it makes no sense, such as before reading the first record of a data set, it is simply ignored in most systems.

The BACKSPACE statement will find limited usefulness in most Fortran programs. If it were not so extremely costly in terms of execution time, it might be handy for things like reading a record once to determine what kind of information is in it, then rereading it by whichever part of the program is appropriate to its contents. But the time penalty is usually too great to permit extensive use in this way.

The REWIND statement, where meaningful, returns a data set to its beginning, ready for the first record to be accessed again.

The END FILE statement is used to place an indication in a data set that no more valid records follow. This is useful when information is being written out that is to be reread later, and we wish to have something in the data set to signal its end—without ourselves providing a sentinel record. The marker that is placed in the data set by the END FILE statement is recognized by the routines that handle reading. If we attempt to read a record that turns out to be the end-of-file mark and have not indicated that we expected this to happen, our program stops execution.

The END and ERR parameters

If nothing is done to specify differently, when the program runs out of data it is simply removed from execution. That is acceptable if there is nothing more for the program to do when the end of data is detected, but what if at that point there are some wrap-up chores to be done? This is the situation for which the END option is provided in a number of Fortran systems. We are permitted to write, for example,

```
READ (5, 100, END=80) X, Y, Z
```

This means that when the end-of-file mark is detected in attempting to read a record, statement 80 will be executed next.

This is a logical place to mention another optional parameter that can be used in the READ statement on a number of Fortran systems, the ERR parameter. This refers to the detection of errors in the recording or transmission of data. If the system detects an error in reading, it usually attempts to read the record again, on the possibility that the error was transient—possibly caused by dust on a tape, for instance. If the error does go away, it is usual not even to inform the object program that anything happened. If the error persists, either some indication is passed to the object program or, in the usual Fortran case, program execution is terminated with an error message. If the programmer wishes to provide his own error-handling routing in such a case, and if the particular Fortran system permits it, he can write, for instance,

```
READ (5, 100, ERR=3000) X, Y, Z
```

to indicate that if an uncorrectable error occurs during transmission the program should transfer to statement 3000, where he will have provided a program segment to take whatever appropriate action he desires.

The END and ERR parameters may both be used in the same READ:

```
READ (5, 100, END=80, ERR=3000) X, Y, Z
```

Unformatted input and output

Until now we have assumed that every READ or WRITE statement names a FORMAT statement that describes the external form of the information. However, if we wish to write out some information for temporary storage for later rereading, without ever printing or punching it, it is possible to transmit the information in essentially the same form as it is represented within the computer, and not name a FORMAT statement.

The form of the READ or WRITE is just as before, except that no FORMAT statement number appears. We can write

```
WRITE (9) ARRAY
```

for example, where ARRAY might be a large array of data. The data set reference number in such a statement must not name a data set that is to be printed; the latter must always be associated with formatting information. All that can legitimately be done with a record that was written without formatting is to read it back, also without formatting:

```
READ (9) ARRAY
```

The primary advantage of unformatted I/O is speed. It turns out that the actions that have to be taken to format information according to the descriptions contained in a FORMAT statement require a lot of time. In a program in which large quantities of data are being manipulated many times, the difference can definitely be appreciable.

Where is the data?

In many practical situations we would like to be able to write a Fortran program without knowing in advance where the data for it will be physically located, whether on regular punched cards, on magnetic tape or disk, directly from a time-sharing console connected to the computer, or from some other device. Using Fortran in conjunction with an *operating system* provides ways of postponing the decision until later in the process.

The facility can be used in several ways. Suppose, for instance, that we have written a Fortran program in which data set 5 was used by default to stand for a data set coming from cards. Now we want to modify things so that the information instead comes from a magnetic disk. The precise form of the command needed for this purpose is different for different computers and different operating systems, but there is almost always some simple way to handle it. In the time-sharing system used to prepare programs for this book it is necessary only to enter a command like this:

```
FILEDEF 5 DSK FIG5 DATA
```

"FILEDEF" stands for "file definition," 5 is the data set reference number, "DSK" tells the system that the data will be coming from a disk, "FIG5" is a name that had been made up by the programmer to identify the data set, and "DATA" is a requirement of the particular time-sharing system to identify the type of file.

In Operating System 360, used for the 360 and 370 series of computers from IBM, specifying that data set 5 comes from disk might be as simple as writing:

```
//GO.FT05F001 DD DSNAME=FIG5
```

The details vary greatly for various computers and their operating systems, and we make no pretense of covering the subject completely. You will be told by your instructor or computer center people how to write the necessary commands, which usually are not very complicated.

A small example program

To see some of these ideas in application, suppose that all of the data of the table on pages 92-93 is on a magnetic disk. Each "record" on the disk corresponds to one card, and there is no harm in thinking of the character positions in the disk record as if they were card columns. Thus we think of positions 1-5 as containing the year (NYEAR), positions 6-10 as containing the Gross National Product in current prices (GNP) etc.

We are required to read three items of data from each line: the year, the civilian labor force, and the unemployment percentage. These items, for all years in the table, are to be stored in arrays for presumed later processing. As the data is being read we shall check that the records are not out of sequence, by doing a *sequence check* on the item NYEAR: if any immediately previous year is greater than or equal to the one just read, there is trouble: we print an error comment and stop.

We expect to find exactly 37 records in this file, and we shall use a suitable DO loop to read the values into the three arrays. As a further guard against bad data, however, we use the END parameter in the READ, so that if there are too few records we get an error indication.

The printing of the values from the three arrays is done using an implied DO in the READ, just to show how this works out in a realistic application.

When this program was run on a time-sharing system, it was necessary to execute the system command

```
FILEDEF 12 DSK PAUL DATA
```

This identified or gave a file definition (FILEDEF) to data set 12, specified a magnetic disk with the "DSK," gave the name of the file as being PAUL, and specified the file type as DATA, a detail that need not detain us.

```
C A PROGRAM TO ILLUSTRATE INPUT/OUTPUT CONCEPTS
C
      DIMENSION NYEAR(37), LABOR(37), UNEMP(37)
C
C SET UP TO CHECK SEQUENCE OF YEARS
C
      NPREV = 0
C
C READ THE DATA
C
```

```
        DO 30 K = 1, 37
            READ (12, 10, END=60) NYEAR(K), LABOR(K), UNEMP(K)
10          FORMAT (I5, 35X, I5, F5.1)
            IF ( NPREV .GE. NYEAR(K) ) WRITE (6, 20) NYEAR(K)
20          FORMAT (1X, 'SEQUENCE ERROR AT YEAR  ', I5)
            IF ( NPREV .GE. NYEAR(K) ) STOP
            NPREV = NYEAR(K)
30      CONTINUE
        WRITE (6, 40)
40      FORMAT ('1', ' YEAR    LABOR    UNEMPLOYMENT'/
     1      1X, '         FORCE    PERCENTAGE'/)
        WRITE (6, 50) (NYEAR(J), LABOR(J), UNEMP(J), J = 1, 37)
50      FORMAT (1X, I5, I8, F11.1)
        STOP
60      WRITE (6, 70)
70      FORMAT ('0', 'UNEXPECTED END OF FILE ON UNIT 12')
        STOP
        END
```

Here is the output when the program was run.

YEAR	LABOR FORCE	UNEMPLOYMENT PERCENTAGE
1929	49180	3.2
1931	50420	15.9
1933	51590	24.9
1935	52870	20.1
1937	54000	14.3
1938	54610	19.0
1939	55230	17.2
1940	55640	14.6
1941	55910	9.9
1942	56410	4.7
1944	54630	1.2
1945	53860	1.9
1946	57520	3.9
1948	60621	3.8
1949	61286	5.9
1950	62208	5.3
1951	62017	3.3
1952	62138	3.0
1953	63015	2.9
1954	63643	5.5
1955	65023	4.4
1956	66552	4.1
1957	66929	4.3
1958	67639	6.8
1959	68639	5.5
1960	69628	5.5
1961	70459	6.7
1962	70614	5.5
1963	71833	5.7
1964	73091	5.2
1965	74455	4.5
1966	75770	3.8
1967	77347	3.8
1968	78737	3.6
1969	80734	3.5
1970	82715	4.9
1971	84113	5.9

A typical file processing example

To show some more of these ideas at work we turn to one of the most common applications of computers, the updating of a master file of information. The example will take advantage of several assumptions that would never be acceptable in actual practice in order to make this first contact simple and understandable.

We are to think of a hardware store that keeps its inventory records on magnetic tape. For every item the store stocks there is one *record* in a *master file* that contains the identification number of the item, a short description of it, and the quantity on hand. This tape, in real life, would have thousands of records; we shall deal with a sample file that has – as it happens – 19. The records appear in the file in ascending sequence of the item number, which we shall call the *key*. A glance at Figure 8.3 will show, for instance, that the first item has a key of 127, the next 128, then 129, then 1106, etc. Note the gaps: not all possible keys are present. Those that there are, however, are in strictly ascending sequence. The first simplifying assumption, and one that would never do in actual practice, is that there are no errors of sequence in this file or in the transaction file that is discussed next. We also assume that in this master file there are no duplicate keys.

The format of a record in the master file is that the first five positions are the integer key, the next 25 contain an alphanumeric description, and the next 10 contain the amount of the stock item on hand.

The purpose of the application is to make sure that the master file is always relatively up to date on the amount of each item there is on hand. Naturally, the store sells items and receives new supplies from warehouses, distributors, etc. At the end of each day – or perhaps each week – the data processing department is required to produce an updated file that reflects all the *transactions* that have occurred since the last updating. This information would then normally be used to order more supplies for items that are in short supply; we shall not attempt to show that part of the operation.

The transaction file would normally be much shorter than the master file, since not all items have "activity" (sales or receipts) every time the master file is updated. In our sample data there are 13 transaction items. Here it is quite natural to expect multiple records with the same key: a given stock item may have been bought by several customers, and there may have been sales and receipts on the same day. We do once again assume, however, that the transaction tape is in correct ascending sequence on the keys. It is also essential to assume that for every transaction there does exist a matching master; otherwise there could be trouble.

The format of the transaction file records is that the first five positions contain the key, just as in the master file. But next comes a code that specifies whether the transaction was an *issue* (sale) which is indicated by a code of 1, or a receipt from a supplier, with a code of 2. This code takes up just one column. Then there is a ten-column quantity field just as with the master. There is no alphanumeric description in the transaction.

The task we approach, stated briefly, is to produce a new master file that takes into account the transactions. The old master is not to be changed. And any record from the old master file for which there is no corresponding transaction record is simply to be written to the new master unchanged.

Figure 8.1 is a flowchart of the method that will be used.

We begin by reading a transaction record, then read a master record and ask if it has the same key as the transaction. If it is not the same, that merely means that there was no activity for the first master record. We accordingly write the master record out of the new master file without change.

If they do match, we pause to ask whether the key is 99999, which is used as a sentinel at the end of each file. This manner of testing makes sure we will not stop until *both* input files have been completely read; we surely do not want to stop merely because the transaction file is exhausted because there could still be master records for which there was no activity. When the sentinel is detected at the end of the old master file our final action is just to put a sentinel at the end of the new master. (Today's new master will be tomorrow's old master, as the cycle repeats.)

If the keys match and they are not sentinels, we are ready to process. At this point we want to subtract the transaction amount from the master amount if this is a code 1 (issue), and add if it is a code 2 (receipt). If it is neither of these, there is a coding error which we will "flag," i.e., write an

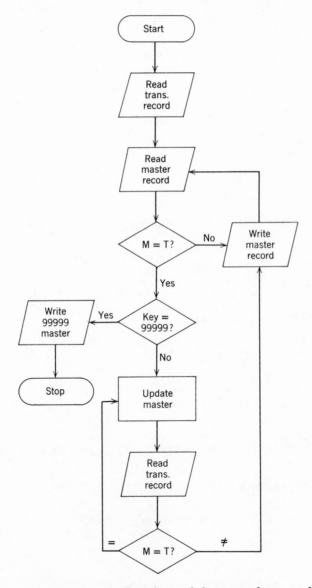

FIGURE 8.1. A flowchart of the procedure used in a simplified file-updating application.

```
C A PROGRAM TO UPDATE A MASTER FILE
C THE INPUT CONSISTS OF AN OLD MASTER FILE AND A TRANSACTION FILE
C THE OUTPUT CONSISTS OF A NEW MASTER; THE INPUT FILES ARE NOT CHANGED
C VARIABLE NAMES
C      ITEMTR   ITEM NUMBER FROM TRANSACTION
C      ITEMMA   ITEM NUMBER FROM MASTER
C      KODE     TRANSATION CODE; 1 = ISSUE, 2 = RECEIPT
C      DESC     DESCRIPTION; AN ARRAY OF 25 CHARACTERS
C      COUNTT   COUNT FROM TRANSACTION
C      COUNTM   COUNT FROM MASTER
C      NDUMMY   DUMMY DO INDEX
C
       DIMENSION DESC(25)
C
C              ... READ A TRANSACTION RECORD TO GET STARTED
C
       READ (3, 10) ITEMTR, KODE, COUNTT
  10   FORMAT (I5, I1, F10.0)
C
C              ... READ A MASTER RECORD
C
  20   READ (4, 30, END = 110) ITEMMA, DESC, COUNTM
  30   FORMAT (I5, 25A1, F10.0)
C
C              ... MASTER AND TRANS SAME ITEM NUMBER?
C              ... IF NOT, WRITE MASTER UNCHANGED
C              ... AND GO BACK FOR ANOTHER
C
  40   IF ( ITEMMA .NE. ITEMTR ) WRITE (7, 50) ITEMMA, DESC, COUNTM
  50   FORMAT (I5, 25A1, F10.0)
       IF ( ITEMMA .NE. ITEMTR ) GO TO 20
C
C              ... THEY ARE EQUAL;  CHECK FOR END OF FILE
C
       IF ( ITEMMA .EQ. 99999 ) WRITE (7, 60)
  60   FORMAT ('99999')
       IF ( ITEMMA .EQ. 99999 ) STOP
C
C              ... RECORDS MATCH: UPDATE MASTER
C
       DO 90 NDUMMY = 1, 100
           IF ( KODE .EQ. 1 ) COUNTM = COUNTM - COUNTT
           IF ( KODE .EQ. 2 ) COUNTM = COUNTM + COUNTT
           IF ( (KODE .NE. 1) .AND. (KODE .NE. 2) ) WRITE (6, 70)ITEMMA
  70       FORMAT (1X, 'CODE FOR ITEM ', I5, '  BAD; TRANS IGNORED')
C
C              ... GET ANOTHER TRANSACTION
C
           READ (3, 80, END = 110) ITEMTR, KODE, COUNTT
  80       FORMAT (I5, I1, F10.0)
C
C              ... IF NOT EQUAL GET OUT OF LOOP
C
           IF ( ITEMMA .NE. ITEMTR ) GO TO 40
  90   CONTINUE
C
       WRITE (6, 100) ITEMTR
 100   FORMAT (1X,'MORE THAN 100 TRANS ITEM ',I7,'; PROBABLE ERROR')
       STOP
C
C              ... WRITE ERROR MESSAGE FOR LACK OF SENTINEL
C
 110   WRITE (6, 120)
 120   FORMAT (1X, 'ONE OF THE FILES HAD NO SENTINEL')
       STOP
       END
```

FIGURE 8.2. A program for updating inventory records, corresponding to the flowchart of Figure 8.1.

error message about. (We are not quite assuming that *everything* will always be correct!)

Having done the update, we next need to see if there are more transactions for this item, which there very well might be. We do not want to write out the master until all the items affecting it have been processed. So we read another transaction and if it has the same key, simply repeat the processing loop. If the keys are now different, we have a new item number, in which case we want to write out the updated master record and start hunting for the master that matches this new key.

The program in Figure 8.2 is almost simpler than the flowchart. The comments in the body of the program have been indented and preceded by three dots to provide better clarity. A DO loop has been used to get all the transactions for a given master record; it is assumed that if there were more than 100 transactions for one stock item, it would probably be an error, and the normal exit of the DO is used to signal this fact. The two READs within the main processing portion of the program have the

```
END = 110
```

option in them. If both files are in order and have sentinels as they should, the program would never attempt to read past the end of the records; this provides another small degree of checking.

Observe the data set reference numbers. It is assumed that the transaction file is on data set 3, the old master on 4, and the new master on 7. Data sets 3 and 4 do not have assumed conventional uses, and will have to be defined; data set 7 is normally for punching and will have to be changed unless that is actually desired.

The important thing to realize is that at this point we have not committed ourselves in any way to the device on which the various files are to appear. If we wanted to read the old master from a tape, the transactions from a time-sharing console, and punch the new master on cards, it would be a trivial matter of a few instructions to do it that way.

In point of fact, it served the author's purposes best to have all three files reside on magnetic disks, which required issuing the following commands to the time-sharing system:

```
FILEDEF 3 DSK CH8TRANS DATA
FILEDEF 4 DSK CH8MAST DATA
FILEDEF 7 DSK NEWMAST8 DATA
```

A small program, not shown, to print the three files in a more readable form, produces the output of Figures 8.3, 8.4, and 8.5. You should trace through at least a few of the transactions to see that the new master does represent an updated version of the old master.

In testing such programs it is essential to test all the special circumstances one can think of: whether or not there is a transaction for the first master record; ditto for the last record. It might be good to see what would happen if there were only one transaction.

Chapter Summary

1. The most important concept in Fortran input/output programming is that of the scanning process by which the system keeps READ/WRITE list

MASTER FILE: ITEM, DESCRIPTION, COUNT

```
   127      6 INCH WRENCHES                    12.
   128      8 INCH WRENCHES                    10.
   129      10 INCH WRENCHES                   31.
  1106      LARGE AWNINGS                      21.
  1107      MEDIUM AWNINGS                      4.
 12001      18 GAUGE WIRE - FEET              800.
 12002      16 GAUGE WIRE - FEET             1200.
 12003      14 GAUGE WIRE - FEET             1050.
 12004      12 GAUGE WIRE - FEET              200.
 12005      10 GAUGE WIRE - FEET             2250.
 12006      8 GAUGE WIRE - FEET               63.
 13001      10 PENNY NAILS - POUNDS           80.
 13002      12 PENNY NAILS - POUNDS           62.
 14019      SHOVELS - LONG HANDLE             12.
 14040      SHOVELS - MEDIUM HANDLE            2.
 14051      SHOVELS - SNOW                    43.
 14136      FRICTION TAPE, ROLLS              80.
 15019      SALT - 50 POUND BAGS             125.
 15400      5-10-5 FERTILIZER 25 LB           29.
 99999                                         0.
```

FIGURE 8.3. The input master file to the inventory updating application.

TRANSACTION FILE: ITEM, CODE, COUNT

```
   127    2       77.
  1106    2       10.
 12001    1      100.
 12001    1      100.
 12004    2     1000.
 13001    2       15.
 13001    1       20.
 13001    1       30.
 13001    1       45.
 14136    1        1.
 15019    3       69.
 15400    2       45.
 15400    2      665.
 99999    0        0.
```

FIGURE 8.4. The transaction file for the inventory updating application.

variables in step with FORMAT field descriptors. If it is clearly understood that Fortran always proceeds from left to right in the READ or WRITE, and does the same in the FORMAT except when instructed otherwise with parentheses, most of the rest of the material is easy to understand.

2. Integer variables in a READ/WRITE list can be used elsewhere in the same list as a subscript, with the requirement that in a READ the subscript use must come later than its nonsubscript use.

3. The list of a READ or WRITE can have an implied DO, with the variables so controlled and the indexing information both enclosed in parentheses.

```
NEW MASTER: ITEM, DESCRIPTION, COUNT

   127      6 INCH WRENCHES                  89.
   128      8 INCH WRENCHES                  10.
   129      10 INCH WRENCHES                 31.
   1106     LARGE AWNINGS                    31.
   1107     MEDIUM AWNINGS                    4.
   12001    18 GAUGE WIRE - FEET            600.
   12002    16 GAUGE WIRE - FEET           1200.
   12003    14 GAUGE WIRE - FEET           1050.
   12004    12 GAUGE WIRE - FEET           1200.
   12005    10 GAUGE WIRE - FEET           2250.
   12006    8 GAUGE WIRE - FEET             63.
   13001    10 PENNY NAILS - POUNDS          0.
   13002    12 PENNY NAILS - POUNDS         62.
   14019    SHOVELS - LONG HANDLE           12.
   14040    SHOVELS - MEDIUM HANDLE          2.
   14051    SHOVELS - SNOW                  43.
   14136    FRICTION TAPE, ROLLS            79.
   15019    SALT - 50 POUND BAGS           125.
   15400    5-10-5 FERTILIZER 25 LB        739.
   99999                                     0.
```

FIGURE 8.5. The updated master file for the inventory application.

4. When there are more variables to transmit than there are field descriptors in the associated FORMAT, scanning of the FORMAT returns to the beginning of the last set of open parentheses.

5. When a sign appears in input field, it must be the first nonblank character in the field.

6. Alphanumeric information may be associated with any type of variable, since Fortran has no specific variable type for the purpose. But variables used to hold alphanumeric information should be all real or all integer, to avoid unwanted automatic data type conversions.

7. The complete set of information that will be read by a READ or written by a WRITE can be described as a *file* or, equivalently in different terms, as a *data set*. A file consists of *records*, where a record is one line, one card, one set of characters on a magnetic disk, etc.

8. A slash (/) in a FORMAT statement means to complete the operations with the current record and move to a new one. This could mean to stop reading from one card and go to the next, or to start a new line of printing.

9. Parentheses within FORMAT statements are used to force repetition of groups of field descriptors.

10. The BACKSPACE, END FILE, and REWIND statements, when appropriate for the file medium being used, cause the actions their names describe.

11. Although not a feature of ANSI Fortran, most Fortrans provide some way to indicate what should be done when an attempt is made to read a record after all the records in a file have already been used. One of the most common ways is the END= parameter in the READ statement. The ERR= parameter provides a similar control for unrecoverable physical errors in data transmission.

12. Unformatted input and output is useful for its great gain in speed. Such methods cannot be used for printing, however, and apply only to intermediate data that is being temporarily stored for later reading.

13. Fortran makes certain assumptions about files to be read, printed, or punched, most commonly assigning them to data sets numbered 5, 6, and 7, respectively. But these designations can be changed, and any other numbers given meaning by appropriate commands to the *operating system*, using language that varies greatly from one system to another. The techniques are not difficult but must be obtained locally since they vary so much.

REVIEW QUESTIONS

1. In the statement

```
WRITE (6, 200) A
```

exactly what does the 6 mean?

2. Suppose that three numbers of ten columns each are on a card, representing values for the variables A, B, and C, respectively. Is there any way we could write a statement such as

```
READ (5, 300) B, C, A
```

and then tell Fortran in the FORMAT that the order in which variables were named in the READ is not the same as the order in which they appear on the card?

3. What would this program fragment do?

```
      DIMENSION (SAM)
      ...
      L = 4
      WRITE (6, 300) L, SAM(L)
300   FORMAT (I5, F12.4)
```

4. What would this fragment do?

```
      DIMENSION GOODMN(20), AND(20), STEINR(20)
      ...
      WRITE (6, 400) (GOODMN(K), AND(K), STEINR(K), K = 1, 20)
400   FORMAT (1X, 3F12.3)
```

5. What would this fragment do?

```
      DIMENSION RAY(17)
      ...
      DO 510 JERRY = 1, 17, 2
          WRITE (5, 500) JERRY, RAY(JERRY)
500       FORMAT (1X, I5, F10.1)
510   CONTINUE
```

6. What would this fragment do?

```
      DIMENSION WEXLER(50)
      ...
      WRITE (6, 600) WEXLER
600   FORMAT (1X, 10F8.2)
```

7. What would this fragment do?

```
      DIMENSION JON(33)
      ...
      WRITE (6, 700) JON
  700 FORMAT (1X, 3I8/(1X, 6I8))
```

8. Consider the example on page 144, where we read a 20-character name into an array named NAME, one character per element. Suppose that we know that an integer variable in this machine can in fact hold four characters. Will this program fragment produce the same results as the text example?

```
      DIMENSION NAME(5)
      READ (5, 220) NAME
  220 FORMAT (5A4)
      WRITE (6, 230) NAME
  230 FORMAT (1X, 5A4)
```

9. Assuming that your Fortran permits both the Hollerith field descriptor and the use of quoted literals in a FORMAT, state the pros and cons of each.

10. What does this statement mean?

```
READ (5, 5000, END=5010, ERR=6000) A, B, C
```

11. What is the point of using unformatted input and output? What is its use restricted to?

12. In the file processing example, what would happen if the first two transaction records were reversed? What does this tell you about the desirability of checking the input?

13. In the file processing example, suppose that through error there were a transaction record with a key greater than the key of the last master record. What would happen?

14. In the file processing example, what would happen if there were two identical old master records? Would there necessarily be any indication of the error?

15. The file processing example permits duplicate transaction records. If there are both issues and receipts for some item, does it make any difference in which order they are processed?

ANSWERS

1. To be perfectly precise, it means whatever I/O device you or your computer center says it means. If you issue your own definition for it, it can mean any type of input or output device available on your computer. *Usually* it means a printer attached to the computer, that definition having been established by the computer center.

2. Absolutely not. The impossibility of doing this is at the heart of the scanning process that keeps the data values, the list variable names, and the FORMAT field descriptors in step with each other.

3. It would print, on one line, the number 4 and the fourth element of SAM.

4. It would print 20 lines. On each line there would be an element from GOODMN, one from AND, and one from STEINR. The successive lines would correspond to the values of K from 1 to 20, but these numbers would not be printed.

5. It would print nine lines. Each line would contain one of the odd integers from 1 to 17, together with the corresponding element from the array RAY.

6. It would print five lines, containing the 50 elements of WEXLER in order, ten to a line.

7. It would print one line consisting of the first three elements of JON, followed by five more lines containing the rest of the elements of JON.

8. The results would be identical.

9. *Pro Hollerith:* you don't have to worry about forgetting the closing quote, and if you ever want to run the program on a system that does not permit quoted literals, you are ahead. *Con Hollerith:* you have to count the characters, and errors in counting can be very damaging. *Pro quoted literals:* no counting, less space in FORMAT. *Con quoted literals:* forget the closing quote and you're in trouble; not all systems accept them.

10. It says to read values for A, B, and C, whatever they are (they could be arrays, for all we know on the basis of the information given) under control of FORMAT statement 5000, which is not shown. If the program attempts to read a record after all the valid data, there will be a jump to statement 5010. If the equipment makes an error, there will be a jump to statement 6000. Not all Fortrans accept these END and ERR options, but the majority do.

11. Unformatted I/O is generally very much faster than formatted, since the formatting and deformatting is a highly time-consuming process. The restriction is that, except in very special circumstances, nothing can be done with unformatted output except to read it back later. In other words, it is ordinarily unprintable.

12. Big problems. The transaction for 1106, now first, would be processed correctly. But then the program would start looking through the master file, searching for item 127. Since that record would already have been passed, it would never find it. This is just one of many possible types of errors that a complete program would need to check for.

13. This would lead to a nonexistent master record and eventually produce the message that one file did not contain a sentinel. This would not be the true explanation, of course, which might confuse things a bit. Another argument for more checking.

14. There would definitely be no error indication if there was no matching transaction. The duplicate masters would both be written out to the new file, with no hint of trouble. If there were a matching transaction, the first master would be updated correctly, and the second one would be written out without any changes. Another reason for more checking!

15. You would always want to process the receipts first, so that if there were more issues than had previously been in stock, there would not be a false out-of-stock indication. (This program does not produce such messages in any event, but in real life it probably would.)

This might argue for coding the issues and receipts differently, so that the issue/receipts code could be made a part of the sorting key.

EXERCISES

Note. In this and the two following chapters there are rather fewer exercises than in preceding chapters. This is done on the assumption that by this point in the course you are working on problems from your other courses or your work situation, or else you are engaged in a term project—possibly one of those suggested at the back of the book. These exercises, accordingly, are only to give you a bit of practice in the basics.

*1. Write WRITE/FORMAT combinations to do the following.
   a. Print three numbers identified by the variable names R, S, and T, each with an F10.2 field descriptor, but in reverse order from the way they are written here.
   b. Print the integer value associated with the variable LAST, together with the element of ARRAY identified by the subscript LAST.
   c. Write out the values of the array SAMPLE identified by the subscripts 1, 10, and JOYCE.

2. Write READ/FORMAT combinations to do the following.
   a. Read values of K, MEAN, and LIMIT from a card, each number being punched in five columns with K beginning in column 11.
   b. Read a value of J from columns 1-3 of a card, then use that value to assign the value in columns 4-10 to ARRAY(J). (Recall that this practice is not recommended.)
   c. Read a value of K from columns 11-13, a value of J from columns 1-3, a value of X from columns 4-10, and a value of Y from columns 14-20.

*3. Write a WRITE/FORMAT combination to print all 50 values of XARRAY, ten to a line, with F8.2 field descriptors.

4. Write a WRITE/FORMAT combination to write all 50 values of XARRAY, one to a line, with five blank spaces before each value. Use an F10.5 field descriptor for the printed values.

*5. Write WRITE statements to do the following:
   a. Print the first 20 elements of an array named GREEK.
   b. Print the odd-numbered elements of TROJAN; the array has 100 elements in all.

6. Write WRITE statements to do the following:
   a. Print the last 20 elements of GREEK, which has 100 elements.
   b. Print the even-numbered elements of TROJAN; the array has 100 elements.

*7. Write a program fragment, including any necessary DIMENSION statement, to read the first 20 columns of a card as alphabetic data, and immediately print that data at the left side of a line.

8. Write a program fragment to read the alphabetic data in columns 41-70 of a card, and print it in printing positions 11-40 of a line.

*9. Write statements to print the word UNDERLINE, then underline it. This will require use of the carriage control feature for suppressing spacing.

10. Write statements to print the words DOUBLE PRINTING, then print the same words again in the same place, in order to give the effect of bold face printing.

*11. An array named SAM has 21 elements. Write the WRITE and FORMAT statements necessary to print the first element of SAM on a line by itself, then the rest of the elements five to a line. Use only one WRITE statement.

12. An array named SAM has 21 elements. Using only one WRITE and one FORMAT, print the elements of the array on four lines, the first three of which have five elements and the last of which has six.

*13. Write a READ statement to get a value of X from columns 1-10 of a card, and transfer to statement 180 if there are no cards still to be read.

14. Write a READ statement that will read a value from a card, but transfer to statement 350 if there is an error in card reading.

*15. Write suitable statements to write an entire array named HARRAY on a magnetic disk that has a data set reference number of 12, without formatting. Assume that this data set has already been defined by operating system commands that you do not have to write.

16. Referring to Exercise 15, write a READ statement to get HARRAY back into storage.

*17. Modify the program of Figure 8.2 so that it includes a check that the transaction file is in correct sequence, that is, that there is never a record with a key smaller than the one that preceded it. See Case Study 4 for guidance on how to do this.

18. Modify the program of Figure 8.2 so that it makes a sequence check on both the transaction and old master files.

CHAPTER NINE
FORTRAN FUNCTIONS AND SUBROUTINES

Introduction

Fortran provides several techniques for reducing the effort of writing a program and increasing the chances that it is correct.

The first new feature that we shall study here is the facility for using pre-programmed functions that carry out common mathematical operations. Since most readers of this book are assumed not to be closely concerned with mathematical applications of computers, we shall move rather quickly over this part.

The second new topic is that of the Fortran SUBROUTINE statement and several statements associated with it. One function of a subroutine is to reduce the effort of writing a program that has some frequently used operations that we can put in one place and call into use whenever needed. The second use is to break a program up into pieces in a way that makes it easier to understand how the program works. We shall devote most of the chapter to this general subject area.

Fortran Supplied Functions

Fortran provides for quite a number of prewritten functions to carry out common operations, mostly mathematical. Each function has a name, such as SQRT for square root, or ALOG10 for a logarithm to the base 10. Whenever we wish to call one of these functions into play, we simply write its name followed by parentheses enclosing an arithmetic expression. For example, if we wanted to take the square root of the quantity X + 2.0, add Y to the result, and assign the whole thing to Q, we would merely write

    Q = SQRT(X + 2.0) + Y

We recall from earlier chapters that a square root can also be found by raising the quantity to the 0.5 power, like this:

    Q = (X + 2.0)**0.5 + Y

Since square roots are so common in some applications, however, and since the square root function turns out to be faster in the object program, a separate function is supplied for it.

Definitions

It will be helpful in what follows to have a certain small amount of new terminology: the expression that is written within parentheses in the use of a function is called its *argument*. The value that is returned is called the *function value*. These terms, like so many others in Fortran, come from mathematics.

Other functions

A list of the supplied functions available in Fortran appears as Appendix 6. Here we shall sample a few that have usefulness even in applications that are not primarily mathematical.

One function that is frequently handy is one that picks the largest of a set of expression values. When used with real arguments to produce a real function value, the correct function is named AMAX1. Now if we want the larger of A and B we can simply write

```
Q = AMAX1(A, B)
```

For an example of the usefulness of this function in a business calculation, consider this instruction from a tax form:

"Line 8: Enter the sum of lines 6 and 7, or the Standard Premium, whichever is greater." Using the obvious variable names we could write

```
XLINE8 = AMAX1(XLINE6 + XLINE7, STNDRD)
```

Finally, let us look at our old friend, the overtime pay calculation. This statement will look quite different from what we did before but will accomplish the same result:

```
PAY = RATE * (HOURS + 0.5*AMAX1(0.0, HOURS-40.0))
```

Look at the AMAX1 function first. This says to subtract 40.0 from HOURS to get the second argument of the function. If HOURS is greater than 40.0, the difference will be a positive number, but if HOURS is less than 40.0, the difference will be a negative number. Now the maximum function works with algebraic values, according to which zero is greater than any negative number. Thus, if HOURS −40.0 is negative, indicating that the person worked fewer than 40 hours, the AMAX1 function will return the value zero. Zero times 0.5 is still zero, so in this case the formula reduces, in effect, to

```
PAY = RATE * HOURS
```

If HOURS − 40.0 is positive, indicating that the person worked more than 40.0 hours, the AMAX1 function will return this value, which will be multiplied by 0.5 to get the "and-a-half" that is added to HOURS before multiplying by RATE.

Conversion Between Real and Integer

Two functions are provided for converting the form of representation of numbers. FLOAT takes an integer argument and returns it in real form: IFIX does the reverse. (The names come from historical usage, when real and integer used to be called floating and fixed, respectively.) The most common usage is to convert an integer variable to real form for use with a function that requires a real argument. If we want the square root of K, for instance, we cannot write

```
R = SQRT(K)
```

because a program containing such an expression would be a syntax error in most systems. Instead, we write

```
R = SQRT(FLOAT(K))
```

It is always possible to convert in advance, utilizing the fact that when the two sides of an assignment statement involve different variable types an automatic conversion is made. We might say

```
XK = K
R = SQRT(XK)
```

If only one such conversion is needed, however, the FLOAT function is simpler.

Truncation

Finally, we have two functions that *truncate* real arguments, which means to discard the fractional part of the argument and return the result in either real (AINT) or integer (INT) form. INT and IFIX actually have the same result. Case Study 7, the simulation of the game of craps, uses the INT function.

The Idea of a Subroutine

The basic idea of a subroutine is that it is possible to write a program in one place, then call it into action many times, usually with different arguments each time, and have control return from the subroutine to the point in the main program where it was called. In a graphical sort of way we can represent the situation thus:

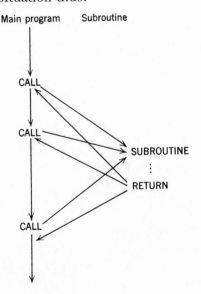

The basic idea is that there is only one copy of the subroutine, but it can still be used many times at different points in another program that calls it into action. This concept, which goes back to the earliest days of the computer era, is still one of the most fundamental intellectual inventions in the usage of computers.

The details of subroutine use in Fortran

A Fortran subroutine is a complete separate program. It can be compiled all by itself if one so desires. It must begin with the word SUBROUTINE and end with an END. There must be a RETURN statement in the subroutine to tell Fortran when we are ready to go back to the calling program. Typically there will be only one RETURN, just before the END.

When a subroutine is to be called into action, one writes a CALL statement that lists the name and the arguments.

An Example

Let us turn quickly to an example to try to make these ideas clearer. Suppose that in a certain program it is frequently necessary to find the area and hypotenuse of a right triangle, given the lengths of its other two sides. The complete subroutine could be as follows:

```
SUBROUTINE TRINGL(A, B, AREA, HYP)
AREA = A * B / 2.0
HYP = SQRT(A**2 + B**2)
RETURN
END
```

Now in a main program we can call this subroutine into action with a CALL statement giving suitable arguments. Maybe the length of the sides are 2.5 and Q, and the area and hypotenuse are to be assigned to variables named Y and Z:

```
CALL TRINGL(2.5, Q, Y, Z)
```

This statement calls the subroutine into action, tells it what the actual arguments are, and what to do with the results. Perhaps later in the program we need to use the same subroutine for a triangle having sides given by HH-3.48 and ABC, with the area and hypotenuse to be assigned to R and SS:

```
CALL TRINGL(HH-3.48, ABC, R, SS)
```

In each case, after the subroutine has been executed, control returns to the statement after the CALL.

Dummy arguments

It is important to realize that the arguments used in defining the subroutine are only dummies, which tell the Fortran compiler what to do with actual arguments. To show what is meant, the subroutine could have been written thus:

```
SUBROUTINE TRINGL(D, E, F, G)
F = D * E / 2.0
G = SQRT(D**2 + E**2)
RETURN
END
```

The program is a bit harder to follow, since the variable names no longer suggest what they stand for, but the effect of the subroutine when called would be exactly the same.

Another example

Suppose that we are writing a program in which it is frequently necessary to find the largest value in an array of 50 values. We need not only the largest value but its element number as well. We know how to write a few statements to do the job but we assume it occurs frequently, so why not set it up as a subroutine? Here is one simple way it could be done.

```
      SUBROUTINE BIGGST (ARRAY, BIG, NBIG)
      DIMENSION ARRAY(50)
      BIG = ARRAY(1)
      NBIG = 1
      DO 10 K = 2, 50
          IF ( ARRAY(K) .GT. BIG ) BIG = ARRAY(K)
          IF ( ARRAY(K) .GT. BIG ) NBIG = K
  10  CONTINUE
      RETURN
      END
```

Now we can use this subroutine with calls like these:

```
CALL BIGGST (X, Y, M)
```

or

```
CALL BIGGST (ARRAY8, BIG, N)
```

Observe that in the second call we have used an actual argument name that is the same as the dummy used in the definition. No problem.

For an example of a subroutine that we can compile and run, consider this job. We have a main program in which it is frequently necessary to find the average of the elements in an array. The arrays are of different sizes. For illustrative purposes we shall have three arrays, of maximum sizes 100, 50, and 200. The first one we shall fill halfway: the first 50 elements will be the first 50 integers. The second will have its first 20 positions filled with the

```
C A SUBROUTINE TO ADD THE FIRST N ELEMENTS OF AN ARRAY
C AND FIND THEIR AVERAGE
C
      SUBROUTINE ADDER (ARRAY, N, AVER)
      DIMENSION ARRAY(1000)
      SUM = 0.0
      DO 10 K = 1, N
          SUM = SUM + ARRAY(K)
  10  CONTINUE
      AVER = SUM / N
      RETURN
      END
```

FIGURE 9.1. A program to illustrate the SUBROUTINE concept.

```
C A PROGRAM TO EXERCISE THE ADDING ROUTINE OF FIGURE 9.1
C
C FIRST APPLICATION: THE SUM OF THE FIRST 50 INTEGERS
C
        DIMENSION X(100), Y(50), DATA(200)
        DO 10 K = 1, 50
            X(K) = K
  10    CONTINUE
        CALL ADDER(X, 50, FIRST)
        WRITE (6, 20) X(1), X(50),   FIRST
  20    FORMAT (1X, 3F12.3)
C
C SECOND APPLICATION: THE CUBES OF THE FIRST 20 INTEGERS
C
        DO 30 L = 1, 20
            Y(L) = L**3
  30    CONTINUE
        CALL ADDER (Y, 20, SECOND)
        WRITE (6, 40) Y(1), Y(2), SECOND
  40    FORMAT (1X, 3F12.3)
C
C THIRD APPLICATION: DATA READ FROM CARDS
C
        READ (5, 50) N
  50    FORMAT (I3)
        IF ( N .LT. 1 ) STOP
        IF ( N .GT. 200 ) STOP
        DO 70 J = 1, N
            READ (5, 60) TEMP
  60        FORMAT (F10.0)
            IF ( TEMP .LT. -1000. ) STOP
            IF ( TEMP .GT.  1000. ) STOP
            DATA (J) = TEMP
  70    CONTINUE
        CALL ADDER (DATA, N, THIRD)
        WRITE (6, 80) DATA(1), DATA(N), THIRD
  80    FORMAT (1X, 3F12.3)
        STOP
        END
```

FIGURE 9.2. A program to "exercise" the subroutine of Figure 9.1.

cubes of the first 20 integers. The third array will have a number of elements determined by reading data from a card; the first N elements will consist of numbers read from subsequent cards.

The subroutine for this job is shown in Figure 9.1. After the identifying comments comes the word SUBROUTINE followed by the name of the sub-routine, ADDER, then parentheses enclosing the arguments. The subroutine contains a DIMENSION statement, as it must to process arrays. We have made it larger than any legitimate size that we expect to process. The adding and averaging contains no new ideas.

A program that "exercises" this subroutine is shown in Figure 9.2. It can be read straight through, to the point that at this stage of the book you should be able to read the program about as easily as you could read a description of it. Validity checks are made on the value of N read from cards, and the values are tested to be sure that they fall between limits that would presumably have been established as reasonable for the application.

These two programs—the main program and the subprogram—were compiled at separate times, then both loaded into the computer and the system was instructed to begin executing the main program. Here is the output produced.

```
              1.000       50.000        25.500
              1.000        8.000      2205.000
     005
     12.3
     23.4
     34.5
     45.6
     56.7
             12.300       56.700        34.500
```

As a matter of fact, the programs were run on a time-sharing system, and the column of figures at the left between the second and third lines produced by the program are the data input, enabling us to see that the output is correct.

The exam grades with a subroutine

To see how a subroutine might be useful in a fairly realistic situation, let us return to the examination grade application of Chapters 6 and 7 once again.

This time there is still a grade in column 1-10 of the card, but in addition there is a code in column 11 that specifies whether the student was an undergraduate (code = 1) or graduate (code = 2). The requirement is that the program produce statistics on the class as a whole, on the undergraduate students as a separate group, and on the graduate students as a separate group. The statistics are to be as in Chapter Seven: lowest and highest grades, mean and median. Since the same operations are to be carried out on three arrays, it is natural to think of writing a subroutine to carry out the common operations.

To be specific, here is what the subroutine is to do. It will accept the name of an array containing a set of grades, ranging from 1 up to a count of the total number of valid elements in the array. The maximum array size is 100, the maximum number of grades specified as legitimate in the application. The subroutine must sort the array to find the median; this sorting simplifies finding the lowest and highest scores as well.

The subroutine is shown in Figure 9.3. Since it is very similar to the program of Figure 7.2, we can pass over most of its features rather quickly.

Observe that the program proper, after the initial comments, begins with the word SUBROUTINE followed by the chosen name and a list of the arguments. This pattern must be followed for all subroutines. Next there is a DIMENSION statement; any subroutine that processes subscripted variables must include a DIMENSION statement for any arrays that are processed. We will be calling this subroutine three times, each time with a different array, but in each case there will be only one array transmitted to the subroutine so the subroutine needs only one DIMENSION. Its size must be as large as the largest array that will be processed. The name chosen for the array in the subroutine is immaterial, so long as what appears in the SUBROUTINE statement at the beginning of the subprogram matches what appears in the body of the subprogram. This is a dummy variable just as all the others are.

```
C A SUBROUTINE TO SORT AN ARRAY, FIND MEAN AND MEDIAN,
C    AND LOCATE THE LARGEST AND SMALLEST ELEMENTS
C
C       VARIABLES
C       A        THE ARRAY TO BE SORTED, ETC.
C       N        THE NUMBER OF ELEMENTS IN THE ARRAY, UP
C                TO MAXIMUM OF 100
C       SMALL    SMALLEST ELEMENT IN ARRAY
C       BIG      THE LARGEST ELEMENT IN THE ARRAY
C       NM1      N - 1: OUTER LOOP INDEXING PARAMETER
C       I        OUTER LOOP INDEX
C       IPLUS1   I + 1: INNER LOOP INDEX PARAMTER
C       J        INNER LOOP INDEX
C       TEMP     TEMPORARY STORAGE IN SORTING
C       AMEAN    MEAN OF THE ARRAY ELEMENTS
C       AMEDN    MEDIAN OF THE ARRAY ELEMENTS
C       NMEDN    ELEMENT NUMBER OF MEDIAN; SEE TEXT
C
C
        SUBROUTINE GRADER (A, N, SMALL, BIG, AMEAN, AMEDN)
        DIMENSION A(100)
        NM1 = N - 1
        DO 20 I = 1, NM1
            IPLUS1 = I + 1
            DO 10 J = IPLUS1, N
                IF ( A(I) .LE. A(J) ) GO TO 10
                    TEMP = A(I)
                    A(I) = A(J)
                    A(J) = TEMP
   10       CONTINUE
   20   CONTINUE
C
C       ... FIND SUM OF GRADES
C
        SUM = 0.0
        DO 30 K = 1, N
            SUM = SUM + A(K)
   30   CONTINUE
C
C       ... GET MEAN AND MEDIAN
C
        AMEAN = SUM/N
        NMEDN = N/2
        AMEDN = ( A(NMEDN) + A(NMEDN+1) ) / 2.0
        IF ( 2*NMEDN .NE. N ) AMEDN = A(NMEDN+1)
        SMALL = A(1)
        BIG = A(N)
        RETURN
        END
```

FIGURE 9.3.   A subroutine to find examination statistics, closely related to the program of Figure 7.2.

Note at the end of the program the RETURN and END statements. The
RETURN says to go back to the calling program; in other circumstances it
might not appear at the end of the program, just as the STOP statement is
not always at the end of a main program. The END tells us that a subprogram
is a complete program, which in fact may be compiled entirely separately
from the main program.

The main program in Figure 9.4 is a little more involved, since it has to
separate the graduate from the undergraduate grades, as well as to carry out

```
C A PROGRAM TO PRODUCE STATISTICS ON AN EXAMINATION
C SIMILAR TO THE PROGRAM OF FIGURE 7.2, BUT HANDLES GRADUATE
C AND UNDERGRADUATE GRADES SEPARATELY, AS WELL AS COMBINED.
C
C USES A SUBROUTINE TO AVOID REPETITION OF PROGRAM SEGMENTS
C AND TO SIMPLIFY PROGRAM LOGIC
C
C      VARIABLE NAMES
C
C      GRADE    AN ARRAY OF UP TO 101 ELEMENTS TO HOLD THE
C               UNSORTED GRADES BEFORE PROCESSING
C      GRAD     GRADUATE GRADES
C      UNDER    UNDERGRADUATE GRADES
C      KGRAD    INDEX OF GRADUATE GRADE ARRAY
C      KUNDER   INDEX OF UNDERGRADUATE GRADE ARRAY
C      KTOTAL   COUNT OF THE TOTAL NUMBER OF CARDS READ
C      KODE     A CODE: 1 = UNDERGRADUATE, 2 = GRADUATE
C      TEMP     TEMPORARY STORAGE
C
C
       DIMENSION GRADE(101), GRAD(101), UNDER(101)
C
C INITIALIZE POINTERS
C
       KTOTAL = 1
       KGRAD = 1
       KUNDER = 1
  5    READ (5, 10) TEMP, KODE
 10    FORMAT (F10.0, I1)
C
C CHECK FOR SENTINEL
C
       IF ( TEMP .LT. 0.0 ) GO TO 50
C
C TEST DATA FOR VALIDITY
C
       IF (        TEMP .LE. 100.0
     1     .AND.   KODE .GE. 1
     2     .AND.   KODE .LE. 2 ) GO TO 30
C
C IF HERE, BAD DATA
C
               WRITE (6, 20) TEMP
 20            FORMAT ('0', 'BAD DATA ON CARD WITH GRADE = ', F10.1)
               GO TO 5
 30    GRADE(KTOTAL) = TEMP
       IF ( KODE .EQ. 1 ) UNDER(KUNDER) = TEMP
       IF ( KODE .EQ. 1 ) KUNDER = KUNDER + 1
       IF ( KODE .EQ. 2 ) GRAD(KGRAD) = TEMP
       IF ( KODE .EQ. 2 ) KGRAD = KGRAD + 1
C
C INCREMENT AND TEST COUNTER FOR TOTAL
C THIS IS SKIPPED FOR BAD DATA
C
       KTOTAL = KTOTAL + 1
       IF ( KTOTAL .LE. 101 ) GO TO 5
C
C IF WE FALL THROUGH THIS LOOP, THERE WERE TOO MANY DATA CARDS
C
       WRITE (6, 40)
 40    FORMAT ('0', 'THERE WERE TOO MANY DATA CARDS--JOB STOPPED')
       STOP
```

FIGURE 9.4.   A program to find examination statistics, utilizing
the subroutine of Figure 9.3.

```
C
C PROCESS COMPLETE SET OF GRADES FIRST
C
  50    N = KTOTAL - 1
        CALL GRADER (GRADE, N, SMALL, BIG, AMEAN, AMEDN)
        WRITE (6, 60) N, SMALL, BIG, AMEAN, AMEDN
  60    FORMAT ('0', 'THERE WERE ', I5, '  GRADES IN ALL, RANGING FROM',
       1     F6.1, '  TO', F6.1/1X, 'WITH A MEAN OF', F6.1,
       2     '  AND A MEDIAN OF', F6.1/)
C
C PROCESS UNDERGRADUATE GRADES
C
        CALL GRADER (UNDER, KUNDER-1, SMALL, BIG, AMEAN, AMEDN)
        N = KUNDER - 1
        WRITE (6, 70) N, SMALL, BIG, AMEAN, AMEDN
  70    FORMAT ('0', 'THERE WERE  ', I5, '  UNDERGRADUATE GRADES',
       1     ' RANGING FROM', F6.1, '  TO', F6.1/
       2     'WITH A MEAN OF', F6.1, '  AND A MEDIAN OF', F6.1/)
C
C PROCESS GRADUATE GRADES
C
        CALL GRADER (GRAD, KGRAD - 1, SMALL, BIG, AMEAN, AMEDN)
        N = KGRAD - 1
        WRITE (6, 80) N, SMALL, BIG, AMEAN, AMEDN
  80    FORMAT ('0', 'THERE WERE', I5, '  GRADUATE GRADES, RANGING FROM',
       1     F6.1, '  TO', F6.1/1X, 'WITH A MEAN OF', F6.1,
       2     '  AND A MEDIAN OF', F6.1/)
        STOP
        END
```

FIGURE 9.4.   *Continued*

the checking that was done in the earlier version. Still, it is almost possible
to read the program from top to bottom in sequence, since there are only
three GO TO statements and only one of these goes back to an earlier statement. Let us study the operation of the program.

There are three arrays to fill. First, there is one called GRADE, which
receives all the grades except those that fail two simple validity checks. This
array, named GRADE, need have only 100 elements in this version of the program, since a grade is not read directly into the arrays but is first checked to
see if it is a sentinel and if it passes the validity tests. A second array named
UNDER will hold all the undergraduate grades, starting with 1 and running
up though however many there are. These must be placed in the array in
sequence, without gaps, so the index variable that points to the next location in GRADE will not also be pointing to the next location in UNDER except in the unusual circumstance that there are only undergraduate grades.
Finally there is an array for the graduate grades, GRAD.

For each of these arrays we need a pointer, or index, that points to where
the next element is to be placed. These are called KTOTAL, KUNDER, and
KGRAD. The scheme is that KTOTAL is incremented for every card except
error cards; KUNDER is incremented for every undergraduate card, and
KGRAD for every graduate card.

The sentinel is simply a negative grade. Naturally, if there is an erroneous
card with a negative grade that was not intended as a sentinel, the program
will fail—but you would want to be informed of such a flaw anyway, so perhaps that is not all bad. The validity check is to be sure that the grade is not
greater than 100.0 and that the undergraduate/graduate code is either 1 or

2. Any card that fails either of these tests will result in a message that states the fault and gives the grade; this latter will help track down the erroneous card in the deck before it is rerun.

Since this time we are interested in getting the statistics from all the good cards even if there are data errors, it is not possible to use the DO statement. We would need to redefine the DO index within the range, and although some compilers would accept this and even give correct results, it is highly risky and cannot be recommended as general practice. Accordingly the pointer that goes with the grade array is initialized, incremented, and tested using separate statements. These statements do just what the DO would do, but permit us to skip over the incrementation instruction for bad data.

It is also true that the testing is skipped for bad data, so that if there are a great many error cards we may accept a total deck of more than 101 cards. This was not thought to be a serious enough problem to require correction. But in other applications of this type it might be worthwhile to keep a separate count of the good and bad cards, and require that the total — counting the sentinel — not to exceed 101. It could certainly be done.

If there were more than 101 good cards, counting the sentinel, we still "fall through" the end of the loop, even though it is not a DO loop this time.

With all the good grades in GRADE, with an integer variable pointing to the *next* element position, we are ready to subtract 1 from KTOTAL to get the actual number of elements and go into the subroutine.

Going to the subroutine involves the CALL statement, in which we name the subroutine to be called and provide the information it needs. In the first call of the subroutine we are dealing with the array GRADE that contains all the good grades, so the first item in the CALL list is GRADE. Here we have computed N in advance, so it is the second parameter. The other four parameters are the names of the results that are to be returned to the main program by the subroutine. We happen to have chosen the same names as used in the subroutine definition; this is permitted, but has no special significance.

One of the essential concepts of the subroutine idea is that control returns from the subroutine to the statement immediately after the CALL. When we come back from the subroutine we are ready to print the results for the total class. The variables in the WRITE are the same as those in the subroutine CALL (except for the array, which is not named in the WRITE), and they are in the same order. Both facts are immaterial and essentially accidental.

The processing of the undergraduate grades is much the same, with one small change to illustrate an idea. Observe that instead of computing

```
N = KUNDER - 1
```

before the CALL, we have simply placed the expression itself in the CALL. This illustrates that the arguments in a Fortran function or subprogram call can be any expressions of the proper type, that is, real or integer. It turns out, of course, that we have to write a separate statement to subtract 1 from KUNDER anyway, since most versions of Fortran do not permit anything but single variable names in the list of a WRITE. The FORMAT here is a bit different, as needed to provide identification of the results as being for the undergraduates only.

There is nothing new in the handling of the graduate grades.

Here is the output when the programs were run with 30 data cards, two of which were in error.

```
BAD DATA ON CARD WITH GRADE =        34.0

BAD DATA ON CARD WITH GRADE =       780.0

THERE WERE     28  GRADES IN ALL, RANGING FROM  34.0   TO   97.0
WITH A MEAN OF  71.1  AND A MEDIAN OF  76.5


THERE WERE      16  UNDERGRADUATE GRADES RANGING FROM  34.0   TO   93.0
WITH A MEAN OF  69.8  AND A MEDIAN OF  74.5


THERE WERE   12  GRADUATE GRADES, RANGING FROM  36.0   TO   97.0
WITH A MEAN OF  73.0  AND A MEDIAN OF  77.0
```

This program may appear forbidding, just because of its size, but it really isn't. Taking one central part and making a subroutine of it permits the study to be done in logical pieces. Both the main program and the subroutine can be read almost entirely from top to bottom. Take them one statement at a time, and you can follow the whole program!

Summary

1. To use a Fortran-supplied function it is only necessary to write its name followed by parentheses enclosing the argument(s). Commas are used to separate multiple arguments in those functions that use more than one.

2. Every function takes either a real or an integer argument, and these conventions must be followed in use. One cannot write

```
Q = SQRT(12)
```

because the SQRT function expects a real argument.

3. The argument of a function can be any expression of the proper type, utilizing other functions if desired. We can write things like

```
Z = 2.0 + SQRT(12.0 + SQRT(14.0*SQRT(X)))
```

4. The manual for every Fortran system will contain a listing of the supplied functions available on that system. Virtually all Fortrans will contain the functions listed in Appendix 6, often with a few others added to handle special situations of local interest.

5. A Fortran subroutine is *defined* by a separate subprogram that begins with the word SUBROUTINE followed by the name of the subroutine and that followed by parentheses enclosing the list of arguments. There must be at least one RETURN statement in the subroutine, and it must end with an END, just like any other separately compilable program.

6. A subroutine is *used* by writing a CALL statement that gives the name of the subroutine followed by parentheses enclosing a list of arguments. There must be the same number of arguments in the CALL as in the definition, and each must be of the same type (real or integer) as the corresponding dummy variable in the definition. The arguments for quantities being sent to the subroutine when called may be any Fortran expressions of the proper

type. The arguments for output values being returned to the main program should be single variable names.

7. After completing its work, a subroutine returns control to the statement in the main program after the CALL that brought it into operation. A subroutine may be called as many times as the programmer wishes, from none on up. Sometimes the advantages of breaking a program up into manageable pieces is sufficient reason to want to use subroutines that are then called only once. More commonly, perhaps, a subroutine is used to avoid duplication of similar sections of code.

8. A subroutine in Fortran may not call itself, and two subroutines may not call each other. With this restriction, subroutines may include calls of other subroutines to any depth one desires.

REVIEW QUESTIONS

1. What does a Fortran function do? How is it called into action?
2. What may the argument of a function consist of?
3. May the argument of a function involve another function?
4. What is the difference in effect of these two statements?

```
Q = SQRT(X)
Q = X**0.5
```

5. Is there a Fortran function named MIN1? How would you find out?
6. Where may the name of a function be written?
7. State in words what this statement does:

```
QQ = AMIN1(12.0, R, T-V)
```

8. How could this statement be rewritten to accomplish the same result?

```
MINMUM = MIN1(FLOAT(J), FLOAT(K))
```

9. What is wrong with these statements?

```
a.  SQRT(2.0) = 2.0**0.5
b.  Y = AMAX1(12.0)
c.  ZZ = FLOAT(K + 12)
d.  Q = SQRT(2.0 + (A - B)/2.0
e.  CUBERT = CUBRUT(X + 15.7)
```

10. How is a Fortran SUBROUTINE defined? How is it called into action?
11. For the Fortran supplied functions such as SQRT, there is a complete "library" of functions already programmed and ready to be called into use simply by writing their names. Is there any equivalent library of SUBROUTINE programs?

12. Is this combination of main program and subroutine legal?

```
SUBROUTINE ADDER(A, B, C, D, ANS)
ANS = A + B + C + D
RETURN
END

...

CALL ADDER(12.0, B, D/2.0, T, ANS1)
CALL ADDER(A, B, C, D, ANS2)
CALL ADDER(6.0, 12.0, 24.0, 48.0, ANS3)
CALL ADDER(A+B+C+D, A/B, SQRT(D), 0.0, ANS4)
```

The main program is of course only a fragment, but the SUBROUTINE is complete.

13. If a main program and a SUBROUTINE are to be compiled at the same time, is it permissible to omit the END at the end of the SUBROUTINE?

14. Why is this SUBROUTINE illegal?

```
SUBROUTINE SUB(A, B, C, D, E)
C = A - B
CALL SUB(C, D, E)
RETURN
END
```

15. Is it ever legal for one subroutine to include a CALL of another subroutine?

16. Interpret the error indications in the following listing. Did the compiler catch all the errors?

```
            C PROGRAM FOR REVIEW QUESTION 16
            C
0001                SUBROUTINE SUB(A, B, C

       01)   IEY0131 SYNTAX
0002                ANS1 = A + B + C
0003                ANS2 = A + B - C
0004                ANS3 = A - B - C
0005                RETURN
                       $
       01)   IEY0151 NO END CARD
```

ANSWERS

1. A Fortran function accepts a value called an *argument*, and performs a predefined operation on it to produce a *function value*. It is called into action simply by writing its name where its action is desired, together with parentheses enclosing a suitable argument or arguments.

2. The argument of a function may consist of any expression of the proper type, that is, real or integer, as the particular function may require.

3. Certainly.

4. The two statements are equivalent, although because of differences in the way the operations are done there can be very small differences in the last digit of the result. The SQRT function is considerably faster.

5. There is indeed such a function, as you can determine by looking at Appendix 6.

6. The name of a function may be written wherever a variable name is legal, with the exceptions of the list of a READ or WRITE, or the left side of an assignment statement.

7. The statement says to compute the value of the expression T-V, then to assign the smallest of the values of the three arguments to the variable named QQ.

8. The statement says to convert J and K to real (floating) form, then to assign the smaller to MINMUM. There happens to be a function, named MINO, that expects integer arguments, so the statement can be simplified to

```
MINMUM = MINO(J, K)
```

9. a. A function name may not be written on the left side of an assignment statement.
   b. The AMAX1 function, as it happens, demands at least two arguments.
   c. Not really an error, but the same result can be achieved without the FLOAT, simply by taking advantage of the automatic-type conversion in writing

   ```
   AA = K + 12
   ```

   d. A right parenthesis is missing.
   e. There is no function named CUBRUT. If the cube root was intended, write

   ```
   CUBERT = (X + 15.7)**0.3333333
   ```

10. A Fortran SUBROUTINE is defined by writing a program that begins with the word SUBROUTINE, followed by the name that is desired, followed by parentheses enclosing the arguments, followed by the defining program itself, which must end with an END statement. It is called into action by the command CALL, followed by the name of the subroutine, followed by parentheses enclosing the arguments.

11. There is no library that can be called into action simply by writing the name, but most computer installations do have libraries of subroutines, available on cards or tape, that may be borrowed. When such are available, it is a wise idea to make good use of them, because they save time and because they may generally be assumed to be completely debugged.

12. Everything is completely legal.

13. Absolutely not. A subroutine is a complete program requiring an END, regardless of how and when it is compiled.

14. Because it calls itself. To add insult to injury, the illegal CALL does not have the proper number of arguments.

15. It is completely legal so long as one subroutine does not call itself and no two subroutines call each other.

16. The closing parenthesis is missing in the definition, and there is no END statement. It certainly did not catch all the errors, since ANS1, ANS2, and ANS3 are not arguments and the results would never be sent back to the calling routine.

EXERCISES

*1. Write a statement that will take the square root of the expression X/12.0, add 12.0 to the result, and assign the resulting value to the variable named ANSWER.

2. Write a statement that will take the square root of X, add 12.0 to the result, then take the square root of that sum and assign it to FOURTH.

*3. Write a statement that will assign to GREAT the largest of the values of the variables named SAM, BEN, and AARON

4. Write a statement that will assign to LITTLE the smaller of the values of the variables named JANELL and MARY.

*5. Write a statement that will put the square root of X or the square root of Y, whichever is smaller, in SMALL.

6. Write a statement that will do the same thing as Exercise 5, but using the two functions in the opposite sequence.

*7. Write a SUBROUTINE that will accept three arguments and return both the sum of their squares and the sum of their cubes. Then write a statement to get the sum of the squares, calling it SUMSQ, and the sum of the cubes (SUMCUB), of 15, 37, and 89.

8. Write a SUBROUTINE that accepts four arguments and returns an integer value of 1 if they are all positive but zero if any one or more is negative.

*9. Write a SUBROUTINE that will accept an array of 100 real elements and return an integer value stating how many of the elements were zero.

10. Write a SUBROUTINE that will accept an array of up to 100 elements, a number N giving the number of actual elements, and return the element number of the first zero in the array.

*11. Write a SUBROUTINE that will accept an array of 100 elements and return the sum of all the elements.

12. Write a SUBROUTINE that will accept an array of 100 elements, add them, and divide by the number of nonzero elements to give an average of the nonzero elements.

*13. Write a main program that will use whatever subroutines from the exercises above are appropriate to find the sum of the 100 elements of an array named GEORGE and to store that sum in SUM.

14. Drawing on the subroutines in the previous exercises, write a segment of a main program to put in NZERO the number of elements of the 100-element array named ARRAY that were zero. Then, further, find the number of nonzero elements of the 100 elements of ZORRO and assign it to NZORRO.

CHAPTER TEN
ADDITIONAL FORTRAN FEATURES

Introduction

There are a number of useful Fortran features that have not been appropriate for the development of this book so far, considering the reader background and interest that we have assumed. This chapter, accordingly, consists of assorted topics, not all of which are related to each other.

The REAL and INTEGER Statements

The presentation to this point has assumed that variables' names must always follow the IJKLMN convention for distinguishing between real and integer variables. Actually, any name can be used for either one, by providing an appropriate REAL or INTEGER statement. For instance, if we write

        REAL INCOME

then INCOME will be treated by the compiler as a real variable even though it begins with one of the letters that would otherwise designate it as an integer variable. Likewise,

        INTEGER X, YZ, A12233

would make the variables named integers. It is quite permissible to include in a REAL or INTEGER statement variables that would already be correctly defined by their initial letters, as in

        REAL A, IJK, RST

The fact that A and RST would be taken as real variables anyway makes no difference.

Some authors find the IJKLMN rule so restrictive that they recommend always writing REAL and INTEGER statements and including all program variables in them. The IJKLMN rule can then be forgotten about.

No major programming language other than Fortran imposes any restriction on the choice of the initial letters of variable names, so perhaps the authors and instructors who insist on including all variable names in REAL and INTEGER statements have a point. It has not seemed best for this presentation.

Logical Variables and Operations

Fortran provides a variable type entirely different from anything we have seen so far, called *logical*. A logical variable, constant, or operation, is one that can take on only the values *true* and *false*.

A logical variable is one that has been so declared in a LOGICAL statement, such as

LOGICAL OK, GOOD, I29, LOG

The initial letter convention has no meaning at all, since a variable is never considered to be of the logical type unless it has appeared in a LOGICAL statement.

There are exactly two logical constants, .TRUE. and .FALSE.. They may appear in logical expressions, which are formed using the logical operators .AND., .OR., and .NOT.. These have been introduced briefly in Chapter 7, where the .AND. was used only in connection with combinations of relations, such as

IF (A .GT. 5.0 .AND. A .LT. 10.0) GO TO 50

For review, the .AND. operation gives a .TRUE. result if and only if both of the expressions it connects are .TRUE.. The .OR. gives a .TRUE. result if *any* (one or more) of the expressions it connects are .TRUE.. The .NOT. reverses the truth value of any expression, changing .TRUE. to .FALSE. and .FALSE. to .TRUE..

There are occasional computer applications where the computation to be done directly involves logical variables. Most commonly in the kinds of applications presented in this book logical operations would be used only to "remember" the value of a relational test to avoid having to repeat the test.

For an example, suppose that we are reading data and testing it for validity before carrying out various other operations; certain things need to be done in case the data value is not valid. A section of the program might look like this:

```
      LOGICAL OK
      READ (5, 130) K, TEMP
130   FORMAT (I5, F10.0)
      OK = (K .GT. 0) .AND. (K .LT. N) .AND. (TEMP .LT. 1000.0)
      IF ( OK ) A(K) = TEMP
      IF ( OK ) B(K) = TEMP
      IF ( OK ) KGOOD = KGOOD + 1
      IF ( .NOT. OK ) WRITE (6, 140) K, TEMP
140   FORMAT (1X, 'CARD WITH K = ', I5, ' VALUE = ', F10.3, ' BAD')
      IF ( .NOT. OK ) KBAD = KBAD + 1
```

Observe in the fourth line a statement in which a value of .TRUE. or .FALSE. is assigned to a logical variable. This is accordingly called a *logical assignment statement*. This logical variable is then used in the five IF statements that follow. The IF statement requires a logical expression in the parentheses; here we have used a logical variable, where before we have always had a relation test that gives a .TRUE. or .FALSE. value.

There are many other ways to handle this kind of problem, but this way is about as good as any, and provides an easily readable and clear indication of what the program action is. Furthermore, the testing of a single logical variable is a very fast operation in the object program, so that we are not giving up much speed for the sake of understandability.

The input and output of logical values is not often required, but when it is there is a special field descriptor for it, the L format code. On input the first T or F encountered in the field is taken to mean .TRUE. or .FALSE., and on output the letter T or F is produced in the output field.

Double Precision Operations

(Readers with minimum mathematical background may skip this section.)

There sometimes arise operations that require greater precision in the representation of numbers than is provided by Fortran real quantities. For such situations we have the *double precision* operations, constants and variables. A double precision variable is one that has been named in a DOUBLE PRECISION statement; therefore the initial letter has no effect.

In most Fortran systems any constant written with more than some specified number of digits is automatically taken to be double precision. In Fortran for the IBM 360 and 370, for instance, any constant of more than seven decimal digits is taken to be double precision. Double precision constants can also be written in an exponent form similar to that discussed in Appendix 3.

The name "double precision" obviously implies that twice as many digits are used in the representation of a double precision quantity as in the representation of a single precision (i.e., real) quantity. That is *approximately* true. The exact facts depend on how information is represented within the particular computer, which is a matter outside the scope of the present chapter.

For an example of a situation where double precision quantities can make a difference, consider this little system of equations:

$$12.3098x + 23.0945y = 47.7141$$
$$1.6062x + 3.0134y = 6.2258$$

This system involves no quantities with more than six digits in them, which puts them in the available size range for a real variable. The simple exact solution, as can be verified by hand, is $x = 2$ and $y = 1$. Yet when a program to solve this system by Cramer's Rule[1] using single precision values was run, it produced the results $x = 3.5$ and $y = 0.0$! The intermediate quantities produced during the arithmetic of the solution could not be represented accurately enough to permit the exact solution to be found.

Here is the program after it was modified to include a DOUBLE PRECISION statement.

---

[1] Cramer's Rule says that the system of equations
$$ax + by = c$$
$$dx + ey = f$$
has the solution

$$x = \frac{ce - bf}{ae - bd}$$

$$y = \frac{af - cd}{ae - bd}$$

```
C A PROGRAM THAT FAILS WITHOUT DOUBLE PRECISION
      DOUBLE PRECISION A, B, C, D, E, F, DENOM
5     READ (5, 10) A, B, C, D, E, F
10    FORMAT (6F10.0)
      DENOM = A*E - B*D
      X = (C*E - B*F)/DENOM
      Y = (A*F - C*D)/DENOM
      WRITE (6, 20) A, B, C, D, E, F, X, Y
20    FORMAT (1X, 3F10.6)
      STOP
      END
```

This program produced the exactly correct results.

Observe in this program that X and Y were *not* included in the DOUBLE PRECISION statement. This means, in this case, that all the arithmetic was done in double precision, then converted to single precision for assignment to the real variable.

Double precision operation should be used with care and with a full understanding of the numerical mathematics of what is being done. The little system of equations used as an example above was deliberately designed to make a point, but it contains a trap: the results cannot really be too reliable in any event because of the characteristics of the system of equations. Double precision should not be used routinely in a vain hope of staying out of trouble without knowing what is going on.

Nevertheless, it is useful to know about double precision just to understand the error messages you will sometimes get. Take this statement:

```
Z = SQRT(12.345678)
```

This will be thrown out by some compilers as illegal use of the function! The function is real (single precision) but we have used a double precision constant by writing eight digits. The double precision square root, which is named DSQRT, should be used to take square roots of double precision quantities.

Complex operations

Just to round out the discussion, it may be mentioned that there is a fifth class of Fortran variable, called COMPLEX, in which every variable and constant has two parts, which are handled separately. It is considered unlikely that any readers of this book would have need for this rather mathematical feature, and we shall accordingly not discuss it further.

The Arithmetic IF statement

Fortran provides another type of IF statement that is quite different from the logical IF that we have used so far in this book. The logical IF has a *logical* expression and, if its value is .TRUE., it carries out the statement that follows the parentheses. The arithmetic IF, on the other hand, has an *arithmetic* expression within parentheses, then lists three statement numbers after the parentheses. It is of the form

IF (arithmetic expression) n_1, n_2, n_3

where n_1, n_2, and n_3 are valid statement numbers. If the value of the expression is negative, statement n_1 is carried out next; if the value of the expression is zero, statement n_2 is carried out next; and if the value of the expression is positive, statement n_3 is carried out next.

The arithmetic IF has little use in well-constructed programs. It is something like a combination of three logical IF statements, all having GO TOs as the statement to be carried out if the expression is true. Heavy use of the arithmetic IF leads to intricate programs that are very hard to read and understand.

We shall have no occasion to use the arithmetic IF in this text. It is mentioned here for the benefit of readers who may have to deal with it in reading other peoples' programs.

The Computed GO TO

The Fortran computed GO TO is of the form

GO TO $(n_1, n_2, \ldots, n_m)$, i

where the n's are statement numbers and i is an integer variable. The value of i must be between 1 and the number of statement numbers listed within parentheses. And don't forget the comma after the parentheses!

It is hard to find good examples of the legitimate use of the computed GO TO that do not involve mathematics. One example might be a salesman's commission formula, where we can imagine that there are, say, seven different formulas that are used for different classes of products. If these classes have been assigned codes in the range of 1 to 7, then a computed GO TO could be used to branch to the section of the program appropriate to each class.

The DATA Statement

More frequently than one might imagine, it turns out to be useful to compile data into the object program from source program statements. Any time there is data that *might* change, so that we do not like to write numbers as constants in the body of the program, we think of the DATA statement. An alternative is to read such data from a card, but if the data is not expected to change very often that is a bother.

In a DATA statement we simply list the names of the variables that are to receive values, then write a slash, then write the values in the corresponding order. For example, if we want to give A the value 14.7, B the value zero, and KAT the value -12, we could write

```
DATA A, B, KAT/14.7, 0.0, -12/
```

There is more flexibility than this example shows. For one thing, there is no limit to the number of groups of variables and values we can have. If, in the example given, we also wished to make DOG equal to 2.0, we could write:

```
DATA A, B, KAT/14.7, 0.0, -12/, DOG/2.0/
```

This also means that if we wish we can write every variable right next to the value it is to receive:

```
DATA A/14.7/, B/0.0/, KAT/-12/, DOG/2.0/
```

Next, if a number of variables are to receive the same value, that one value can be written with a repetition factor in front of it, with an asterisk, like so:

```
DATA R, S, T, U, V/5*0.0/
```

This example hints at one excellent way to use the DATA statement, namely, to initialize variables without the boredom of writing long lists of statements like this:

```
R = 0.0
S = 0.0
T = 0.0
U = 0.0
V = 0.0
```

Finally, most Fortrans permit an array to be named without listing all its elements. For example, if all 17 elements of ARRAY are to be set equal to 1.0, we can write

```
DIMENSION ARRAY(17)
DATA ARRAY/17*1.0/
```

The COMMON statement

We saw in the previous chapter how to send values from a main program to a subprogram, by writing them as arguments in parentheses following the name of the subroutine. We did not make a point of it before, but every program, whether main program or subprogram, has its own storage allocation. That is, a variable named in a subprogram, if it is not an argument, is assigned a separate storage location even though there may be a variable of the same name in other program segments. This is as we ordinarily want it.

But suppose that it became convenient to communicate information to a subprogram without making arguments out of everything? Then is would be nice to be able to say, in effect, "The names that follow represent the same variable in the main routine as in the subroutine." That is essentially what the COMMON statement does. If we write, for instance,

```
COMMON A, B, K, L
```

in a main program *and* in the subprogram that it calls, the variables named will be assigned to a block of storage in such a way that A in the main program *is* the same variable as A in the subprogram.

The COMMON statement, like the DIMENSION and DATA statements, must appear before the first executable statement of a program in which it appears.

The EQUIVALENCE statement

The COMMON statement establishes that two variable names in *different* subprograms are really the same quantity. The EQUIVALENCE statement provides a way to inform the compiler that two different names in the *same* program or subprogram are the same. Thus, if we write

```
EQUIVALENCE (A, B, C)
```

the three variables named A, B, and C will all be assigned to the same location. This might be done to conserve space if no two of the three variables are ever needed at the same time.

A more likely usage of the statement involves the larger amounts of storage involved with arrays, where we are permitted to state which element of an array is equivalent to another variable. Suppose, for example, that the array X has 100 elements, and that Y and Z have 50 each. We assume that the variable X is never needed at the same time as Y and Z, so there is duplication of storage. We write

```
EQUIVALENCE (X(1), Y(1)), (X(51), Z(1))
```

In this way the elements of Y coincide with the first 50 elements of X and 50 elements of Z coincide with the second 50 elements of X.

Or suppose that G is an array of 10 elements, H is an array of eight elements, and that R and S are nonsubscripted variables. We can write

```
EQUIVALENCE (G(1), H(1)), (G(9), R), (G(10), S)
```

Now assuming that there are appropriate DIMENSION statements for G and H, we have a free choice whether to write

```
      WRITE (6, 20) H, R, S
20    FORMAT (1X, 10F8.2)
```

or

```
      WRITE (6, 20) G
20    FORMAT (1X, 10F8.2)
```

The same ten values will be printed, in the same order, either way. The second method turns out to be faster, and in some programs situations arise where rather large amounts of time can be saved by this technique. This is one of the most common reasons for using the EQUIVALENCE statement.

The FUNCTION subprogram

There is another type of subprogram in Fortran, which is like a SUBROUTINE subprogram in all respects except this one: there is a value associated with its name, which is returned to the calling program. The initial letter naming convention therefore applies, although it can be overridden by a REAL, INTEGER, LOGICAL, DOUBLE PRECISION, or COMPLEX statement.

For a simple but realistic example, suppose that in some program we very frequently needed to find the sum of all the values of an array, which is then needed in an arithmetic expression in the program. We could write this subprogram:

```
      FUNCTION SUM(ARRAY, N)
      DIMENSION ARRAY(1000)
      SUM = 0.0
      DO 10 K = 1, N
          SUM = SUM + ARRAY(K)
10    CONTINUE
      RETURN
      END
```

Now, for any array having no more than 1000 elements, we can write statements like these

```
Q = 2.57*SUM(X, 20)
QQ = SUM(A12, L)
```

The main program that brings the subprogram into action with statements like these would have to have its own DIMENSION statements.

Adjustable dimensions

The previous example brings up a point that occurs so frequently that a special way of handling it was devised. That is the situation where we need to send to a subprogram the name and size of an array. With the techniques so far available we have no recourse but to make the array in the subprogram DIMENSION statement as large as any array that would ever be passed to it. This can result not only in great waste of space but also in a loss of flexibility.

The solution to the problem is to let the size of the array be specified as one of the arguments of the subroutine, so that the array size in the DIMENSION statement is a variable. The FUNCTION subprogram shown above would have as its DIMENSION statement

```
DIMENSION ARRAY(N)
```

Within the main program an actual size would be given to the array, and that size would become the size of the array in the subprogram as well.

This feature can be used with both FUNCTION and SUBROUTINE programs. And in a situation where one subprogram calls another, dimensions can be "passed through" as many subroutines as one pleases.

Programmer-Defined Statement Functions

(This section is optional.)

All the functions in Chapter Nine were *supplied* functions, that is, functions that come with the compiler and can be called into action simply by writing their names. We have now seen, in the FUNCTION subprogram, how we can write our own functions. But the FUNCTION method is, after all, a somewhat elaborate way to do things if the task to be accomplished requires only one statement. For that purpose the programmer-defined functions are available.

The scheme is that we *define* the function at the beginning of the program, in a statement that does not cause any processing to occur, then *use* the function later by writing its name followed by appropriate arguments. The general form of the definition is:

Name (arg$_1$, arg$_2$, . . .) = Expression

The name is formed according to the initial letter convention unless overriden by a type statement (REAL, INTEGER, DOUBLE PRECISION, LOGICAL, or COMPLEX). There may be as many arguments as are needed. The only limitation on the expression is that it must not contain subscripted variables. It is also obvious that there can be only one statement here; for situations requiring more than one statement we turn to the FUNCTION subprogram.

The argument names must also follow the naming convention unless overridden. Just as with subprograms, the arguments are only dummy variables, having no relation whatever to any actual variables that might happen to have the same name.

Let us take as an example a function that will be used in Case Study 9. We have a problem to solve that will require repeated evaluation of the mathematical expression

$$f(x) = x^3 - 11.5x^2 + 10.5x + 45$$

Rather than writing out this complete expression every time it is needed we instead write, at the beginning of the program

```
FUNC(X) = X**3 - 11.5*X**2 + 10.5*X + 45.0
```

The X here is a dummy variable, having nothing to do with any variable of the same name that might appear elsewhere in the program. What this expression says might be translated this way:

"Whenever you see the name FUNC followed by parentheses enclosing a real-valued expression, do this: evaluate the expression, then cube it, subtract 11.5 times its square, add 10.5 times it, and finally add 45.0. Do with the result whatever the statement in which the function name appears says to do with it."

For instance, we will want to apply this formula to the value of a variable named A and assign the result to the variable named FA, so we write

```
FA = FUNC(A)
```

The effect of this statement, together with the function definition earlier in the program, is just as if we had written

```
FA = A**3 - 11.5*A**2 + 10.5*A + 45.0
```

After that we will want to evaluate the formula for the value B and assign that result to FB, so we write

```
FB = FUNC(B)
```

Once again, the result is precisely the same as if we had written

```
FB = B**3 - 11.5*B**2 + 10.5*B + 45.0
```

For a second example suppose that a certain program frequently requires us to find one of the roots of the quadratic equation

$$ax^2 + bx + c = 0$$

According to the familiar formula the roots are

$$x = \frac{-b \pm \sqrt{b^2 - 4ac}}{2a}$$

We choose the root with the positive sign before the radical and define a function that we shall call ROOT1:

```
ROOT1(A, B, C) = (-B + SQRT(B**2 - 4.0*A*C))/(2.0*A)
```

Now we can use this function wherever we need a root, simply by writing the name ROOT1 with parentheses enclosing expressions for the three coefficients (a, b, and c) which are the arguments. If we need a root of the equation

$$22.97x^2 - 14.09x + 0.63 = 0$$

to be assigned to R1 we can write

```
R1 = ROOT1(22.97, -14.09, 0.63)
```

If we need a root of the equation

$$qx^2 - 2x + a - v = 0$$

which is to be added to the square root of $2g$ and the result assigned to ANS, we can write

```
ANS = ROOT1(Q, -2.0, A-V) + SQRT(2.0*G)
```

The A here is completely unrelated to the A in the function definition.

A closing word

There is no major illustrative program in this chapter, since so many unrelated topics have been taken up and since there are nine case studies in the material that follows.

REVIEW QUESTIONS

1. What does the REAL statement make it possible to do that is otherwise impossible?

2. What happens if a variable that already begins with I, J, K, L, M, or N is listed in an INTEGER statement?

3. What are the advantages and disadvantages of requiring that every variable in a program be included in a REAL or INTEGER statement, instead of using the IJKLMN rule?

4. How does Fortran know that a variable is to be considered to be of logical type?

5. Consider this program fragment:

```
LOGICAL A, B, C, D
C = A .AND. B
D = A .OR. B
```

State that values will be assigned to C and D in terms of the possible combinations of values of A and B.

6. What value will be given to QUESTN by this fragment:

```
LOGICAL QUESTN, TWOB
QUESTN = TWOB .OR. .NOT. TWOB
```

7. What will this program fragment do?

```
LOGICAL GOOD
...
GOOD = .TRUE.
IF ( X .GT. 1000.0 ) GOOD = .FALSE.
IF ( GOOD ) WRITE (6, 10) X
```

```
10      FORMAT (1X, 'A VALUE OF', F12.6, ' FOR X IS GOOD')
        IF ( .NOT. GOOD) WRITE (6, 20) X
20      FORMAT (1X, 'A VALUE OF', F12.6, ' FOR X IS NO GOOD')
```

8. What is the result of listing a variable in a DOUBLE PRECISION statement?

9. Does the use of double precision guarantee that there will never be a problem with the approximate values of numbers that are used in computers?

10. What is the effect of this program fragment?

```
        IF ( X - 12.0 ) 10, 10, 20
10      Y = 23.0
        GO TO 30
20      Y = 43.0
30      ...
```

11. What is the effect of this program fragment?

```
        IF ( X) 10, 10, 20
10      STOP
20      ...
```

12. What is the effect of this program fragment?

```
        READ (5, 10) K
10      FORMAT (I1)
        GO TO (10, 20, 30, 40), K
```

13. Is this DATA statement syntactically correct?

```
DATA A/12/ B/23.0/ C/34.0/
```

14. What does this DATA statement do?

```
DATA A, B, C, D, E, F/6*0.0/
```

How would you do the same thing without a DATA statement? Would there be any difference between the two methods from a program execution standpoint?

15. What does a COMMON statement do? Can you think of any reason to use a COMMON statement in a program that has no subprograms?

16. Does proper use of the COMMON statement ever make it possible to write a SUBROUTINE without an argument list?

17. What is the difference between a SUBROUTINE and a FUNCTION?

18. In discussing the arguments of a FUNCTION or SUBROUTINE, the phrase "appropriate arguments" often crops up. What does it mean?

19. Is this program structure legal?
Main program:

```
DIMENSION ARRAY(100)
...
CALL SUB(ARRAY, 40, ANSWER)
...
```

Subprogram:

```
SUBROUTINE SUB (ARRAY, N, ANSWER)
DIMENSION ARRAY(N)
...
```

20. If a FUNCTION or SUBROUTINE deals with arrays, is it always necessary to have a DIMENSION in both the main program and in the subprogram?

21. Suppose we have this programmer-defined function at the beginning of a program:

```
OPER(A, B, C) = SQRT(A**2 + B**2 + C**2)
```

Would these subsequent uses of the function be legal?

```
QQQ = 12.0 + OPER(A, B, C)
QQQQ = OPER(1.0, 2.0, 3.0)
QQQQQ = OPER(X-1.0, Y+2.0, Z/3.0)
```

22. What is the matter with this programmer-defined function?

```
OPERA(X) = IF ( X .LT. 10.0 ) OPERA = 24.5
           IF ( X .GE. 10.0 ) OPERA = 40.9
```

ANSWERS

1. The REAL statement makes it possible to use variable names beginning with the letters I, J, K, L, M, and N for real variables, which is otherwise impossible.

2. No problem. Some programmers like to do this to make sure every variable is listed in either a REAL or an INTEGER statement, as a guard against forgetting to list variables that are required to be listed.

3. The advantage is as just noted: there is less likelihood of forgetting to name a variable that must be named in order to have the right attributes. It also fits generally with a habit of precision in one's programming. The disadvantages are the extra writing and space.

4. Fortran considers a variable to be of the logical type if and only if it is listed in a LOGICAL statement.

5. C will be assigned the value .TRUE. if A and B are *both* .TRUE., and .FALSE. otherwise. D will be assigned the value .TRUE. if *either* A or B (or both) is .TRUE., and .FALSE. only if A and B are both .FALSE..

6. If TWOB is .TRUE. then .NOT. TWOB is .FALSE., and vice versa. Therefore, one or the other will always be .TRUE., and the .OR. of the two will always be .TRUE..

7. If X is less than or equal to 1000.0, the program will print the value of X together with the remark that it is an acceptable value. If X is greater than 1000.0, the program will print the value of X with the remark that it is not acceptable.

8. Twice as much space is assigned to the variable, which generally means that about twice as many digits are used in its representation. Expressions in which such a variable appears will be done using double precision arithmetic.

9. Not at all. It postpones or minimizes many problems with number precision, but programs can be written using DOUBLE PRECISION variables throughout that produce utter nonsense.

10. If X is less than or equal to 12.0, Y is assigned the value 23.0; if X is greater than 12.0, Y is assigned the value 43.0. The program then proceeds in sequence with whatever comes next.

11. If X is less than or equal to zero, the program stops; otherwise it proceeds in sequence.

12. It is assumed that the value of K is in the range of 1 to 4 (a good assumption to check before using it in this way). Then if K is 1 a jump to 10 is made; if it is 2, to 20, etc.

    In many Fortran systems, if the controlling integer variable is not in the proper range, control passes to the next statement after the computed GO TO. Unless one is absolutely certain that his system works this way, however, it is a good idea to have a programmed check.

13. It is incorrect, for two missing commas. It should be

```
DATA A/12.0/, B/23.0/, C/34.0/
```

14. The statement gives the value zero to the six constants named. The alternative would be six assignment statements. The latter could be re-executed throughout the course of program operation, whereas the DATA statement is not "executed" at all.

15. A COMMON statement places the variables named in it in a special section of storage in the order named. It is not obvious that there would ever be an advantage to doing this unless subprograms were being used.

16. Certainly.

17. There is a value associated with the name of a FUNCTION, so that it is called into play simply by writing its name with appropriate arguments. The SUBROUTINE requires the use of the CALL statement since no value is associated with its name. Also, the initial letter naming convention does not apply to the SUBROUTINE.

18. There must be the same number of arguments in the call as in the definition, the arguments in the call must be listed in the same order as in definition, and the real/integer character of the arguments must correspond. Finally, expressions other than a single variable name are permitted only for input to the subprogram.

19. Yes. The main program specifies a maximum size of 100 elements for the array; the call says there are in fact 40 in this case, which becomes the size of the array in the SUBROUTINE. This is the essence of adjustable dimensions.

20. Yes, absolutely.

21. All are correct. Observe, however, that there is no correspondence between the A, B, and C of the first usage, and the A, B, and C in the definition. All variables used in calling the function would have to be defined within the program.

22. A programmer-defined function can consist of no more than one statement.

EXERCISES

*1. Write statements to make the variables named SAM1, GEORGE, and DON all integer variables, and LARRY a real variable.

2. Write statements to make JOYCE and JON real variables and DAN an integer variable.

*3. Write statements to set the logical variable SAVE equal to .TRUE. if the sum of X and Y is greater than 190., and .FALSE. otherwise.

4. Write statements to set the logical variable VALID to .TRUE. if A, B, and C are each greater than 50.0, and to .FALSE. otherwise.

*5. Write a DATA statement to give the value −12.3 to CAT and the value +12.3 to DOG. Write the statement in two different but equivalent ways.

6. Write a DATA statement to assign the values shown to the variables named.

    A   99.0
    B   12.3
    C   −123.0
    D   0.0012

*7. Write a DATA statement to initialize to 1 all the variables named KAT1, KAT2, and KAT3, using a repetition factor.

8. Write a DATA statement to initialize to zero all the variables named DOG1, DOG3, DOG5, and DOG7, using a repetition factor.

*9. Write a DATA statement to initialize to zero all the 39 elements of the array named JACK.

10. Write a DATA statement to initialize to 1.0 all 79 elements of the array named BENNY.

*11. Write a COMMON statement to go in both a main program and in a SUBROUTINE subprogram, that will assign the variables HORSE and COW to COMMON storage, in that order.

12. Write a COMMON statement to go in both a main program and in a SUBROUTINE subprogram, that will assign the variables A1B, A2B, and A3B to COMMON storage.

*13. Write an EQUIVALENCE statement that will assign the elements of the ten-element array SAM to the last ten elements of the array GEORGE, which has 30 elements.

14. Write an EQUIVALENCE statement to assign A to the same storage location as the first element of HARRY, the variable B to the same storage as the second element of HARRY, and the 18 elements of DICK to the last 18 elements of HARRY. HARRY has 20 elements in all.

*15. Write a FUNCTION subprogram that will accept as arguments the arrays named X and Y and produce as the value associated with its name (SUM2) the sum of all the elements of both arrays.

16. Write a FUNCTION subprogram named SUMCUB that accepts the names of three arguments and returns the sum of their cubes.

CASE STUDIES

CASE STUDY 1: Printing Three Columns with Headings

(For use with Chapter Four or later)

This simple case study deals with elementary computer operations in a way that is typical of some of the things that are commonly done with computers.

We begin with a table of data punched on cards in a prescribed format. To be specific, we have the United States economic data on pages 92-93. We are required to produce a table of the following form.

Three columns are to be printed: the year, the Gross National Product in current prices, and the Gross National Product in terms of 1958 prices. The columns should be headed YEAR, GNP, and GNP58, and the columns should be spaced apart by a few columns for ease of readability.

The data cards are punched with all of the information shown in the table, with every data item taking up five card columns. The year, therefore, is punched in columns 2-5, the GNP in current prices in 6-10, and the GNP in 1958 prices in columns 16-20.

The program below begins by writing the column headings, the spacing of which was determined using a printer spacing chart like this:

```
        0                   1                   2
 1 2 3 4 5 6 7 8 9 0 1 2 3 4 5 6 7 8 9 0 1 2 3 4 5 6 7 8 9 0 1 2 3

   Y E A R       G N P       G N P 5 8

   1 9 5 8       4 3 2 . 1   4 3 2 . 1
```

After printing the headings we come to a READ statement that has a statement number so that we can return to it repeatedly. This reads the three numbers from a card, in cooperation with a FORMAT statement that has a 5X field descriptor to skip over the unwanted information in columns 11-15. After reading the data we check to see if the year is zero, which serves to indicate the end of the deck; if so, we simply stop—the job is done. If not, we write the three numbers in a properly spaced manner and then return to read another card.

```
C CASE STUDY 1: PRINTING THREE COLUMNS WITH HEADINGS
C
      WRITE (6, 10)
   10 FORMAT ('1',' YEAR     GNP     GNP58'//)
   20 READ (5, 30) NYEAR, GNP, GNP58
   30 FORMAT (I5, F5.1, 5X, F5.1)
      IF ( NYEAR .EQ. 0 ) STOP
      WRITE (6, 40) NYEAR, GNP, GNP58
   40 FORMAT (1X, I5, 2F8.1)
      GO TO 20
      END
```

Here is the output when the program was run.

YEAR	GNP	GNP58
1929	103.1	203.6
1931	75.8	169.3
1933	55.6	141.5
1935	72.7	169.5
1937	90.4	203.2
1938	84.7	192.9
1939	90.5	209.4
1940	99.7	227.2
1941	124.5	263.7
1942	157.9	297.8
1944	210.1	361.3
1945	212.0	355.2
1946	208.5	312.6
1948	257.6	323.7
1949	256.5	324.1
1950	284.8	355.3
1951	328.4	383.4
1952	345.5	395.1
1953	364.6	412.8
1954	364.8	407.0
1955	398.0	438.0
1956	419.2	446.1
1957	441.1	452.5
1958	447.3	447.3
1959	483.7	475.9
1960	503.8	487.7
1961	520.1	497.2
1962	560.3	529.8
1963	590.5	551.0
1964	632.4	581.1
1965	684.9	617.8
1966	749.9	658.1
1967	793.9	675.2
1968	864.2	706.6
1969	930.3	725.6
1970	976.4	722.1
1971	1050.4	741.7

CASE STUDY 2: A Self-Checking Number Routine

(For use with Chapter Four or later)

A great many applications require the use of some kind of identification number, from credit cards to library cards. Very frequently these numbers are made to be—in some sense or other—"self-checking," to help detect error and fraud. In this brief case study we shall show one way how this might be done.

We assume that the application in question has something to do with college registration, and that the number in question is a seven-digit student number, constructed as follows.

The first digit identifies an undergraduate (if it is a 1) or a graduate (if it is a 2). No other beginning digit is permissible, which already provides one small degree of checking. Next come five digits that identify the student. Finally, there is a check digit that reflects the others in the following way. First, identify the seven digits of the number with the variable names N1, N2, etc., counting from the left. Then the seventh (and last) digit is the unit's digit of this expression:

N1 + N3 + N5 + 3(N2 + N4 + N6)

For example, if the first six digits are 123456 then the check digit is 5, since

1 + 3 + 5 + 3(2 + 4 + 6) = 45

and we take only the unit's digit of the expression.

This checking method reduces the chance of error and fraud by a factor of ten, because there is only one chance in ten that a "made-up" number will have the correct check digit, assuming of course that the perpetrator of intended fraud does not know the scheme.

Furthermore the checking system guards against certain kinds of unintentional errors, one of the most common of which is the interchange of two digits. A legitimate number with adjacent digits interchanged will always fail this test. Try it on 213456, for example:

2 + 3 + 5 + 3(1 + 4 + 6) = 43

The check digit of 3 does not match the correct digit of 5.

What does all this require from a programming standpoint? For one thing, It requires that we have access to all seven digits of the number separately. If we were to read the seven digits by a combination like this:

READ (5,10) NUMBER
10 FORMAT (17)

we would have to go to the trouble of a series of divisions, keeping the remainders, to separate out the seven digits to seven variables. We shall take the alternative approach of reading them separately, then putting them back together for use later in a complete program. This latter step can be done by remembering what the decimal notation means, using the long expression shown in the program. In reading this remember that a number like 123 really means

1*100 + 2*10 + 3

In the program shown we arrange to read a series of numbers, check each one for a zero value as a sentinel, then check each to see if it passes the test, printing an appropriate comment in each case.

```
C CASE STUDY 2: A SELF-CHECKING NUMBER ROUTINE
C
   10    READ (5, 20) N1, N2, N3, N4, N5, N6, N7
   20    FORMAT (711)
         NUMBER = N1*1000000
      1        + N2*100000
```

```
      2          + N3*10000
      3          + N4*1000
      4          + N5*100
      5          + N6*10
      6          + N7
        IF ( NUMBER .EQ. 0 ) STOP
C
C CHECK FOR CORRECT INITIAL DIGIT -- ONLY 1 AND 2 ARE VALID
C
        IF ( N1 .EQ. 1 ) GO TO 40
        IF ( N1 .EQ. 2 ) GO TO 40
        WRITE (6, 30) NUMBER
   30   FORMAT (1X, 'THE NUMBER', I9, ' IS NOT LEGITIMATE')
        GO TO 10
   40   NCHECK = N1 + N3 + N5 + 3*(N2 + N4 + N6)
        JUNITS = NCHECK - 10*(NCHECK/10)
        IF ( JUNITS .EQ. N7 ) WRITE (6, 50) NUMBER
   50   FORMAT (1X, 'THE NUMBER', I9, ' PASSES THE TEST')
        IF ( JUNITS .NE. N7 ) WRITE (6, 60) NUMBER
   60   FORMAT (1X, 'THE NUMBER', I9, ' DOES NOT PASS THE TEST')
        GO TO 10
        END
```

One feature of the program is a bit different, and that is the provision for getting the unit's digit of the expression for the check digit. The way we shall do it is to divide by 10, which produces an integer quotient, discarding the remainder if any. If we multiply this quotient by 10 and subtract from the original number we shall have the unit's digit. Try it on 45, with this expression:

$$UNITS = 45 - 10*(45/10)$$

The quotient 45/10 gives just 4, since the remainder of 5 is discarded. Ten times 4 is 40, and 45 minus 40 is 5—the desired check digit.

With the explanation as background, the program shown should be readable without further verbiage.

```
THE NUMBER  1234565  PASSES THE TEST
THE NUMBER  2134565  DOES NOT PASS THE TEST
THE NUMBER  3123456  IS NOT LEGITIMATE
THE NUMBER  2233441  DOES NOT PASS THE TEST
THE NUMBER  2233446  PASSES THE TEST
THE NUMBER  2345678  DOES NOT PASS THE TEST
THE NUMBER  2342345  DOES NOT PASS THE TEST
THE NUMBER  1122330  DOES NOT PASS THE TEST
THE NUMBER  2122330  DOES NOT PASS THE TEST
THE NUMBER  3122330  IS NOT LEGITIMATE
THE NUMBER  2333440  DOES NOT PASS THE TEST
THE NUMBER  2033440  PASSES THE TEST
THE NUMBER  9876543  IS NOT LEGITIMATE
THE NUMBER  8765432  IS NOT LEGITIMATE
THE NUMBER  7654321  IS NOT LEGITIMATE
```

CASE STUDY 3: An Ecological Model of Two-Species Interaction

(For use with Chapter Four or later)

This case study is based on a rather simple model from ecology, involving the interaction of two species, here called foxes and pheasants. The example has been used in several other books, perhaps in part because it is fun, as well as timely.

We assume for the purposes of the problem that the pheasants eat only vegetation and insects, but are no threat to the foxes. The foxes, on the other hand, eat mostly pheasants, and are therefore partially dependent on the pheasant population for something to eat and thereby to stay alive.

We take the approach of computing the number of foxes and the number of pheasants alive at the end of each of many time periods. The time period can be thought of as a year, if one wishes. During any year some pheasants would be hatched and some would die. We take the difference and call it the net growth rate if there were no losses to the foxes. This growth factor is taken as 4% in the example that is worked out below. But of course some pheasants are eaten during the year, too. The number depends both on the availability of pheasants to be eaten and the number of foxes to do the eating. This decrease is therefore the product of a constant times the number of pheasants times the number of foxes. In the example the constant here is 0.0005.

We further assume that if there were no pheasants to eat there would be a net decrease of foxes: more would die than would be born and survive. This decrease factor is taken to be 3%. Finally, there is a growth of foxes depending on a constant (0.00025 below) times the number of pheasants available to be eaten. The formulas for the numbers of pheasants and foxes are therefore:

$$\text{PHEAS} = \text{PHEAS} + \text{A}\star\text{PHEAS} - \text{B}\star\text{PHEAS}\star\text{FOX}$$
$$\text{FOX} \quad = \text{FOX} \quad + \text{C}\star\text{FOX} \quad + \text{D}\star\text{PHEAS}\star\text{FOX}$$

The program shown below applies these formulas repeatedly, with no provision for stopping the program: that was done at a time-sharing terminal after determining that the cycle was repeating as expected. Since the change in any one year, using these figures, is rather small, we arranged to print only every tenth time. The IF statement that makes this decision takes advantage of the fact that integer division drops any remainder, so that $10\star(\text{N}/10)$ is equal to N only if N is a multiple of 10.

```
C CASE STUDY 3: AN ECOLOGICAL MODEL OF TWO-SPECIES INTERACTION
C
C      VARIABLES AND THEIR MEANINGS
C
C      FOX      THE NUMBER OF FOXES ALIVE AT THE BEGINNING
C               OF A TIME PERIOD
C      PHEAS    THE NUMBER OF PHEASANTS ALIVE AT THE BEGINNING
C               OF A TIME PERIOD
C      A        THE PHEASANT GROWTH-FACTOR IN ABSENCE OF FOXES
C      B        THE PHEASANT DECREASE-FACTOR BECAUSE OF BEING EATEN
C               BY FOXES
C      C        THE FOX DEATH-FACTOR IF THEY COULD EAT NO PHEASANTS
C      D        THE FOX GROWTH-FACTOR FROM EATING PHEASANTS
C
C
       READ (5, 10) PHEAS, FOX, A, B, C, D
   10  FORMAT (6F10.0)
       WRITE (6, 20) PHEAS, FOX, A, B, C, D
   20  FORMAT('1', 'WE STARTED WITH ', F5.0, ' PHEASANTS AND ', F5.0,
      1    ' FOXES'//1X, 'THE FOUR CONSTANTS WERE', 4F10.5//
      2    1X, 'PHEASANTS    FOXES'//)
C
C INITIALIZE COUNTER FOR PRINTING EVERY TENTH TIME
C
```

```
         N = 1
C
C GO INTO THE COMPUTING CYCLE
C
  30     PHEAS = PHEAS + A*PHEAS - B*PHEAS*FOX
         FOX =   FOX   - C*FOX   + D*PHEAS*FOX
         IF ( N .EQ. 10*(N/10) ) WRITE (6, 40) PHEAS, FOX
  40     FORMAT (1X, F7.0, F10.0)
         N = N + 1
         GO TO 30
         END
```

Here is the output when the program was started and allowed to run for a few cycles. It seems clear that the pattern repeats itself over and over.

WE STARTED WITH 300. PHEASANTS AND   50. FOXES

THE FOUR CONSTANTS WERE   0.04000   0.00050   0.03000   0.00025

PHEASANTS	FOXES
327.	81.
293.	130.
201.	177.
116.	192.
67.	176.
44.	149.
33.	121.
28.	96.
27.	76.
29.	60.
33.	48.
39.	39.
49.	32.
63.	27.
82.	24.
108.	23.
143.	23.
189.	26.
243.	33.
297.	49.
327.	79.
297.	127.
208.	175.
121.	192.
69.	178.
45.	151.
33.	123.
29.	98.
27.	77.
29.	61.
33.	49.
39.	40.
48.	33.
62.	28.
80.	24.
106.	23.
141.	23.
185.	26.
239.	33.
294.	47.
327.	76.
301.	123.
215.	173.

These results are even more interesting if plotted on a graph:

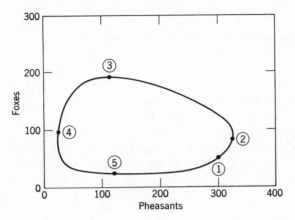

We began the process at a time when foxes and pheasants were both increasing; this is point 1. Since there were lots of pheasants to eat, the fox population rose. This led to point 2, where there were so many foxes that the pheasant population began to decline. The number of foxes still increased however, until reaching point 3, where so many pheasants had been eaten that the fox population finally began to drop also. At this stage both populations decreased to point 4, where there were so few foxes that the pheasant population could start growing again. But there were still rather few pheasants, and the fox population accordingly kept dropping until reaching point 5. The steady growth of pheasants then led back to point 1 and the whole process repeated.

CASE STUDY 4: Account and Grand Totals with Sequence Checking

(For use with Chapter Four or later)

This case study presents, in about the simplest possible form, one of the most common types of business data processing, the production of a set of totals from a group of records that are in sequence on an account number. You could think of the input data as being purchases by customers, or commissions due salesmen, or sales totals for various districts. In any event we begin with input data that is in ascending sequence on an account number (AC). For each account number there may be one or more records. We are to read that data, produce a total for each account, and a grand total for all records. Here is some typical input; see page 202 for some typical output.

```
123       5.40
123     100.69
123      67.40
127     170.00
129      15.00
129       7.78
129     105.09
129      66.66
129       4.12
130      61.12
130     109.10
131       6.99
132     140.12
132      12.12
134      99.12
```

Note that there are three lines for account 123, one for 127, etc. In the output there is to be one line for each account, containing the total for that account.

Let us develop the logic of the algorithm for this task in two stages. First is a narrative description of what is to be done, followed then by a rigorous, correct, and complete flowchart, and finally a program that embodies the flowchart logic. This is typical of the series of stages of thinking that many programmers use in developing a final program.

A narrative description might go like this:

"First I have to read one record to get the process started. The account number goes to a variable named PREVAC ("previous account"), which is what this record will be when we read the next record. The dollar amount from the first record goes into both totals, the one for this account and the grand total.

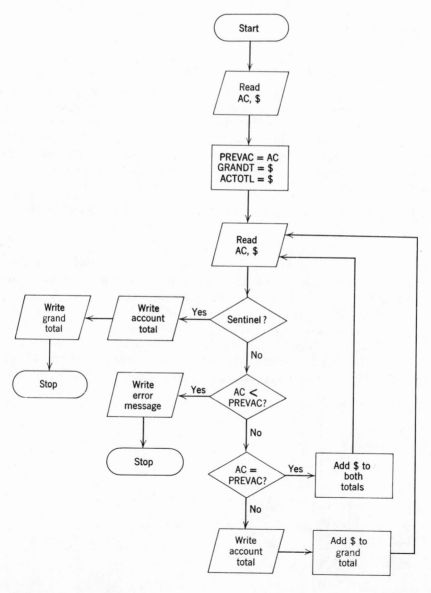

"Now I come to the part of the program that will be repeated. I read a record and transfer to the wrapup section if it is a zero sentinel. If the account number from this record is *less* than PREVAC the input is out of sequence; I'll write an error message and stop.

"If the present account (AC) is the same as the previous account (PREVAC), then I need to add the dollar amount from this record to the account total and to the grand total, then go back for another record.

"If the present account is neither less than nor equal to the previous, then it must be greater, and I have read the first record of a new account. I therefore need to write out the total for the previous account, set the account total to the dollar amount from this new record, and add the dollar amount to the grand total. I must set PREVAC to the account number from this record so that I can get the comparison going again. Having done all this I can transfer back to read another record.

"The wrapup section is a simple matter of writing the total for the final account and the grand total."

This narrative description is one possible form for an algorithm. The flowchart is another way, representing the exact same operations as the narrative description, bearing in mind that the order in which the different aspects of the algorithm are described is unimportant. There is accordingly no need to explain the flowchart.

The program is worked out in precisely the same sequence as the narrative description, so its operation should be simple to follow. One feature is used that is not explained in the text until Chapter Ten; that is the INTEGER statement, which is used to inform Fortran that AC and PREVAC are integer variables even though their initial letters are those of real variables. This handy feature, together with the similar REAL statment, is a benefit in many situations.

```
C CASE STUDY 4: ACCOUNT AND GRAND TOTALS, WITH SEQUENCE CHECKING
C
C     VARIABLES
C     AC      ACCOUNT NUMBER OF CURRENT RECORD
C     PREVAC  ACCOUNT NUMBER OF PREVIOUS RECORD
C     DOLLAR  DOLLAR AMOUNT OF TRANSACTION
C     GRANDT  GRAND TOTAL FOR ALL ACCOUNTS
C     ACTOTL  TOTAL FOR ACCOUNT
C
C NOTE USE OF INTEGER STATEMENT TO MAKE AC AND PREVAC INTEGER VARIABLES
C
      INTEGER AC, PREVAC
C
C READ FIRST RECORD
C
      READ (5, 10) AC, DOLLAR
   10 FORMAT (I3, F10.2)
      PREVAC = AC
      GRANDT = DOLLAR
      ACTOTL = DOLLAR
C
C READ ANOTHER RECORD--PROGRAM REPEATS FROM HERE
C
   20 READ (5, 30) AC, DOLLAR
   30 FORMAT (I3, F10.2)
C
C CHECK FOR SENTINEL
C
```

```
      IF ( AC .EQ. 0 ) GO TO 60
C
C MAKE SEQUENCE CHECK; WRITE ERROR MESSAGE AND STOP IF OUT OF SEQUENCE
C
      IF ( AC .LT. PREVAC ) WRITE (6, 40) AC
  40  FORMAT (1X, 'SEQUENCE ERROR ON ACCOUNT NUMBER ', I5/)
      IF ( AC .LT. PREVAC ) STOP
C
C CHECK FOR SAME ACCOUNT NUMBER AND ADD TO BOTH TOTALS IF SO
C
      IF ( AC .EQ. PREVAC ) GRANDT = GRANDT + DOLLAR
      IF ( AC .EQ. PREVAC ) ACTOTL = ACTOTL + DOLLAR
      IF ( AC .EQ. PREVAC ) GO TO 20
C
C IF WE GET TO HERE, SEQUENCE OK BUT NEW ACCOUNT STARTING
C PRINT ACCOUNT TOTAL, START NEW ACCOUNT TOTAL, ADD TO GRAND TOTAL
C SET 'PREVIOUS ACCOUNT' TO CURRENT ACCOUNT NUMBER, TO PREPARE
C FOR NEXT COMPARISON OF ACCOUNT NUMBERS
C
      WRITE (6, 50) PREVAC, ACTOTL
  50  FORMAT (1X, 'TOTAL FOR ACCOUNT ', I5, ' = ', F10.2)
      ACTOTL = DOLLAR
      GRANDT = GRANDT + DOLLAR
      PREVAC = AC
      GO TO 20
C
C THIS IS THE WRAPUP, AFTER DISCOVERING SENTINEL
C MUST STILL PRINT TOTAL FOR FINAL ACCOUNT, ALONG WITH GRAND TOTAL
C
  60  WRITE (6, 50) PREVAC, ACTOTL
      WRITE (6, 70) GRANDT
  70  FORMAT ('0', 'TOTAL FOR ALL ACCOUNTS = ', F12.2)
      STOP
      END
```

Observe that the program logic follows the phrasing of the narrative description in testing for AC less than PREVAC and taking appropriate action ending with a STOP, then testing for equality and taking appropriate action ending with a GO TO. If neither of these conditions have been met, the only possibility left is that AC is greater than PREVAC. There is no need, therefore, to place these last actions within logical IF statements.

Here is the output of the program when it was run with the data shown earlier as input. Observe that the program operated correctly with a "group" consisting of only one item—always a good thing to check. A separate run, not shown here, established that the program does properly detect a sequence error.

```
TOTAL FOR ACCOUNT    123  =      173.49
TOTAL FOR ACCOUNT    127  =      170.00
TOTAL FOR ACCOUNT    129  =      198.65
TOTAL FOR ACCOUNT    130  =      170.22
TOTAL FOR ACCOUNT    131  =        6.99
TOTAL FOR ACCOUNT    132  =      152.24
TOTAL FOR ACCOUNT    134  =       99.12

TOTAL FOR ALL ACCOUNTS =         970.71
```

CASE STUDY 5: Elementary Descriptive Statistics

(For use with Chapter Six or later.)

One of the most common uses for computers is in the development of statistics that describe collections of data. Terms like mean, standard deviation, and correlation coefficient are familiar to students of economics, psychology, and education, to mention only a few.

In this case study we shall devise a program to read in two sets of data having a presumed relationship to each other. For each set we shall compute its mean and standard deviation, and then compute the coefficient of correlation between the two.

Here is a brief sketch of the mathematical theory involved.

A basic idea is that of a summation, represented by the Greek letter capital sigma, which means to add up all the values of the type indicated. If we write

$$\Sigma x$$

for instance, we mean to form the sum of all the values described by the letter x. In our numerical example below, one of the variables will be the Gross National Product in current prices, for each of 37 years. The formula

XMEAN = Σ GNP / 37.0

would say to add up all the GNP values, and divide the sum by 37, giving the mean (average).

To simplify the notation, we shall call the two sets of numbers X and Y, after reading them under their more descriptive names of GNP (Gross National Product) and FRBNDX (Federal Reserve Board Index of Industrial Production, 1967 = 100). Using the shorter names, here is the task we have.

For each we are to compute the mean, given by the formula already stated. Then we are to compute the standard deviation of each, which for the X values is given by

$$\text{XSTDEV} = \frac{\sqrt{N \Sigma x^2 - (\Sigma x)^2}}{N}$$

Here we have written the formula in the more common form in which the number of items in the set is called N; this will be 37 in our case. Reading through the formula, it says to add up all the values of x squared, and multiply that sum by N. From this product we are to subtract the square of the sum of all the x values. We then take the square root of the result and divide it by N.

The formula for the coefficient of correlation is somewhat more complex, but still involves just the concept of a summation. The usual symbol for this quantity is r, and the formula is

$$r = \frac{N \Sigma xy - \Sigma x \, \Sigma y}{\sqrt{N \Sigma x^2 - (\Sigma x)^2} \; \sqrt{N \Sigma y^2 - (\Sigma y)^2}}$$

Notice that the two quantities in the denominator also appear in the formulas for the standard deviation; we shall take advantage of this fact in writing the program.

The formation of the various sums can be done as each x and y value is read; there is no need to store the entire array of numbers in each set in the computer, which would require the use of subscripted variables as discussed in Chapter Seven.

The program is actually not very complicated. A simple DO loop is used to read the 37 pairs of numbers. The data in this table is used in many examples throughout the book, so we assume that it has been thoroughly checked. We shall therefore not concern ourselves about such problems as missing or mispunched data, etc. This is a questionable procedure for a real-life program, but as in some of our early examples it seems necessary in order to learn to walk before we run.

As each pair of numbers is read it is treated appropriately for producing the five sums that are needed. When all of these have been formed, an application of the formulas stated above produces the results we want, which are then written out with descriptive comments. Note the use of the intermediate variables XFACTR and YFACTR to avoid recomputing these factors that occur twice each in the various formulas.

```
C CASE STUDY 5: ELEMENTARY DESCRIPTIVE STATISTICS
C
C THIS PROGRAM READS TWO SET OF NUMBERS, AND COMPUTES THE MEAN
C AND STANDARD DEVIATION FOR EACH.  IT ALSO COMPUTES THE COEFFICIENT
C OF CORRELATION BETWEEN THE TWO SETS.
C
C      VARIABLES
C      SUMX     THE SUM OF THE X VALUES
C      SUMY     THE SUM OF THE Y VALUES
C      SUMXSQ   THE SUM OF THE SQUARES OF THE X VALUES
C      SUMYSQ   THE SUM OF THE SQUARES OF THE Y VALUES
C      SUMXY    THE SUM OF THE PRODUCTS OF THE X AND Y VALUES
C      XMEAN    THE MEAN OF THE X SET
C      YMEAN    THE MEAN OF THE Y SET
C      XFACTR   A FACTOR NEEDED IN TWO FORUMULAS
C      YFACTR   DITTO
C      XSTDEV   THE STANDARD DEVIATION OF THE X SET
C      YSTDEV   THE STANDARD DEVIATION OF THE Y SET
C      CORRLN   THE COEFFICIENT OF CORRELATION BETWEEN THE SETS
C
C
C SET THE VARIOUS ACCUMULATION VARIABLES TO ZERO
C
       SUMX = 0.0
       SUMY = 0.0
       SUMXSQ = 0.0
       SUMYSQ = 0.0
       SUMXY = 0.0
C
C READ THE DATA AND FORM THE VARIOUS SUMS
C
       DO 20 I = 1, 37
          READ (5, 10) GNP, FRBNDX
   10     FORMAT (5X, F5.1, 25X, F5.1)
          X = GNP
          Y = FRBNDX
          SUMX = SUMX + X
          SUMY = SUMY + Y
          SUMXSQ = SUMXSQ + X**2
          SUMYSQ = SUMYSQ + Y**2
          SUMXY = SUMXY + X*Y
   20  CONTINUE
C
C COMPUTE THE VARIOUS STATISTICS
C
       XMEAN = SUMX / 37.0
       YMEAN = SUMY / 37.0
       XFACTR = (37.0*SUMXSQ - SUMX**2) ** 0.5
       YFACTR = (37.0*SUMYSQ - SUMY**2) ** 0.5
       XSTDEV = XFACTR / 37.0
       YSTDEV = YFACTR / 37.0
       CORRLN = (37.0*SUMXY - SUMX*SUMY) / (XFACTR * YFACTR)
C
       WRITE (6, 30) XMEAN, YMEAN, XSTDEV, YSTDEV, CORRLN
```

```
30    FORMAT (1X, 'MEAN OF X SET = ', F10.1/
  1         1X, 'MEAN OF Y SET = ', F10.1/
  2         1X, 'STANDARD DEVIATION OF X SET = ', F10.1/
  3         1X, 'STANDARD DEVIATION OF Y SET = ', F10.1/
  4         1X, 'COEFFICIENT OF CORRELATION = ', F10.4//)
      STOP
      END
```

Here is the output when the program was run. The closeness of the co-efficient of correlation to 1.0 indicates a very close connection between the two sets of values.

```
MEAN OF X SET =           400.9
MEAN OF Y SET =            55.7
STANDARD DEVIATION OF X SET =       278.5
STANDARD DEVIATION OF Y SET =        28.7
COEFFICIENT OF CORRELATION =      0.9866
```

CASE STUDY 6: A Program to Graph the GNP from 1929 to 1971

(For use with Chapter Seven or later.)

There are many applications in which presenting the results as a stack of pages containing only numbers would not be very meaningful, and where we would much prefer to see the output in some sort of graphical form.

The preparation of a program to do a realistic job of graphing is a sizeable undertaking, and in real life the wise programmer will take advantage of the pre-programmed routines that are available for the purpose. Here we shall take a simple case to demonstrate the basic ideas in the same spirit as a chemistry student does an experiment to produce oxygen by electrolysis even though no practicing chemist would ever do it that way.

We take as our input one of the columns of economic data from the table on pages 92-93, specifically the United States Gross National Product in 1958 prices.

The basic scheme in our graphing method will be as follows. We set up an array, unimaginatively called ARRAY in the program, containing 81 elements. We shall print the entire contents of this array once for each year for which we want the graph printed, with a bar in the leftmost position. The row of bars thus produced will become the horizontal axis, because the final printed graph is to be turned one-quarter of a turn counter-clockwise for viewing. Before starting the graphing proper we fill the entire array with minus signs and print it, to provide what becomes the vertical axis.

The basic idea of the routine we shall write is that the numbers to be printed all fall in the range of zero to 800 billion dollars, and are stated in billions. If we divide the figures as given by 10, we shall have a number between zero and 80. We add 0.5 to this to provide for rounding, then use the integer function, named INT, to take just the portion of the result that is to the left of the decimal point, i.e., the integer portion. This integer is tested to be sure that it is greater than zero and no greater than 81, and if so an X is placed in ARRAY in that position and the whole array is printed.

Next the X is removed by replacing it with a blank, in preparation for printing the next line. This sequence is repeated for every input value.

Notice in the table that six years are skipped—1930, 1932, 1934, 1936, 1943, and 1947. Zeros will be entered for these years, which, under the logic described above, will produce blank lines for those years.

The main programming matter to be considered is how to get the alpha-numeric characters to use for printing. Fortran does not provide for a data type "alphanumeric," but permits any type of variable to be so used. There are only two problems: getting the values into variables, and watching out for unintended data type conversions.

The simplest way to get the values is to use the DATA statement described in Chapter Ten. If you have not studied that chapter yet, simply be assured that this statement will do the job:

```
DATA DASH/'-', BAR/'|', X/'X', BLANK/' '
```

Now, whenever we write something like

```
ARRAY(K) = DASH
```

the result will be to place in the specified position of the array the alpha-numeric representation of a dash, that is, the minus sign.

The Fortran compiler, as noted, makes no notice of our usage of a variable as alphanumeric. However, if we were to write this statement

```
LINE(K) = DASH
```

the compiler would arrange for a conversion from real to integer form — which would mess up the whole arrangement. We therefore have to be sure that all the variables we are using in this way are of the same type, using a REAL or INTEGER statement if necessary. (See Chapter Ten on these statements.)

(In the case of certain computers and compilers, it may be better to use integer variables throughout to hold alphanumeric variables. The reasons are too complex to be worth the trouble of explaining them.)

The complete program is shown. There are only about two dozen statements here altogether — the rest being comments — and the program is actually not very hard to follow.

After the DIMENSION and DATA statements we start by filling the array with dashes and printing the line. This will become the vertical axis when the page is turned. After doing this we have to clear the array, and then place a bar in the first position for producing the horizontal axis when the page is turned. Now comes a loop, using the years in question as the indexing parameters. Nothing is actually ever done with the DO index.

Within this DO loop we repeatedly read values of the GNP from cards. For each we divide it by 10.0, add 0.5 for rounding, and convert to integer form. The result, assuming that there was correct data for that year, is an integer between 14 (as it happens) and 74. If there was no data, the result is zero and we certainly don't want to try to place something in array position zero. Also, if a data value is incorrect, we don't want to try to place anything in array positions beyond 81. Accordingly, a test is made before placing an X in the array. The same test has to be applied to the reblanking of the position that held the X.

At the end we skip to a new page so that the complete graph will come out on one sheet of the output.

Since this example is so very greatly simplified from a real-life graphing routine, it might be well to list some of the special features of this program. Seldom would data convert from the values given to the position in an array with such a simple formula as dividing by 10.0 and adding 0.5. One of the

```
C CASE STUDY 6: A PROGRAM TO GRAPH THE GNP FROM 1929 TO 1971
C
C       VARIABLES
C
C       ARRAY    AN ARRAY OF 81 ELEMENTS, HOLDING ALPHANUMERIC DATA
C       DASH     ALPHA DASH FOR VERTICAL AXIS
C       BAR      ALPHA BAR FOR HORIZONTAL AXIS
C       X        ALPHA X FOR PRINTING THE POINT
C       BLANK    BLANK FOR CLEARING ARRAY
C       K        DO INDEX
C       M        POINTS TO POSITION IN THE ARRAY
C       GNP      GROSS NATIONAL PRODUCT FOR THE YEAR
C
C  NOTE USE OF INT (INTEGER) FUNCTION TO GET INTEGER PORTION OF
C       THE QUOTIENT OF GNP AND 10.0; THIS PICKS POINT FOR 'X' IN ARRAY
C
C NOTE ALSO USE OF DATA STATEMENT TO GET ALPHANUMERIC CONSTANTS
C
        DIMENSION ARRAY(81)
        DATA DASH/'-'/, BAR/'|'/, X/'X'/, BLANK/' '/
C
C       ... PUT DASHES IN ARRAY; PRINTS VERTICAL AXIS WHEN PAGE IS TURNED
C
        DO 10 K = 1, 81
             ARRAY(K) = DASH
   10   CONTINUE
        WRITE (6, 20) ARRAY
   20   FORMAT ('1', 81A1)
C
C       ... CLEAR ARRAY
C
        DO 30 K = 1, 81
             ARRAY(K) = BLANK
   30   CONTINUE
C
C       ... PUT A BAR IN THE FIRST ELEMENT, FOR HORIZONTAL AXIS
C
        ARRAY(1) = BAR
C
C USE DO LOOP TO GO THROUGH THE YEARS
C
        DO 60 K = 1929, 1971
C
C            ... READ A VALUE OF THE GNP
C
             READ (5, 40) GNP
   40        FORMAT (F10.0)
C
C            ... DECIDE WHERE TO PUT THE X
C
             M = INT(GNP/10.0 + 0.5)
C
C            ... PUT AN X IN THAT POSITION IN ARRAY, IF IN RANGE
C
             IF ( M .GT. 0 .AND. M .LE. 81 ) ARRAY(M) = X
C
C            ... PRINT THAT LINE, EVEN IF BLANK
C
             WRITE (6, 50) ARRAY
   50        FORMAT (1X, 81A1)
C
C            ... CLEAR THAT POSITION IN THE ARRAY, UNLESS IT WAS BLANK
C
             IF ( M .GT. 0 .AND. M .LE. 81 ) ARRAY(M) = BLANK
   60   CONTINUE
C
C       ... SKIP TO NEW PAGE
C
        WRITE (6, 70)
   70   FORMAT ('1')
        STOP
        END
```

inputs to a complete routine would be the permissible range of values, from which the routine itself would derive the conversion formula. This remark applies to both axes.

We have not printed axis identifications, scale markings, grid lines, curve identifications, or provided for a choice of the plotting symbol. There is no provision for indicating or otherwise treating bad data. There is no provision for negative values.

With all this being admitted, the program does illustrate some basic concepts, in an application that is not quite like any other in this book.

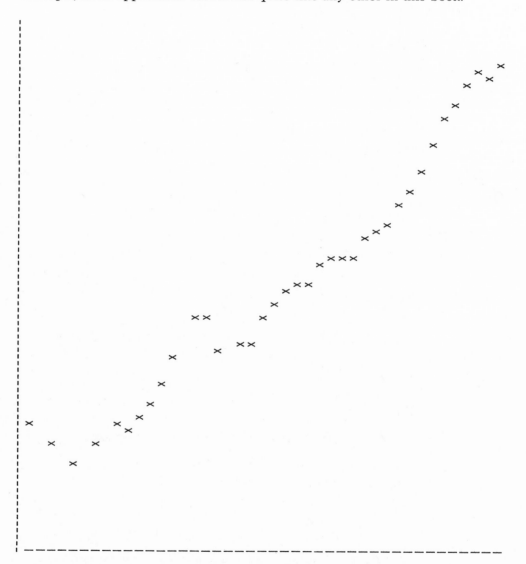

CASE STUDY 7: A Program to Simulate Ten Games of Craps

(For use with Chapter Nine or later.)

The game of craps, as most everybody knows, is played with two dice, each of which has six sides numbered from 1 to 6. The roll of two dice therefore produces a total between 2 and 12.

The simple rules of craps are as follows.

If on your first roll you get 2, 3, or 12, you lose.

If on your first roll you get 7 or 11, you win.

If on your first roll you get none of these, the number you do get is called your *point*. You then continue rolling until either repeating your point—you win—or getting a seven—you lose.

The odds of winning can be analyzed by the methods of probability and are just slightly less than one-half. That little bit is enough to keep the gambling casinos in business.

Simulation of this game is quite simple, provided the Fortran system has a way to generate *random numbers*, which are used to simulate the roll of the dice.

A random number, as we shall use the term, is a fraction between zero and one. The fact that it is random means that any number within that range is as likely as any other number, and there is no connection between successive numbers. If one number is 0.92, the next might be 0.12 or .50 or perhaps 0.92 again—in other words, there is no pattern.

In the Fortran system used to prepare programs for this book, the random number generator is a function named RAN. As its first letter indicates, it produces a real value. Its argument must be an integer, which handles the following problem. Suppose you have run a program that involves a random number generator, and have now made some changes. You would like to try it again to see if it produces the same results—but how is that possible when there are random numbers in the program? The solution is to be able to specify a starting point, called a *seed*, so that the *same* sequence of random numbers will be generated. Or, in other situations, we might want to be able to guarantee that we are *not* getting the same sequence of random numbers. That will be the case with our program. It will be set up to play ten games of craps, then to stop. If we want to play ten more, it would do no good simply to run the program again, starting with the same initial random number, because the exact same sequence would be generated and we would get identical results.

How do we make a random number between zero and one into a random integer between 1 and 6? The process is actually fairly simple. The random number generator produces a number as small as zero but less than 1.0. Six times such a number is a product between zero and something less than 6.0. Adding 1.0 to that gives a number that might be as small as 1.0 but is definitely less than 7.0. We take the integer portion of that number to get one of the six integers 1 through 6, with each digit having equal probability.

All that last remark means is that if we ran a program until it produced many such numbers, there would be approximately the same number of each of the numbers 1, 2, 3, 4, 5, and 6. The process therefore simulates the roll of one die. Doing it twice and adding the results gives the same result as rolling two dice and adding up the spots on the two of them.

The program should be nearly self-explanatory, with this much background. The first argument of the random number generator, the seed, is read from a card so that it is possible to decide whether to repeat a run or try a new one. The program makes good use of the .OR. function.

Here is the output of three runs, with a first line in each case showing what the seed was; this is done merely to demonstrate that they were different. The method by which the function RAN generates a sequence of random numbers is beyond the scope of this book.

Notice that out of 30 games we won 14, which is within a few percentage points of the theoretical expectation of winning. This degree of closeness to theory in only 30 tries is accidental.

```
123456
YOU WIN BY MAKING YOUR POINT
YOU LOSE ON FIRST ROLL
YOU WIN BY MAKING YOUR POINT
YOU WIN BY MAKING YOUR POINT
YOU WIN BY MAKING YOUR POINT
YOU LOSE BY FAILING TO MAKE YOUR POINT
YOU LOSE BY FAILING TO MAKE YOUR POINT
YOU WIN ON FIRST ROLL
YOU WIN BY MAKING YOUR POINT
YOU LOSE ON FIRST ROLL


987654
YOU LOSE ON FIRST ROLL
YOU LOSE BY FAILING TO MAKE YOUR POINT
YOU WIN BY MAKING YOUR POINT
YOU WIN ON FIRST ROLL
YOU WIN ON FIRST ROLL
YOU LOSE BY FAILING TO MAKE YOUR POINT
YOU LOSE BY FAILING TO MAKE YOUR POINT
YOU WIN BY MAKING YOUR POINT
YOU LOSE BY FAILING TO MAKE YOUR POINT
YOU LOSE ON FIRST ROLL


334556
YOU WIN BY MAKING YOUR POINT
YOU LOSE BY FAILING TO MAKE YOUR POINT
YOU LOSE BY FAILING TO MAKE YOUR POINT
YOU WIN ON FIRST ROLL
YOU LOSE BY FAILING TO MAKE YOUR POINT
YOU LOSE BY FAILING TO MAKE YOUR POINT
YOU WIN BY MAKING YOUR POINT
YOU LOSE BY FAILING TO MAKE YOUR POINT
YOU LOSE BY FAILING TO MAKE YOUR POINT
YOU WIN ON FIRST ROLL
```

```
C CASE STUDY 7: A PROGRAM TO SIMULATE 10 GAMES OF CRAPS
C
      READ (5, 5) NSEED
    5 FORMAT (I10)
      KOUNT = 1
C
C     ... ROLL THE DICE
C
   10 K1 = INT(6*RAN(NSEED)+1)
      K2 = INT(6*RAN(NSEED)+1)
      K = K1 + K2
C
C     ... CHECK FOR WIN OR LOSS ON FIRST ROLL
C
      IF ( K .EQ. 2 .OR. K .EQ. 3 .OR. K .EQ. 12 ) GO TO 30
      IF ( K .EQ. 7 .OR. K .EQ. 11 ) GO TO 50
C
```

```
C      ... NOT A WIN OR LOSS ON FIRST ROLL -- SET 'POINT' AND ROLL AGAIN
C
       KPOINT = K
  20   K1 = INT(6*RAN(NSEED)+1)
       K2 = INT(6*RAN(NSEED)+1)
       K = K1 + K2
C
C      ... CHECK FOR MAKING POINT OR CRAPPING OUT -- GO BACK IF NEITHER
C
       IF ( K .EQ. KPOINT ) GO TO 70
       IF ( K .EQ. 7 ) GO TO 90
       GO TO 20
C
C      ... WRITES AND FORMATS FOR VARIOUS OUTCOMES
C
  30   WRITE (6, 40)
  40   FORMAT (1X, 'YOU LOSE ON FIRST ROLL')
       GO TO 110
  50   WRITE (6, 60)
  60   FORMAT (1X, 'YOU WIN ON FIRST ROLL')
       GO TO 110
  70   WRITE (6, 80)
  80   FORMAT (1X, 'YOU WIN BY MAKING YOUR POINT')
       GO TO 110
  90   WRITE (6, 100)
 100   FORMAT (1X, 'YOU LOSE BY FAILING TO MAKE YOUR POINT')
 110   KOUNT = KOUNT + 1
       IF ( KOUNT .LE. 10 ) GO TO 10
       STOP
       END
```

CASE STUDY 8: Printing a Properly Spaced Index from a Memo File

(For use with Chapter Ten.)

It is possible to get the impression that computers and Fortran are used exclusively for the manipulation of numbers, which is by no means the case. Fortran can also be used for graphing, as we have seen, and can be used in a wide variety of applications that involve the manipulation of data that consists only of symbolic information such as letters of the alphabet. Fortran is not the ideal language for such work, but it certainly can be done. This case study shows how Fortran may be used to prepare the index of a book, and in fact the index of this book was prepared using the program shown below.

The program shown is heavily commented, so that to some degree the program explains itself, but a few additional comments may be helpful.

The program was set up as a main program and a subroutine. The function of the subroutine is simply to print one line and determine whether the maximum number of lines on a page has been reached. This function needs to be done at several places in the main program, and the subroutine method is a good way not only to reduce duplication of segments, but also to improve the readability of the main program. The subroutine is set up with no arguments: all communication between the main program and the subroutine is done by having identical COMMON statements in each that include all the data items that the two routines both need to know about.

These programs use almost all of the features of Fortran that we have discussed in this book, plus one or two that have not been mentioned. One of the latter is the INTEGER*2 statement near the beginning of the program proper, that is, after the introductory comments. It turns out that in the IBM computer used for this work an integer variable can be set up to use either 2 or 4 of the basic units on information in the computer, which are called *bytes* and consist of eight *binary digits*, usually called *bits*. The way this program has been written we would be content with *one* byte per element, so it seemed reasonable to save a bit of space by using the two-byte option; not that it matters in a small program of this type, but in other instances it can be quite important. Notice also that the INTEGER statement can be used to give the information that we have usually placed in a DIMENSION statement, namely, that the variable is subscripted and how many elements it has.

A DATA statement is used to give values to the three variables that are used to hold alphanumeric information. We recall that Fortran has no variable type specifically for this purpose. We may use either integer or real, but it is important to be consistent to avoid unwanted automatic data type conversions.

```
C CASE STUDY 8: PRINTING A PROPERLY SPACED INDEX FROM A MEMO FILE
C
C
C      THE PROGRAM ACCEPTS 80-CHARACTER RECORDS FROM A FILE ON DISK.
C THE FILE CONTAINS BOTH UPPER AND LOWER CASE CHARACTERS, HAVING
C BEEN ENTERED FROM A TIME-SHARING TERMINAL IN 'MEMO' MODE.
C THE PURPOSE OF THE PROGRAM IS TO PREPARE CAMERA-READY COPY FOR THE
C INDEX OF A BOOK.  IT WAS USED TO PREPARE THE INDEX FOR THIS BOOK.
C      THE PROGRAM MUST BE ABLE TO ACCEPT NUMBERS DEFINING THE MAXIMUM
C LINE LENGTH AND THE MAXIMUM PAGE LENGTH, SO THAT THE DECISION ON
C THESE PARAMETERS CAN BE LEFT TO THE LAST MINUTE TO COORDINATE
C PROPERLY WITH THE REQUIREMENTS OF THE PUBLISHER.
C      THE MAJOR PROBLEM THAT THE PROGRAM MUST DEAL WITH IS THE CASE
C OF INPUT LINES THAT ARE LONGER THAN THE MAXIMUM LINE LENGTH; THESE
C HAVE TO BE BROKEN AT A POINT WHERE THERE IS A BLANK SPACE, WHICH
C THE PROGRAM MUST LOCATE, AND THEN 'TURN OVER' (A PUBLISHING TERM)
C THE CONTINUATION, I. E., INDENT IT FOUR SPACES.  FURTHERMORE, SOME
C LINES OF INPUT ARE MARKED (IN THEIR FIRST CHARACTER) AS NEEDING
C TO BE INDENTED TWO SPACES, SINCE THEY REPRESENT SECOND-LEVEL ENTRIES.
C (A GLANCE AT THE INDEX WILL SHOW THE APPEARANCE THAT IS REQUIRED.)
C
C VARIABLE NAMES AND USAGES:
C
C      INDENT  LOGICAL; IF TRUE, LINE MUST BE INDENTED 2 SPACES
C      TRNOVR  LOGICAL; IF TRUE, LINE MUST BE INDENTED 4 SPACES
C      TEXT    ALPHABETIC; CONTAINS LINE OF TEXT FROM DISK
C      INDMRK  ALPHABETIC; '>' TO DESIGNATE A LINE TO BE INDENTED
C      EOL     ALPHABETIC; '$' TO MARK END-OF-LINE IN INPUT RECORD
C      BLANK   ALPHABETIC; ' ' USED TO SEARCH FOR PLACE TO BREAK LINE
C      LCOUNT  INTEGER; LINE COUNTER
C      MAXLIN  INTEGER; READ AS CONSOLE DATA; MAX CHARACTERS PER LINE
C      MAXCNT  INTEGER; READ AS CONSOLE DATA; MAX LINES PER PAGE
C      INITL   INTEGER; POINTER TO FIRST CHARACTER OF LINE BEING
C                  PRINTED FROM INPUT RECORD
C      LAST    INTEGER; POINTER TO LAST CHARACTER OF LINE BEING
C                  PRINTED FROM INPUT RECORD
C      LINEL   LINE LENGTH--VARIES BECAUSE OF INDENTS AND TURNOVERS
C
C
C      A SUBROUTINE IS USED TO HANDLE THE PRINTING OF A LINE.
C THIS WAS DONE BECAUSE THERE ARE THREE POINTS IN THE PROGRAM
C AT WHICH OUTPUT IS NEEDED, AND AT EACH OF THESE IT IS NECESSARY
C TO MAKE THE INDENTATION AND LINE COUNT DECISIONS.  A SUBROUTINE
C PERMITS ALL THIS TO BE DONE WITHOUT CONFUSING GO TO STATEMENTS.
C THERE ARE NO PARAMETERS IN THE SUBROUTINE CALL; COMMON STATEMENTS
C HAVE BEEN USED TO MAKE ALL THE VARIABLES KNOWN TO BOTH MAIN AND
C SUBPROGRAMS.
```

```
C     AN ENTRY STATEMENT IS USED TO GET INTO THE SUBROUTINE AT A
C SPECIAL POINT FOR SPACING LINES BETWEEN LETTER-GROUPS; THIS IS
C NOT A FEATURE OF ANSI FORTRAN.
C
      LOGICAL INDENT, TRNOVR
      INTEGER*2 TEXT(80), INDMRK, EOL, BLANK
      DATA INDMRK/'>'/, EOL/'$'/, BLANK/' '/
      COMMON LCOUNT, MAXCNT, INITL, LAST, INDENT, TRNOVR, TEXT
C
C WRITE PROMPT FOR MAXIMUM CHARACTERS PER LINE AND LINES PER PAGE
      WRITE (6, 10)
  10  FORMAT (1X, 'ENTER MAX CHARS AND MAX LINES, PER SAMPLE: 25,55,')
      READ (5, 20) MAXLIN, MAXCNT
  20  FORMAT (2I3)
C
C INITIALIZE LINE COUNTER
      LCOUNT = 0
C
C READ A LINE OF TEXT
  30  READ (4, 40) TEXT
  40  FORMAT (80A1)
C CHECK FOR END-OF-LINE (EOL) MARK IN INITIAL POSITION, SIGNIFYING
C THAT A BLANK LINE IS DESIRED
      IF ( TEXT(1) .EQ. EOL ) CALL BLKOUT
      IF ( TEXT(1) .EQ. EOL ) GO TO 30
C
C CHECK WHETHER LINE IS TO BE INDENTED
      LINEL = MAXLIN
      INDENT = .FALSE.
      INITL = 1
      IF ( TEXT(1) .EQ. INDMRK ) INDENT = .TRUE.
      IF ( INDENT ) INITL = 2
      IF ( INDENT ) LINEL = MAXLIN - 2
C
C SET TURNOVER SWITCH OFF
      TRNOVR = .FALSE.
C
C CHECK WHETHER LINE IS SHORT ENOUGH TO PRINT ON ONE LINE
C PRINT IT AND GO BACK FOR ANOTHER LINE IF SO
  50  DO 60 K = 1, LINEL
          LAST = INITL + K
          IF ( TEXT(LAST) .EQ. EOL ) CALL OUT
          IF ( TEXT(LAST) .EQ. EOL ) GO TO 30
  60  CONTINUE
C
C IF HERE, LINE OF TEXT TOO LONG TO PRINT ON ONE LINE; MUST BREAK IT
  70  IF (TEXT(LAST) .EQ. BLANK ) GO TO 80
C
C BACK UP ONE CHARACTER POSITION
      LAST = LAST - 1
      GO TO 70
C
C HAVE FOUND A PLACE TO BREAK - PRINT LINE
  80  CALL OUT
C
C SET UP TO TURN OVER SUCCEEDING LINES UNTIL FINDING EOL
      TRNOVR = .TRUE.
C
C ALLOW FOR TURNOVER IN CHECKING MAXIMUM LINE LENGTH
      LINEL = MAXLIN - 4
C
C MOVE POINTER TO NEXT CHARACTER AFTER ONE JUST PRINTED
      INITL = LAST + 1
C
C GO BACK TO CONTINUE PRINTING THE LINE THAT HAD TO BE BROKEN
      GO TO 50
      END
```

```
C SUBROUTINE TO DO THE OUTPUT AND CHECK THE LINE COUNTER
C IN CASE STUDY 8.
C USES AN ENTRY STATEMENT TO GET IN FOR PRINTING BLANK LINE
C
C
        SUBROUTINE OUT
        COMMON LCOUNT, MAXCNT, INITL, LAST, INDENT, TRNOVR, TEXT
        INTEGER*2 TEXT(80)
        LOGICAL INDENT, TRNOVR
C
C PRINT A LINE, WITH OR WITHOUT INDENTATION
        M = LAST - 1
        IF (            .NOT. INDENT
     1      .AND. .NOT. TRNOVR ) WRITE (6, 20) (TEXT(J), J = INITL, M)
        IF (                  INDENT
     1      .AND. .NOT. TRNOVR ) WRITE (6, 30) (TEXT(J), J = INITL, M)
        IF (                  TRNOVR ) WRITE (6, 40) (TEXT(J), J = INITL, M)
C
C SKIP AROUND THE ENTRY POINT, WHICH IS FOR BLANK LINE PRINTING
        GO TO 10
        ENTRY BLKOUT
        WRITE (6, 20)
C
C INCREMENT AND CHECK LINE COUNTER
   10   LCOUNT = LCOUNT + 1
        IF ( LCOUNT .LT. MAXCNT ) RETURN
C
C READ A NULL LINE, TO STOP PRINTING WHILE PAPER IS CHANGED
        READ ( 5, 20)
C
C RESET LINE COUNTER
        LCOUNT = 0
C
        RETURN
   20   FORMAT (1X, 50A1)
   30   FORMAT (3X, 50A1)
   40   FORMAT (5X, 50A1)
        END
```

One of the important features of the program is that it must be able to accept numbers defining the maximum number of characters per line and the maximum number of lines per page. ("Per page" means "per column" actually, as there are two parallel columns per page in the printed book.) The program writes a "prompting" line saying that these numbers are needed and telling how to write them.

The program was run from a time-sharing terminal, to get the high print quality that it provides, and to allow for watching the output as it is printed, occasionally making on-the-spot decisions about changing column length by one line to prevent awkward carryovers from one column to another, for instance.

The input data to the program consists of a file on magnetic disk, placed there in a separate operation. This file is read as data set 4, requiring a file definition. (We want to save data set 5 for the time-sharing console, so that it can be used for such things as the maximum characters and column lengths input.)

Now we come to the part of the program that is executed repeatedly, once for each line of the input file. A line of text is read, using the array name TEXT without subscripting, so that it takes the entire line of 80 characters. At the end of the line we are assured that there is a dollar sign; the input data has been thoroughly checked by other methods to be sure this is true. (The program fails in the absence of the end-of-line character on any line.) The "last" character may actually be the first, since the way we handle inserting a blank line between letter groups is to put in a line with just a dollar sign in the first position. If this is the case we call the subroutine by its alternate name of BLKOUT (as indicated by the ENTRY statement in the subroutine). This simply produces one blank line as output and goes back for another line.

Next we check to see if the first character in the line is the symbol '>' which we use to mean "indent two spaces." If this is the first character, we set the logical variable INDENT equal to .TRUE. and subtract 2 from the permitted line length. It is also then necessary to indicate that the "first" (INITL) character is in position 2, since position 1 was taken up with the indent symbol.

Now we need to see if the input line will fit on one line of the maximum length permitted. In order to do this we must start at the left end of the line and look for the dollar sign that signifies the end of the line. This is done with a DO loop that runs from 1 to the line length. If the dollar sign end-of-line (EOL) symbol is found before termination of this DO loop, the line can be printed with a CALL to the subroutine named OUT, and then we return to statement 30 for another line.

If we fall through the end of the range of the DO, the input line was too long for one line on the page. The line must be printed on at least two lines, breaking it where there is a blank space. We start at wherever the DO loop left off, and go back toward the left, looking for a blank. Upon finding it we print that much, set the logical variable named TRNOVR ("turnover") to .TRUE., decrease the line length to compensate for the extra indentation that will be used subsequently, and go back to see if what remains to be printed will fit on one line. If it does we print it and go back for another line. If not, we back up to a blank, etc. This process is carried out over and over until the entire input line has been printed.

There are two potential snags. One is that the input line might need to be more than 80 characters. This is handled by making the entry into two lines, on a sort of hand-tailored basis. The other is that some input line might contain a word longer than the maximum line length; this simply doesn't happen with the normal usage of the program.

The subroutine OUT is fairly simple. About all it has to do is decide whether the line is not indented, is indented two spaces, or is indented four spaces. All this is handled with three IF statements containing WRITEs that refer to appropriate FORMATs. The ENTRY statement allows the subroutine to be used under the name BLKOUT for producing a blank line.

The subroutine also takes care of counting the number of lines in a column. Once that limit is reached it stops, using a READ without a list, to allow time for the paper to be changed. Pressing the carriage return key on the time-sharing terminal starts program execution again.

Here is a sample of the input data, consisting of a few lines from the index of one of the author's previous books.

Observe the extra dollar signs at the end. This is to provide time to get the last page out of the terminal before various other kinds of time-sharing messages start coming out. You may have noticed that the program makes no provision for stopping when the input file is exhausted. This is another matter that can readily be handled from the time-sharing terminal.

```
A field descriptor, 129, 222$
Absolute value, of complex number, 63, 64, 246$
Absolute value function, complex 63, 66, 67, 246$
>double precision, 60, 246$
>integer, 246$
>real, 11, 44, 246$
Ac circuit example, 35, 105-107$
Acceleration, of Gauss-Seidel method, 112, 119, 121$
Access, of records, 137, 141$
Accumulation of error, 42$
Ackoff, Russell L., 119$
Addition, 7, 236, 240, 243$
Adjustable dimension, 175, 176, 222$
Aircraft position exercise, 51$
ALGOL, 173, 227$
Algorithm, 2, 38, 82, 189, 236$
Alphanumeric data, 129, 144, 150,206-215, 222$
Amortization exercise, 164, 165$
Ampersand (&), 135$
AND, 32, 68, 227, 240$
APL, 166, 210$
Apostrophe ('), 58, 130, 140$
Approximate value, 5, 55$
Approximation methods, Gauss-Seidel, 105-114, 119, 121, 150, 151, 156-159$
>Newton-Raphson, 42-48$
Arctangent function, double precision, 61, 246, 251$
>real, 11, 66, 67, 246$
Argument, of function, 11, 170, 181$
Arithmetic, assignment statement, 5, 11, 55, 65, 101$
>expression, 7-10, 30, 55, 243, 244$
>IF statement, 30, 33, 98, 186, 227, 240$
>operation, 7, 243, 244$
Arm movement, disk, 141$
$
$
$
$
$
$
$
```

Following is the output when the program was run with the line length and column length parameters shown. Naturally, the prompt line and the response to it would be cut off before sending the page to the publisher.

Observe the extra space after the entry for Argument; this was where the program stopped after printing 37 lines, to wait for the paper to be changed.

```
ENTER MAX CHARS AND MAX LINES, PER SAMPLE: 25,55,
33,37,
A field descriptor, 129, 222
Absolute value, of complex
    number, 63, 64, 246
Absolute value function, complex
    63, 66, 67, 246
  double precision, 60, 246
  integer, 246
  real, 11, 44, 246
Ac circuit example, 35, 105-107
Acceleration, of Gauss-Seidel
    method, 112, 119, 121
Access, of records, 137, 141
Accumulation of error, 42
Ackoff, Russell L., 119
```

CASE STUDY 9: Finding a Root of an Equation by Interval Halving

(For use with Chapter Ten. Readers with minimum mathematical background should skip this case study.)

One of the common applications of computers is in finding the roots of equations. In a few cases, such as the quadratic equation, there are simple formulas for finding the roots. In most situations of practical interest, however, no such formulas exist, and it is necessary to use iterative (repetitive) methods that lead to an approximate answer. We shall consider the simplest such method, which goes by the name of *interval halving*, for a reason that will become obvious.

Suppose we have some equation, the graph of which might look like this:

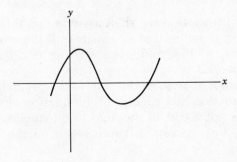

A root of an equation is a point at which the graph crosses the x axis; at such a point the ordinate of the curve (height above or below the x axis) is of course zero. Let us suppose that we have two points, call them a and b, such that the ordinates at a and b are of different signs, like this:

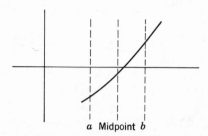

a Midpoint b

We can be sure that in such a case there is at least one root in the interval between a and b. There might be three, of course, or any odd number, but there must be at least one. Let us suppose there is only one.

Now what if we were to evaluate the function at a point midway between a and b. The root would have to fall either between a and the midpoint, or between the midpoint and b. If the ordinate at a and the ordinate at the midpoint have different signs, then the root is in that interval—otherwise it is in the interval between the midpoint and b. Either way, we have halved the interval within which the root must lie. We can accordingly relabel a and b and repeat the process, as many times as we wish. We can thus narrow the interval within which the root could lie as far as we please, and get as close to the root as may be desired, within the limits of the precision of number representation within the particular computer.

There are many ways to decide when to stop the iterative process. One is to decide in advance how small an interval we wish to reach. Another, which we shall use here, is to decide on the basis of the size of the ordinate at the midpoint. After all, if by good luck we get extremely close to the root at an early iteration, there is no need to keep narrowing the interval. Naturally, a small ordinate indicates a closeness to the root only if the graph is not too flat. In this picture the ordinate is small but we are far from the root:

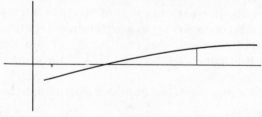

However, for the sake of this illustration we shall assume that this does not happen. (Writing a root-finding program that eliminates *all* the strange possibilities that can occur is impossible, and even writing one that covers most things is a great deal of work.)

A flowchart of the algorithm is shown. At the start of the program we will have a programmer-defined function that specifies the equation of which we want a root. This definition is not a part of the algorithm, since it does not itself call for any processing, but we can still indicate it on the flowchart as shown.

The first action is to read the values of A and B, within which it is specified that a root is known to fall.

We begin by writing headings. Then we immediately compute the ordinates at these points, calling them FA and FB. Now, on the chance that A and B might be in error, so that there is no root between them, or on the chance that anything else might happen to prevent us from finding a root in some reasonable number of iterations, we start an *iteration counter* at 1. This will be used to limit the number of iterations to a maximum of 15. These are all of the preliminary operations.

At the beginning of the part of the algorithm that is applied repeatedly we compute the midpoint between A and B, and compute the corresponding ordinate. Now we want to know whether the ordinate at A and the ordinate at the midpoint have the same sign. The simplest way to find out is to multiply them together and check the sign of the product, which will be negative if the two have different signs and positive if they are both positive or both negative. Suppose first that they have the same sign. Then we have this situation:

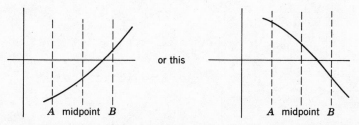

That means that we want to make the new value of A the same as the present value of the midpoint, and likewise for the ordinate at A. On the other hand, if the ordinate at A and the ordinate at the midpoint have different signs, we have this situation:

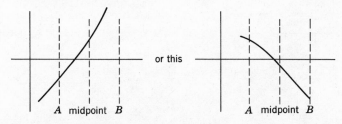

Here we want to narrow the interval by making the new value of B the same as the present midpoint. Either way, we have now halved the interval. In order to be able to watch the halving process we shall now print the value of the midpoint and of the ordinate.

Now we want to know if the iterative process has *converged* to a root, as it is called. We accordingly want to know if the value of the ordinate at the midpoint, FXMID, is sufficiently small — say, less than 0.01. But of course we don't care whether the ordinate is positive or negative, so long as it is small *in absolute value*. Accordingly, we shall be using the absolute value function in the test. If the process has converged, we simply print a remark and stop. If not, we add 1 to the iteration counter.

If the new value of N is less than or equal to 15, we simply go back to

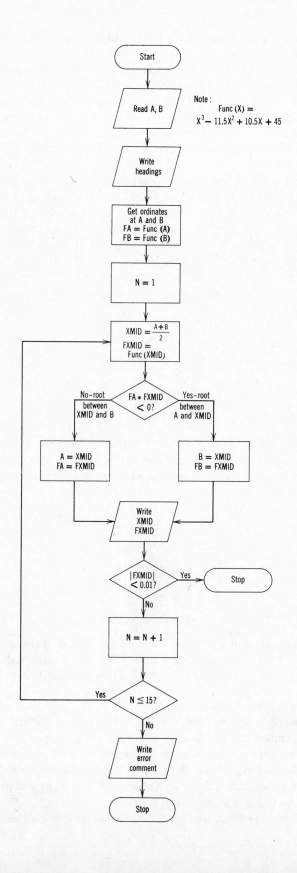

Note :
$$\text{Func (X)} = X^3 - 11.5X^2 + 10.5X + 45$$

repeat the process. Otherwise we write a comment indicating that the process did not converge in 15 iterations and stop.

The program should be quite simple to understand, if the algorithm as defined in the flowchart has been clear. We see the function definition specifies the equation

$$x^3 - 11.5x^2 + 10.5x + 45 = 0$$

and has the name FUNC. The defined function is then brought into action at three subsequent points in the program, for finding the value of the ordinate at A, B, and XMID. The first IF statement, which tests for a small ordinate, uses the absolute value function, ABS, in a simple way.

```
C CASE STUDY 9:   FINDING A ROOT OF AN EQUATION BY INTERVAL HALVING
C USES A PROGRAMMER-DEFINED FUNCTION FOR THE EQUATION
C
C THIS IS THE DEFINED FUNCTION -- MAY BE CHANGED FOR OTHER EQUATIONS
C
      FUNC(X) = X**3 - 11.5*X**2 + 10.5*X + 45
C
C READ THE LEFT AND RIGHT ENDPOINTS OF AN INTERVAL THAT CONTAINS A ROOT
C
      READ (5, 10) A, B
 10   FORMAT (2F10.0)
C
C WRITE HEADINGS
C
      WRITE (6, 15)
 15   FORMAT (1X, '      XMID         FXMID'/)
C
C FIND THE VALUES OF THE ORDINATES AT THOSE POINTS
C
      FA = FUNC(A)
      FB = FUNC(B)
C
C INITIALIZE THE ITERATION COUNTER
C
      N = 1
C
C PROGRAM REPEATS FROM HERE -- GET MIDPOINT AND ITS ORDINATE
C
 20   XMID = (A + B) / 2.0
      FXMID = FUNC(XMID)
C
C SEE WHETHER ROOT IS IN LEFT OR RIGHT HALF-INTERVAL
C
      IF ( FA*FXMID .LE. 0.0 ) GO TO 30
C
C ROOT IS IN RIGHT HALF-INTERVAL
C
      A = XMID
      FA = FXMID
      GO TO 40
C
C ROOT IS IN LEFT HALF-INTERVAL
C
 30   B = XMID
      FB = FXMID
C
C WRITE THE LATEST MIDPOINT
C
 40   WRITE (6, 50) XMID, FXMID
 50   FORMAT (1X, 2F12.6)
```

```
C
C CHECK WHETHER ORDINATE AT XMID IS SMALL IN ABSOLUTE VALUE
C
      IF ( ABS(FXMID) .LT. 0.01 ) STOP
C
C INCREMENT THE ITERATION COUNTER AND GO BACK IF NOT TOO LARGE
C
      N = N + 1
      IF ( N .LE. 15 ) GO TO 20
C
C WRITE ERROR COMMENT AND STOP
C
      WRITE (6, 60)
   60 FORMAT (1X, 'PROCESS DID NOT CONVERGE IN 15 ITERATIONS')
      STOP
      END
```

Let us see how the program behaved in action. Here is the output when it was run with a card giving A = 9.5 and B = 19.0. These numbers were chosen because the graph does have different signs at those points, because this interval was known to contain only one root, and because they produced the interesting iterative behavior that follows:

XMID	FXMID
14.250000	753.046875
11.875000	222.568359
10.687500	64.412842
10.093750	7.710205
9.796875	-15.596680
9.945313	-4.347168
10.019531	1.579346
9.982422	-1.409424
10.000977	0.078613
9.991699	-0.666748
9.996338	-0.294556
9.998657	-0.108093
9.999817	-0.014618
10.000397	0.031998
10.000107	0.008682

Study of the equation will show that there is in fact a root at $x = 10$, so that the last approximation is closer to the true root than the ordinate at that point is to zero. This means only that the graph in the vicinity of this root is quite steep.

Let us take a different equation to indicate that the method works on any equation that does have one root between A and B. The equation used this time is

$$x^4 - 23.01 \sqrt{x + 234} - 199.78 = 0$$

This has a negative value at $x = 0$, and it is positive at $x = 10$, so we shall use those values for A and B.

Entering this equation is a matter of changing the defined function at the beginning of the program, recompiling, and rerunning. Just to prove that the argument used in the function definition is really only a dummy that tells the compiler what rule to follow when the function is later used, we shall use Q as the argument instead of X. Since the only change in the entire program is this one statement, we shall not use up a page to show the modified program. The changed statement is:

```
FUNC(Q) = Q**4 - 23.01*SQRT(Q + 234.) - 199.78
```

Here is the output, when the program was run with a data card giving A = 0.0 and B = 10.0.

```
     XMID          FXMID

  5.000000     69.494171
  2.500000   -514.577637
  3.750000   -356.820068
  4.375000   -188.676727
  4.687500    -72.475555
  4.843750     -4.928192
  4.921875     31.395782
  4.882813     13.015656
  4.863281      3.989532
  4.853516     -0.482880
  4.858398      1.750031
  4.855957      0.632111
  4.854736      0.074005
  4.854126     -0.204559
  4.854431     -0.065155
PROCESS DID NOT CONVERGE IN 15 ITERATIONS
```

We see that the program did not quite manage to converge to an answer in 15 iterations.

An iteration counter is not ordinarily used merely to guard against an iterative process taking a *little* too much time. Changing the limit to 20 or 25 would permit this program to find this root quite readily, and with an even more "tight" test than 0.01. Iteration counters have the more important purpose of preventing a large waste of time because some process might *never* converge. If we were to impose the requirement that the ordinate be less than 0.0000001 in value, for instance, it might be impossible for the program ever to get that close because of limitations of number precision in the computer. Or if the value of A were greater than the value of B, because of a punching error, this program would never stop without an iteration counter. Naturally, that particular error could be tested for—and probably should be—but since it is impossible to anticipate *all* the funny things that can happen, iteration counters are strongly recommended practice.

SUGGESTIONS FOR TERM PROBLEMS

The following list, it is hoped, will be suggestive of projects that a student who has spent several months studying Fortran might consider for a term problem. No attempt has been made to indicate the relative difficulty of the suggestions, largely because the difficulty depends mostly on how much of a complete job is attempted. Almost any of these could easily become far too large for a term problem in a one-semester course. *It is essential that you write down a definition of the precise scope of the task you propose to attempt, and get your instructor's approval before proceeding.* It is sometimes remarkably difficult for the beginner to distinguish between a job that is too simple to be worth term problem status, and one that would be tough for a Ph.D. candidate.

Many of the exercises in the chapters will suggest term problems if suitable scopes are established.

These suggestions are offered only on the thought that some readers may not have better ideas of their own. The goal of a term problem, after all, is to provide a transition from this course of study to the next one or to a realistic work situation. By far the best term problems are those that come from the reader's own field of interest: another course of his work. Even in these cases, however—or perhaps *especially* in these cases—it is essential to get guidance from an instructor or other experienced person before proceeding. Some rather simple-sounding jobs can turn out to be terribly difficult or complicated in ways that are not educational.

1. *Desk calculator simulation.*[1] Using typewriter terminal keys to simulate addition, subtraction, multiplication, and division, write a program that will cause a time-sharing system to act like a desk calculator. This problem may be done in terms of whatever "desk calculator" you wish; hand-held devices using LSI (large-scale integration) technology and costing under $100 are currently available to do considerably more than electromechanical devices costing ten times as much were able to do a few years ago.

2. *Justified typing.* Devise a program that will make Fortran simulate a justifying typewriter, so that after a line of English text has been entered the machine will adjust the spacing between the words that is as even as

---

[1] The first six of these suggestions are adapted from "Problems for Students of Computers," by John W. Carr, III, in *Computers and Automation*, Vol. 4, No. 2 (Feb. 1955). Used by permission of Prof. Carr and *Computers and Automation*.

possible. (Do not try to hyphenate the words, unless you want to get into a very much larger problem.)

3. *Language translation.* Set up a dictionary of a few hundred words in some language you know (some *natural* language, that is, such as French or German) and their English equivalents. Write a routine to accept text in the source language and translate it into the target language.

4. *Musical transposition.* Write a program that will accept a tune, encoded in some suitable form, and transpose it into another key.

5. *Track betting odds.* Find out how the odds are calculated on the win, place, and show pools at a race track, if you don't already know, and write a routine that will calculate the payoff on a given horse given the appropriate information. Recall that all payoffs are *truncated*, that is, any pennies above a multiple of 10¢ are dropped. (This is called the *breakage*. As an extension of the project, estimate what the total breakage amounts to for two months of racing at Aqueduct Racetrack.)

6. *Bridge playing.* Write a program that handles some aspect of the game of bridge. Possibilities: using a random number generator, deal out a hand; get the point-count of a hand; make a legal bid; make a bid according to some system; follow suit if possible, otherwise trump if possible, otherwise discard randomly.

7. *Graphic output.* Write a routine that converts any string of eight or fewer characters to graphic symbols about 2 inches high. Such a routine is used at many computer installations to provide a title page that can be read at a distance by the computer operators.

8. Write a program that will compute the score of a bowling game, given the numbers of pins knocked down with each ball. The number of balls is variable, of course, ranging from twelve tens for a perfect game to 20 zeros for 20 gutter balls. For a description of how to approach this problem, see Problem H6, "The Game of Bowling," in Fred Gruenberger and George Jaffrey, *Problems for Computer Solution*, New York, Wiley, 1965, pp. 266–269.

   Or find out what the league secretary's job is and automate some or all of it. This has been done, of course, and is available as a commercial service from a number of companies.

9. Learn enough about how alphabetic data are represented in your computer to allow you to sort a file of information into alphabetical order. Assume that each item to be sorted consists of a four letter "key" together with four letters or digits of alphanumeric data that is part of the record, and "goes along with" the key but it is not part of the key on which the records are to be sorted.

   (In some computers you will be able to give the key the integer attribute and then treat it as an integer variable; a numeric comparison between two keys considered as integers will serve as an alphanumeric comparison. The same would not likely be true of real variables.)

10. Write a program that will print a real number as a dollars-and-cents amount, with a decimal point, with a comma where appropriate, and with a dollar sign immediately to the left of the first significant digit. Here are samples of the results you are to produce:

$12,345.67
$1,234.56
$123.45
$12.34
$1.23
$0.12
$0.01

You may assume that the amount will be less than $1 million, so that no more than one comma will be required.

11. Extend the program of Figure 8.2 to handle the addition of new records to the master file. These will appear in the transaction stream, properly identified by a code as being additions instead of regular sales or receipts, and in correct sequence. They should be placed in the new master in their proper locations.

It would be possible for a new record to be followed immediately by sales or receipts for that item. Your program should take this into account.

While you are making changes to the program, insert a test for a negative balance, which would indicate some type of data preparation error, since it is not possible to sell more of an item than there are on hand. (The error could also be in the master file, since it might not properly represent all past transactions.) To handle this situation, you might wish to extend the program so that a fourth type of transaction — properly so coded — would correct the number of an item on hand.

12. *Parts Explosion and Summary.* You begin with two files. The first lists, for each of a hundred products that a company manufactures, the parts that are required for its production. For example, a type 1 widget might require one body, four nuts and four bolts, whereas a type 2 widget takes one body, eight nuts, eight bolts, and three lamps. All of the information as to product and part identification is coded in numeric form. This first file is in sequence on model number.

The second file contains a list of the models that are to be manufactured for the week, and how many of each are needed. It is also in sequence on model number. Your job is to produce a list of all the parts that are needed to manufacture all the models that are to be built. This involves running the two files against each other, multiplying the number of models required by the number of each type of part required for one model. This is the "explosion" part of the job. The resulting file will not be in sequence on part number, so you sort it into sequence and then summarize the parts. The final output, the summary part, will show the total number of each part that is required for the week's work of manufacturing.

You are to invent the file contents, using only a few models and parts to keep the project within reasonable bounds.

13. Write a program using a random number generator to simulate playing the game of Bingo.

A sample of a Bingo card is shown in the accompanying figure. In playing the game a caller removes tokens, one at a time, from a container that originally holds 75 tokens numbered from 1 to 75. If the token is between 1 and 15, it will always go in the column under the B, and will be so identified by the caller; if it is between 16 and 30 it will fall under the I, etc. The first player to complete a row of five markers — horizontally, vertically or diagonally — wins.

BINGO

	30			
12	16	39	48	74
14	21	35	54	67
9	18	FREE	49	62
3	24	45	60	65
10	30	41	51	75

MILTON BRADLEY COMPANY
Springfield, Massachusetts

The program should provide for reading in the numbers that go on the card, as well as simulating the random selection of tokens. Remember that once a token has been called, it cannot be called again in the same game.

14. *A management information system.* You are a systems analyst/programmer for the Fizzies Bottling Company. You have been asked to design and implement a small-scale management information system, along the following lines.

The company has four products: a cola, a root beer, a ginger ale, and a lime drink; each product can be packaged in 8-ounce bottles, 12-ounce cans, 12-ounce bottles, 16-ounce cans, and 32-ounce bottles, although not all of the 41 franchisers produce all products in all sizes. Sales history is kept in terms of each product, each size, and each franchiser, for each of the past 60 months, in terms of both cases and dollars.

You are to design a system that will permit any authorized company employee to be able to get rapid answers to questions of the following sort:

- What were the total sales for franchiser N in the last 12 months?
- What were the sales of root beer by all franchisers four months ago?
- How do franchisers M and N compare in sales of ginger ale on a month-by-month basis for the past two years?
- What were total company sales in the last month and in the month before that?
- What franchiser sold the most cola in month 16? What franchiser had the greatest sales of all products in the last year?

Assuming a fairly clean existing data base and experienced programmers, this job might take one to two man-years in a realistic situation, including designing the system, converting the data base to a form suitable for use, providing for weekly or monthly updates of the data, and so on. Cut the job down to something you can hope to finish in however much time you have. You will invent the data, of course, and you should cut the specifications down, by assuming only three or four franchisers, for instance. You should probably ignore the entire question of updating the data once the system is running.

You may assume that requests will be presented in a coded form, and part of your job will be to devise the codes. But it is crucial to observe the requirement that the questions be askable "by anyone." That doesn't really mean anyone in the whole world; a certain amount of intelligence, motivation, and a few hours of training may be assumed. But you may *not* assume any knowledge whatsoever of data processing in general or of programming.

If available to you, the project should of course be set up for interactive (time-sharing) operation, which is how it would be used in real life.

15. As shipping clerk you are responsible for shipping quantities of products from one location to another as cheaply as possible. Since it is generally less expensive to send 50 items in one large carton than 25 in each of two cartons, the problem is filling the biggest boxes first.

    Read cards containing, in any convenient format, the following information:
    (a) Stock number (NSTOCK).
    (b) Number of items to be shipped (NOITEM).
    (c) Maximum number of items that can be contained in the largest-sized box (NSIZE1).
    (d) Maximum number of items that can be contained in the middle sized box (NSIZE2).

(e) Maximum number of items that can be contained in the smallest-sized box (NSIZE3).

It is to be understood that NSIZE1> NSIZE2> NSIZE3, and that there may be only one or two sizes of boxes, which will be signalled by NSIZE3 = 0 if there are only two and NSIZE2 = NSIZE3 = 0 if there is only one size.

For each card, write a line containing:

(a) NSTOCK

(b) NUM1 = number of boxes of NSIZE1

(c) NUM2 = number of boxes of NSIZE2

(d) NUM3 = number of boxes of NSIZE3

A negative NSTOCK will signal the end of the deck.

Your program should place as many of the items as possible in the largest box, then place any remaining items in the smallest box in which they will fit.

(Suggested by Professor H. George Friedman, Jr., Department of Computer Science, University of Illinois.)

16. Write a program to encode and decode messages according to a substitution cipher, as follows.

On the first card of the deck are punched all of the characters that will ever appear in a message. (Remember to include blank as one of the characters!) You might choose to make this card set simply all the characters that can be punched on your input device, or you might limit it to letters only, or letters and punctuation, or whatever you please. The second card contains in each column the character that is to be substituted for the character in the corresponding column of the first card. The second card ought to contain the same number of characters as the first, counting blank as one of the characters on the first. The second card should not contain any character more than once (at least not if you hope to be able to decode the encoded message!). The program must read these first two cards, count the characters to determine how large the character set is and set up the substitution tables. It should then read subsequent cards in the deck, making the appropriate substitution for every character, and write out the encoded message.

The simplest way to see whether the program works is to produce the output as a deck of punched cards except that the output deck should have cards 1 and 2 reversed from the order in which they appear in the input. Rerunning the program with this output deck as the input ought to produce a copy of the original deck.

17. The following familiar puzzle problem leads to the solution of a quadratic equation:

Two ladders, one 20 feet long and the other 30 feet long lean against buildings across an alley, as shown in the figure. If the point at which the ladders cross is 8 feet above the ground, how wide is the alley?

Gruenberger and Jaffrey, in *Problems for Computer Solution* (New York: Wiley, 1965) show that this problem can be formulated to require solution of the following equation;

$$y^4 - 16y^3 + 500y^2 - 8000y + 32{,}000 = 0$$

Then $x = \sqrt{400 - y^2}$.

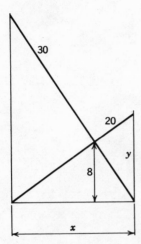

18. Rank difference coefficient of correlation. Given two sets of number u_i and v_i, each consisting of the integers from 1 to n in some order, which are the rank orderings of two other sets of numbers such as scores on two tests, then the rank difference coefficient of correlation between the two sets is

$$R = 1 - \frac{6 \sum_{i=1}^{n} (u_i - v_i)^2}{n(n^2 - 1)}$$

You start with two arrays U and V each containing at most 100 elements. The first N elements have rank orderings in them, and are zero beyond N elements. You must establish N by searching through either one of the arrays for the first zero. You are allowed to assume correct data, i.e., that both arrays have the same number of elements and that each does continue all the integers from 1 to N. The N that your program determines can then be used in the formula. If it is any help, you may also assume that there are no fewer than two elements in each array.

APPENDIX ONE:
THE CARD PUNCH

Most programs are entered into the computer in the form of punched cards. The use of time-sharing terminals is growing, but the bulk of programming—especially that done by students—uses the medium of cards.

There are card punches available from various manufacturers, but the most widely used is the Model 029 Card Punch produced by IBM, so we shall give a description of card punching in terms of this equipment. (The official name is card punch, but the almost universal term is *keypunch*, referring to the keys that are pressed to produce the desired punches.)

Figure 1 shows the basic Model 029. It has a desk-like space for the papers from which punching is being done and a keyboard at the right that can be rotated to the most comfortable position.

The basic idea of card input to computers is that symbols can be represented by one or more holes. A card normally has 80 columns, any of which can hold any of the 64 possible characters that are available on most models. (There is also a 48 character version that eliminates many of the special characters.) Figure 2 shows the combinations of punches that are used to represent letters and special characters. We see, for instance, that the letter A is represented by a punch at the top of the card together with a punch in the "1" position. Similarly, the plus sign is made up of a combination of a punch at the top, a "6" and an "8".

One item of terminology will occasionally be useful. The punches in the top three rows of a card are called the *zone punches*, and the punches from zero to 9 are called *numeric punches*. The zero can thus be either a zone punch, as when it is used to produce the letters in the last third of the alphabet, or a numeric punch as when it is used by itself as a number. The top punch is called the 12-zone and the one below it the 11-zone.

The various combinations are produced automatically by the card punch. When the key for "A" is pressed, for example, both of the two holes used to represent it are punched at the same time.

Most card punches are equipped with a printing device that prints at the top of the card what is punched in each column, which makes working with the cards much simpler.

Let us consider the overall functioning of the major parts of the card punch shown in Figure 1.

At the top right is the *card hopper*, which has space for about 500 blank cards that are to be punched. A plate behind the cards pushes them to the

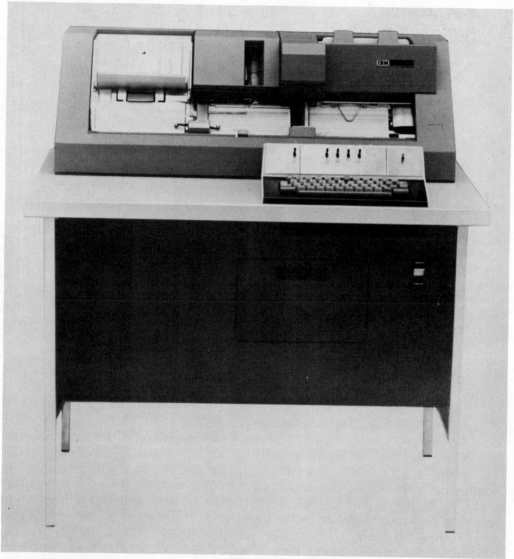

FIGURE 1

front where one card at a time descends to the punching area. When a card descends from the hopper it arrives at the *punch station*, where, as the name implies, holes are punched in the card as it moves through the station. A rotating device above the cards shows the number of the column that is about to be punched. After moving through the punch station, presumably having at least some columns punched, the card reaches the *read station*, where its contents may be read. This is useful when part of a card has a punching error in it. Finally, after leaving the read station, the card is placed in the *stacker*. This has a capacity for approximately 500 cards; if it gets too full, a switch is actuated that prevents further feeding of cards from the hopper until some are removed from the stacker.

The card punch has a device called the *program unit*, which uses a punched card wrapped around a circular drum in about the center of the ma-

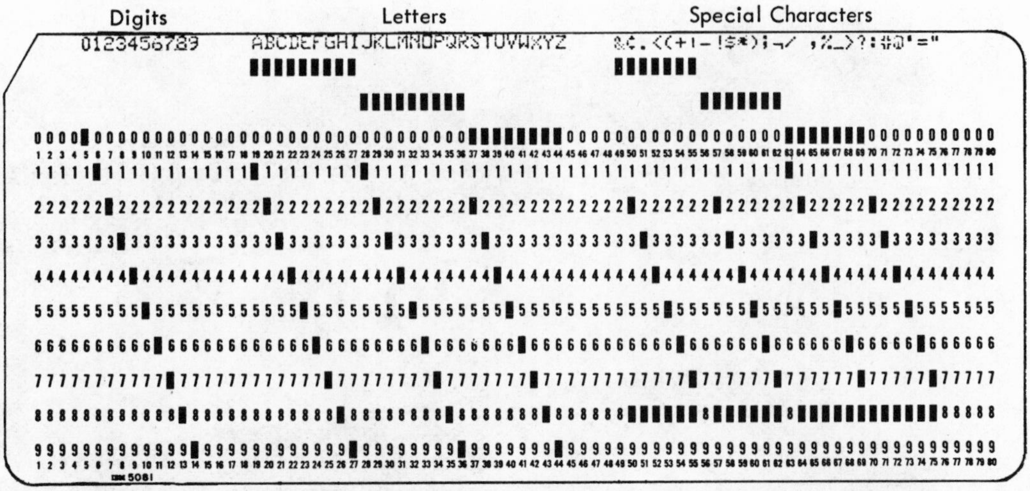

FIGURE 2

chine to control certain aspects of punching action, such as automatic skipping of unpunched columns and automatic duplication. It is doubtful that many student Fortran programmers would have occasion to use the drum card, and we shall assume in what follows that it is not in operation.

Figure 3 shows the *combination keyboard* that would be used to punch Fortran programs. (A model is available that provides only for punching numeric information.) The combination keyboard has many keys that operate differently, depending on whether the machine is in numeric or alphabetic *shift*. Without a drum card the keyboard is normally in alphabetic shift, and punching the key marked 4J, say, would produce the letter J. But if the *numeric shift key* is depressed when the same key is struck, it produces the digit 4. The digits are arranged in a section at the right side of the keyboard, rather than being on the top row as in the fashion that is usual for typewriters. This is done to speed the punching of all-numeric information, which can be done with the right hand only.

The punching of a Fortran program involves material that requires alphabetic shift part of the time and numeric shift part of the time. The numeric shift key is at the lower left of the keyboard, where it can be held down with a finger from the left hand while numeric keys are being pressed with the fingers of the right hand.

The basic alphabetic part of the keyboard is arranged like an ordinary typewriter, so that people who know touch typing can use the keyboard as they would a typewriter. The various special characters (plus, asterisk, etc.) are in various places on the keyboard, some in numeric shift and some in alphabetic. Most students would probably not have sufficient occasion to do keypunching to learn to use the full capability of the keyboard by touch alone.

When less than a full 80 columns of information is to be punched, there is a *release key* that will eject the card at high speed.

There are six keys above the keyboard, some of which are important to us. The Automatic Feed key should be on when cards are being punched continuously, since cards will be then fed automatically from the hopper to the punch station. On the other hand, when individual cards are being

FIGURE 3

punched or corrected it should be off. Cards can be sent from the hopper individually by a Feed key on the keyboard. The Print key should ordinarily be on, to print column contents at the top of the card. Pushing up the Clear key once will remove all cards from the punch and read stations. The other keys have to do with the program card and are therefore of no concern to us.

The main power key is under the desk top, on the right.

APPENDIX 2:
A SKETCH OF COMPUTER HARDWARE

This book is about programming, the preparation of program of instructions that tell a computer what procedure we want it to follow. We have said almost nothing about the computer itself, the wires and transistors that actually do the work. Some readers may have a curiosity about the subject, and some may feel that their understanding of the "software" (programs) side will be enhanced by having at least a little background on the "hardware" (physical machine parts).

The accompanying figure shows in block diagram form how a computer is organized from basic components.

At the center of the collection is the central processing unit (CPU), which holds the instructions that the computer is carrying out, and which in so doing controls the actions of all the rest of the components. The CPU contains, among other things, a central storage for data and instructions.

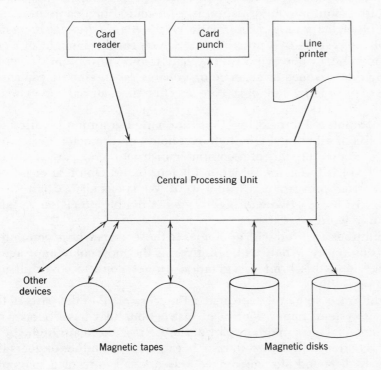

The card reader, line printer, and card punch are the familiar devices that we have been referring to throughout the book. A typical card reader operates at a speed of about 1,000 cards per minute. Card punching is generally slower, and line printers operate at typically 1,200 lines per minute, a line usually being 120 or 132 "characters" (letters, digits, or other symbols).

Magnetic tapes and magnetic disks are used for storage of large amounts of data for varying periods of time. Sometimes they are used to store information for only a few seconds during the execution of a program, but they are also used for long-term storage since a tape or disk can be physically removed from the computer for storage in a separate location. There are several computer installations having libraries of hundreds of thousands of reels of magnetic tape, each tape holding an amount of information equal to several hundred boxes of cards. One magnetic disk unit can hold roughly the same amount of information but information from a disk can generally be retrieved with much less delay. Naturally, these statements are all of a rather general nature, since both tapes and disks come in many different sizes and have differing physical characteristics.

Many specialized types of input and output devices are available, such as visual display units, typewriter-like time-sharing terminals, microfilm recorders, voice response units, devices that can read the magnetic ink characters at the bottom of checks, etc.

A large computing system may have many of these various devices. It would not be unusual to find a computer with two or three card readers, three or four line printers, ten tapes, and 20 disk units, along with other specialized devices such as readers for magnetically encoded information. More than half the cost of the hardware in a typical computer installation is to be found in the input and output devices.

Before we can say very much about the central processing unit it is necessary to say a little about how information is represented in a computer.

The most elementary unit of information is the *binary digit*, abbreviated to *bit*. One bit represents two possibilities, which can be thought of as off and on, zero and one, or however else one may find it convenient. It can be represented by the presence or absence of a charge on an electric capacitor, the direction of magnetization of a core of ceramic material, or in many other ways.

In many computers the next level of information grouping is called the *byte*, and consists of eight bits. One byte can hold one character for printing in a heading, or it may be part of a computer instruction, or part of a number. The next level is the *word*, which holds four bytes. One real or integer variable in a Fortran program takes up a word. We speak also of half words and double words, having two and eight bytes. A double precision variable takes up a double word.

These definitions are used with apologies to those users whose computers are organized differently. What has been given is the most common usage of the terminology, and this brief presentation cannot hope to cover all machines encyclopedically.

The central processing unit coordinates the work of all of the parts of the total computing system, under control of instructions that have been written by programmers. One important part of the CPU is the main high speed storage, which is often called *core storage* because for a number of years the most common high speed storage device was a small core of a magnetic ceramic material. At the present time most high speed storage is based on Large Scale Integration (LSI) devices, in which thousands of transistors and other electronic elements are placed on small chips about one-tenth of an inch square.

A computer large enough to have a Fortran compiler would have to have at least a few thousand words of high speed storage. At the upper end of the range are computers with high speed storage for about a million words. The time to access one word varies from about two *microseconds* (millionths of a second) down to less than one-tenth of a microsecond.

The high speed storage holds not only data that is being processed, but also the coded object program *instructions*. These are machine instructions, each one of which ordinarily does only a part of the actions of a complete Fortran statement. The main function of the Fortran compiler is to translate from the Fortran language to the language of object program instructions of the machine.

In order for instructions to specify what information is to be processed, it is necessary for every word location in high speed storage to have an identifying number associated with it. This number is called the *address* of the words. One of the other functions of the Fortran compiler and of some other parts of the complete system is to associate a specific address with every variable in a program, so that the machine instructions can know, for instance, where to put the new value for the variable on the left side of an assignment statement.

The actual processing of information is done in the part of the CPU called the *arithmetic and logic unit*. It is here that arithmetic is done, numbers are compared, numbers are converted (integer to real and vice versa), etc. All of this is done under the control of instructions that are fetched from the high speed storage and interpreted in the arithmetic and logic unit. To carry out these actions requires having places where information can be held while it is being worked on; these are called *registers*. The IBM 360 and 370 series machines have 16 general purpose registers that can be used for these and other purposes.

One other feature of the arithmetic and logic unit that may be mentioned is the instruction location counter. The arithmetic and logic unit must always know where to find its next instructions in high speed storage. Just as in Fortran, instructions are carried out in the sequence in which they appear unless the machine is instructed otherwise. The machine must therefore be able to keep track of where it is in its program.

In most computers the work of reading and writing information is only *initiated* by instructions from high speed storage. The actual work of making the transfer of information is done under control of devices called *channels*, that are controlled by their own commands. In fact, it is possible (and usual) for there to be several programs in the computer at once, so that while one program is waiting for data, say, another program can be doing operations that do not involve the channels. This method of program execution is called *multiprogramming*.

It is also possible to organize a machine so that there are two or more arithmetic and logic units, each operating independently of the others, working with the same or different high speed storage devices. This method of machine organization and operation is called *multiprocessing*.

Finally, to complete the tour of new terminology, there is *time sharing*, which has been mentioned throughout the book. This is a system where many users are connected to the computer at one time, through typewriter-like terminals or even medium speed input and output devices. The computer is fast enough that it can handle each of the users on a rotating basis by giving each user a "slice" of the time and resources of the system. The computer is so much faster than the user that each user can work as though he had the whole machine to himself. (The computer used to prepare programs for this book can do about 100,000 additions in the time between typing two characters on a typewriter.)

This is all the space we shall be able to devote to this subject here. The reader who wants to know more might begin by obtaining a copy of the manual describing machine organization and language for his computer. This talks about the facilities and methods of machine language programming, which is often the subject taught after a first course in Fortran programming.

APPENDIX THREE:
EXPONENT NOTATION AND THE E FIELD DESCRIPTOR

In this book we have dealt only with numbers within a limited range of size. That is, there have been no numbers that would take more than seven digits to represent, with or without a decimal point. But there arise situations where this restriction is intolerable, and we look for another way to represent numbers. This is the exponent notation.

We begin with a sketch of what the notation is all about.

We need here to deal with only exponents that are integers. Recall that a positive integer exponent tells how many times to multiply a number together. For example, 2^3 means 2 times 2 times 2, and 10^5 means 10 times 10 times 10 times 10 times 10, which is 100,000. When working with positive powers of 10, the exponent gives the number of zeros after the digit 1. We see this in 10^5, which when written out has five zeros.

An exponent of 1 means just the number itself. Thus $8^1 = 8$, and $10^1 = 10$.

Any number (except zero) raised to the zero power is 1, so $2^0 = 1$ and $10^0 = 1$.

If we restrict our discussion to powers of 10 only, it is possible to say that a negative exponent means to move the decimal point left the specified number of places. Therefore $10^{-1} = 0.1$, $10^{-2} = 0.01$, $10^{-3} = 0.001$, etc.

The fundamental idea of the Fortran exponent notation is that any number can be represented in the form of one number times a power of 10. For example, 593 can be written as 5.93×100, which can be written as 5.93×10^2. Likewise, a number like 0.001936 can be written as 1.936×10^{-3}. The exponent notation simply represents quantities in this form. It is possible to use any combination of multiplier and power of 10 that produces the same number. Thus 593 could also be written as 59.3×10^1, or, for the matter, as 593×10^0, although there would be little point to that. On the other hand, if we have decided to write *all* numbers in exponent form, there would be need to write such things as 6.82 in the form 6.82×10^0.

In Fortran it is possible to use the exponent form for constants in a somewhat condensed form. It is assumed that we are writing numbers in the form of a multiplier times a power of 10. We do not write the 10 itself, which is taken for granted, but we do have to write an indication that this form of number representation is being used, which we do with the letter E following the multiplier. Thus if we write the Fortran constant 1.234 E02 we mean 1.234×10^2, which is 123.4, and 1.234E-4 means 1.234×10^{-4}, which is 0.0001234.

The size of exponent that can be written is limited in each Fortran, but the limits are large numbers, typically in the range of 40 to 100. It is very seldom that computer applications require quantities larger than some multipler times 10^{40}, so this is no problem in practice. We do, however, fairly often deal with numbers in the millions and billions, especially in working with economic data. A number like 2.3 billion would have to be written as 2300000000 without the exponent notation; 2.3E9 is not only easier to write but easier to comprehend, in part because commas are not permitted in constants in Fortran.

When working with negative numbers the sign of the number is written in front of the number as usual; the sign of the exponent is written in front of the exponent. Thus -9.03×10^2 is written −9.03E2 and -23.19×10^{-5} is written −23.19E−5.

Fortran provides the E field descriptor for input and output of numbers in exponent form. Its form is E$w.d$ where w is the total number of columns in the number and d is the number of digits after the decimal point in the multiplier. For input, we recommend always punching a decimal point in the multiplier, so the d part then has no effect.

On output the w in the field descriptor still indicates the total number of columns the number is to occupy, while the d tells how many digits should be printed after the decimal point in the multiplier portion of the number. Every number will be printed as a multiplier between 0.1 and 1.0 times a power of 10. Then the exponent represents the power of 10 and is always produced in four printing positions. To be sure of having enough total colums, w should be a least $d + 7$.

Many people prefer to see their output in the form of a multiplier between 1.0 and 10.0 rather than between 0.1 and 1.0. This can be obtained by writing a *scale factor* of 1P in front of the E field descriptor. The exponent is automatically adjusted. There is a precaution, however: that scale factor automatically applies to all E and F field descriptors that follow in the FORMAT. This is generally not desired for the F descriptors, and must be "cancelled" by a scale factor of 0P.

To try to make these points clear, here are some examples of numbers written in several different forms, as we might write them without using a computer, as they might appear with two forms of the F field descriptor, and two forms of the E field descriptor. To be perfectly clear, let it be understood that on each line we have the *same number* represented in five different forms, the last four as produced by a small computer program. The four field descriptors used were F12.2, F12.4, E15.5, and 1PE15.4.

```
5.93                5.93        5.9300     0.59300E 01     5.9300E 00
 -16.01           -16.01      -16.0100    -0.16010E 02    -1.6010E 01
59,300,000   59300000.00************    0.59300E 08     5.9300E 07
621.8469          621.85     621.8469     0.62185E 03     6.2185E 02
0.101               0.10       0.1010     0.10100E 00     1.0100E-01
-0.101             -0.10      -0.1010    -0.10100E 00    -1.0100E-01
0.0009              0.00       0.0009     0.90000E-03     9.0000E-04
-0.0082147         -0.01      -0.0082    -0.82147E-02    -8.2147E-03
```

Careful study of these examples is revealing. We see that simple numbers such as 5.93 are easier to read with the familiar F field descriptor than with the E; in the latter we have to remind ourselves the 0.59300×10^1 is in fact 5.93 in a different form. On the other hand, large numbers such as 59300000 are easier to read in the exponent form, and cannot be represented at all in an F field that has insufficient space. This is why we need the E field descriptor, after all: a more convenient form for representing very large and very small numbers. Speaking of small numbers, we see that a number such as 0.0009 is not represented correctly at all in an F field that has insufficient space for its digits after the decimal point, but that there is no problem with the exponent form.

The exponent form is often called *scientific notation* because it is commonly used by scientists and engineers, but we see that it is useful for commercial data processing in Fortran, too, especially for representing large numbers such as national economic data or world population.

APPENDIX FOUR:
A BRIEF HISTORY OF COMPUTING

If one considers the abacus to be the first mechanical aid to computation, the field is 2500 years old. If one considers the mechanical calculators built by Blaise Pascal and Wilhelm von Leibniz in the 17th century to be the fore-runners of today's computers, the field is three hundred years old. Almost everyone would consider the work of Charles Babbage in England in the last century to be in the main stream of computer development. Babbage, in his machines called the difference engine and the analytical engine, introduced concepts that have their counterpart in computers running today.

The first electronic computer was the Eniac, which stands for Electronic Numerical Integrator And Calculator, which was completed in 1945. It used 18,000 vacuum tubes and was controlled by wires that had to be set up something like a telephone switchboard. The Eniac did not provide for the storage of instructions in the same or similar storage device as used for data, which is the essence of the *stored program* concept used in modern computers. The idea for this type of computer grew out of the Eniac group and is usually credited to the late mathematician John von Neumann. The machine first to go into service using this concept was the Edsac (Electronic Delay Storage Automatic Calculator) which was built at Cambridge University in England in 1949.

The first machine to be built in quantity was the Univac I, produced by a group that became part of the Sperry Rand Corporation. It was used in the preparation of the 1950 United States Census. (The U.S. Census of 1890 had been the spur to the development of punched card equipment by Herman Hollerith, in a company that became IBM.) The Univac I used tanks of mercury for storage, with sound waves travelling through the tanks being the storage technique. Some machines were built shortly thereafter that used TV-like tubes for storage. The most important single contribution to the "hardware" of computers, that is, the devices of which they are built, was the magnetic core storage, developed in the early 1950's at MIT. The change from vacuum tubes to transistors in the mid 1950's was also a major milestone, since it led to much greater reliability of the equipment. Integrated circuits, in which dozens or thousands of electronic components such as transistors are placed on tiny chips, came to the fore in the 1960's.

In 1950 there were a few computers, all one-of-a-kind. In 1960 there were perhaps 5,000 stored program computers. In 1970 there were perhaps 70,000, depending on one's definition of what is a computer. The number continues to rise steadily.

The development of the *software* of computing, which means approximately the programming side of things, was going on at the same time as the improvements in the hardware. In the earliest days it was necessary to do all programming in the language of the machine itself, with the storage locations for data and programs being determined by the programmer. One of the first improvements was what is now called *assembly language programming*, in which the computer, under the control of the assembler program, makes the storage allocation. This contributes much to the ease of programming and makes subsequent modifications a great deal easier.

The first higher level programming language to gain wide acceptance was Fortran, which was first introduced in 1956. With Fortran having demonstrated both what the possibilities were and what some of the limitations to be avoided were, many other languages were rapidly developed. Algol (Alorithmic Language) was first announced in 1958 and Cobol (COmmon Business Oriented Language) in 1960. Algol has had limited acceptance as a language for actual programming, but had been heavily used for publishing algorithms and has had great influence on languages designed after it. Cobol is the most widely used computer programming language of all at the present time, with Fortran second.

A great many other languages have been designed—hundreds in all. Some of the more important ones have names like APL (A Programming Language), Basic (Beginner's All-purpose Symbolic Instruction Code), and PL/I (Programming Language One). Most of these other languages have well-defined, if narrow, ranges of application, and have their enthusiastic supporters. PL/I was designed in the mid 1960's to be an all-purpose language, which, it was hoped by those who designed it, would replace both Fortran and Cobol. It replaced neither, but is now enjoying a renewed interest that could lead to a significant shift to it from other languages.

APPENDIX FIVE:
OPERATOR FORMATION RULES AND HIERARCHIES

Table 1 indicates the types of operands that may be combined by the four arithmetic operations other than exponentiation to form valid arithmetic expressions. If the operation is valid, the type of the result is given. An X indicates that the combination is illegal in all Fortran systems. NR means Not Recommended: the combination is not permitted in the American National Standards Institute (ANSI) standard, and although it is legal in many Fortran systems it should be used with caution. The same analysis for exponentiation is given in Table 2. Table 3 indicates how various types of operands may be combined by the six relational operators to form valid logical expressions.

TABLE 1

+ − * /	TYPE OF RIGHT OPERAND				
	Integer	Real	Double	Complex	Logical
Integer	Integer*	Real (NR)	Double (NR)	Complex (NR)	X
Real	Real (NR)	Real	Double	Complex	X
Double	Double (NR)	Double	Double	X	X
Complex	Complex (NR)	Complex	X	Complex	X
Logical	X	X	X	X	X

(TYPE OF LEFT OPERAND — left margin label)

* Division of an integer by an integer gives a truncated integer quotient, discarding any remainder.

TABLE 2

**	TYPE OF EXPONENT				
	Integer	Real	Double	Complex	Logical
Integer	Integer	Real (NR)	Double (NR)	X	X
Real	Real	Real	Double	X	X
Double	Double	Double	Double	X	X
Complex	Complex	X	X	X	X
Logical	X	X	X	X	X

(TYPE OF LEFT OPERAND — left margin label)

TABLE 3

		TYPE OF RIGHT OPERAND				
	.EQ. .NE. .GT. .GE. .LT. .LE.	**Integer**	**Real**	**Double**	**Complex**	**Logical**
TYPE OF LEFT OPERAND	Integer	Logical	Logical (NR)	Logical (NR)	X	X
	Real	Logical (NR)	Logical*	Logical*	X	X
	Double	Logical (NR)	Logical*	Logical*	X	X
	Complex	X	X	X	X	X
	Logical	X	X	X	X	X

* In many compilers the comparison of anything but two integers may produce unexpected results. For example, two numbers written in the same form, one read from a card and the other written as a program constant, may compare as unequal because of differences in the input conversion routines.

Operator Hierarchy Rules

1. Parentheses always force the operations inside them to be done first.
2. In the absence of parentheses, all exponentiations are done first, then all multiplications and divisions, and then all additions and subtractions.
3. A sequence of additions and/or subtractions, or a sequence of multiplications and/or divisions, that is not governed by the first two rules, results in a left-to-right evaluation in most Fortran systems.
4. The best rule is: *when in doubt parenthesize.* There is no important penalty for extra parentheses used to make absolutely certain of the order in which operations are to be done.

APPENDIX SIX:
MATHEMATICAL FUNCTIONS

Function	Definition	Number of Arguments	Name	Type of Argument	Type of Function
Square Root	$\sqrt{a}$	1	SQRT	Real	Real
Exponential	e^a	1	EXP	Real	Real
Natural Logarithm	$\log_e(a)$	1	ALOG	Real	Real
Common Logarithm	$\log_{10}(a)$	1	ALOG10	Real	Real
Absolute Value	$|a|$	1	ABS	Real	Real
			IABS	Integer	Integer
Trigonometric sine (Argument in radians)	$\sin(a)$	1	SIN	Real	Real
Trigonometric cosine (Argument in radians)	$\cos(a)$	1	COS	Real	Real
Trigonometric tangent (Argument in radians)	$\tan(a)$	1	TAN	Real	Real
Trigonometric arctangent (Function value returned in radians)	$\arctan(a)$	1	ATAN	Real	Real
Choosing Largest Value	$\text{Max}(a_1, a_2, \ldots)$	≥ 2	AMAX0	Integer	Real
			AMAX1	Real	Real
			MAX0	Integer	Integer
			MAX1	Real	Integer
Choosing Smallest Value	$\text{Min}(a_1, a_2, \ldots)$	≥ 2	AMIN0	Integer	Real
			AMIN1	Real	Real
			MIN0	Integer	Integer
			MIN1	Real	Integer
Float	Convert from integer to real	1	FLOAT	Integer	Real
Fix	Convert from real to integer	1	IFIX	Real	Integer
Truncation	Sign of a, times largest integer $\leq a$	1	AINT	Real	Real
			INT	Real	Integer

ANSWERS TO SELECTED EXERCISES

There are several acceptable answers to many of the exercises. The one shown here is sometimes better than other possibilities, but only occasionally is the test of goodness completely clear. For instance, it seldom makes any difference whether one writes $A = B + C$ or $A = C + B$. In short, the answers given here are correct, but they are often not the *only* possible correct answer.

Chapter One

1.   F6.3

3.   F10.0

5.   READ (5, 100) PRICE
  100 FORMAT (F4.1)

7.   EARN = REG + OTIME

9.   WRITE (6, 200) PRICE
  200 FORMAT (1X, F9.1)

11. READ (5, 10) COST, DEPREC
  10 FORMAT (F7.2, F6.2)
    VALUE = COST - DEPREC
    WRITE (6, 20) COST, DEPREC, VALUE
  20 FORMAT (1X, F12.2, F11.2, F12.2)
    STOP
    END

Chapter Two

1. a. X + Y**3

 c. X ** 4

 e. (A + B) / C

 g. 2.0*X - 3.0*Y

2. a. BONUS = 0.5 * OTIME

 c. AVER = (X + Y + Z) / 3.0

 e. SQRT2 = 2.0 ** 0.5

 g. D = D + 2.0

 i. CALC = (X + Y - 2.0) ** 0.5

3. CHECK = GROSS - FICA - FIT - SIT - USSAV - UF

5. VOLUME = X * Y * Z
  AREA = 2.0*(X*Y + X*Z + Y*Z)

7. TAX = 0.12 * (GROSS - 12.00 * DEPEND)

9. ```
   CURRNT = CASH + ACCREC + SUPPLS + RENT
   PLANT = EQUIP - DEPREC
   TOTASS = CURRNT + PLANT
   ```

11. ```
    RATIO = 2.0 ** (1.0/12.0)
    ```

13. ```
    FIFTH = 1.059463 ** 7
    ```

15. ```
         READ (5, 100) ID, A, B, C
    100  FORMAT (I4, F5.1, F5.1, F5.1)
         S = (A + B + C) / 2.0
         AREA = (S * (S - A) * (S - B) * (S - C)) ** 0.5
         WRITE (6, 200) ID, A, B, C, S, AREA
    200  FORMAT (1X, I4, F10.1, F10.1, F10.1, F10.1, F14.1)
         STOP
         END
    ```

Chapter Three

1.
0	-10	0.0	0.
1	1098	1.00	1.
10	****	16.87	17.
-587	-841	-586.21	-586.
90062		0.04	0.
****		12.34	12.

3. a.
```
     WRITE (6, 10) K, A, B
10   FORMAT (1X, I2, F10.3, F9.2)
```

b.
```
     WRITE (6, 20) K, B, A
20   FORMAT (1X, 'K =', I3, '    B =', F6.2, '    A =', F7.3)
```

c.
```
     WRITE (6, 30) K, B, A
30   FORMAT (1X, 'K =', I3, ', B =', F6.2,', AND A =', F7.3)
```

d.
```
     WRITE (6, 40) K, B, A
40   FORMAT (1X, '  K        B          A'/1X, I2, F8.2, F9.3)
```

e.
```
     WRITE (6, 50) K, B, A
50   FORMAT (1X, 'FOR CODE', I3, ', FACTOR 1 =', F6.2,
    1    ' AND FACTOR 2 =', F7.3)
```

5.
```
   TLABOR = 17.50
   TPARTS = 2.40
   ACCESS = 0.0
   OILGRS = 0.0
   SUBTOT = TLABOR + TPARTS + ACCESS + OILGRS
   SALTAX = 0.05 * SUBTOT
   TOTAL = SUBTOT + SALTAX
   WRITE(6, 10) TLABOR, TPARTS, ACCESS, OILGRS, SUBTOT, SALTAX, TOTAL
10 FORMAT ('1', 'TOTAL LABOR', F8.2/
  1        1X,  'TOTAL PARTS', F8.2/
  2        1X,  'ACCESSORIES', F8.2/
  3        1X,  'OIL, GREASE', F8.2/
  4        '0', 'SUBTOTAL   ', F8.2/
  5        '0', 'SALES TAX  ', F8.2/
  6        '0', 'GRAND TOTAL', F8.2)
   STOP
   END
```

7.
```
     READ (5, 100) NAGE
100  FORMAT (33X, I2)
```

9. The FORMAT statements could be modified as follows.

```
60    FORMAT ('1', 49X, 'EXPERIMENT   CENTIGRADE    FAHRENHEIT'/
      1            1X, 49X, ' NUMBER     TEMPERATURE  TEMPERATURE'/
C
C
70    FORMAT (1X, 49X, I6, 2F14.1)
```

11.
```
C CHAPTER 3 EXERCISE 11
C
      READ (5, 50) NCUST, SALES, EXP
50    FORMAT (4X, I7, 2F7.2)
      XNETIN = SALES - EXP
      WRITE (6, 60) NCUST, SALES, EXP, XNETIN
60    FORMAT ('1', 'CUSTOMER', I8/
      1          '0', 'SALES', 19X, F8.2/
      2          ' ', 'EXPENSES', 6X, F8.2/
      3          ' ', 'NET INCOME', 14X, F8.2/
      4          '0', '(DEBITS ARE TOWARD THE WINDOW)')
      STOP
      END
```

Chapter Four

1. a.

```
IF ( DOG .GT. 0.0 ) STOP
```

c.

```
IF ( DAY .GT. 8.0 ) EXTRA = DAY - 8.0
```

e.

```
SHORT = 0.0
IF ( SALES .LT. QUOTA ) SHORT = QUOTA - SALES
```

g.

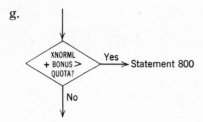

```
IF ( XNORML + BONUS .GT. QUOTA ) GO TO 800
```

i.

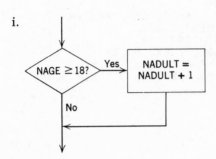

```
IF ( NAGE .GE. 18 ) NADULT = NADULT + 1
```

k.

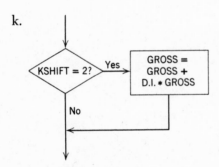

```
IF ( KSHIFT .EQ. 2 ) GROSS = GROSS + 0.10*GROSS
```

2. a.

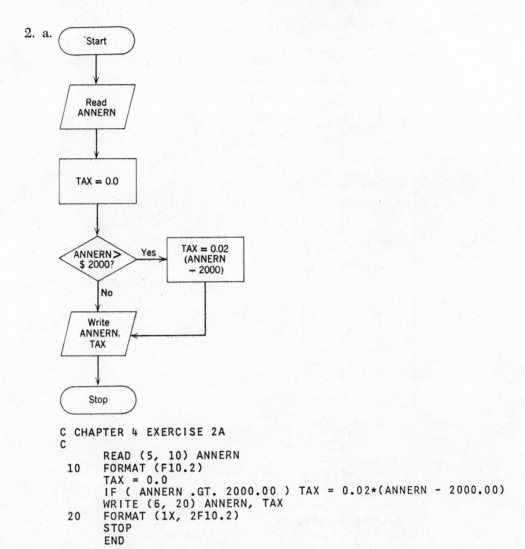

```
C CHAPTER 4 EXERCISE 2A
C
        READ (5, 10) ANNERN
   10   FORMAT (F10.2)
        TAX = 0.0
        IF ( ANNERN .GT. 2000.00 ) TAX = 0.02*(ANNERN - 2000.00)
        WRITE (6, 20) ANNERN, TAX
   20   FORMAT (1X, 2F10.2)
        STOP
        END
```

c.

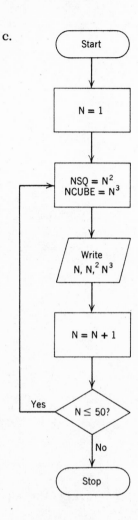

```
C CHAPTER 4 EXERCISE 2C
C
        N = 1
  10    NSQ = N ** 2
        NCUBE = N ** 3
        WRITE (6, 20) N, NSQ, NCUBE
  20    FORMAT (1X, 3I10)
        N = N + 1
        IF ( N .LE. 50 ) GO TO 10
        STOP
        END
```

e.

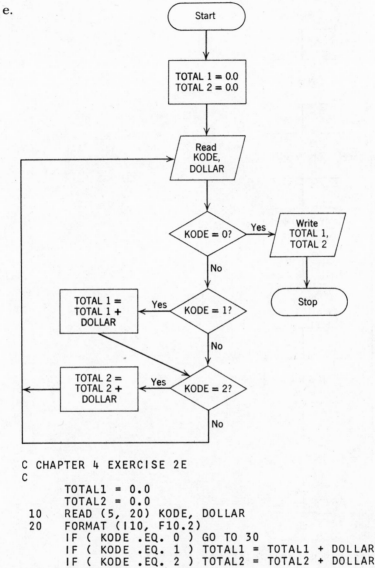

```
C CHAPTER 4 EXERCISE 2E
C
      TOTAL1 = 0.0
      TOTAL2 = 0.0
10    READ (5, 20) KODE, DOLLAR
20    FORMAT (I10, F10.2)
      IF ( KODE .EQ. 0 ) GO TO 30
      IF ( KODE .EQ. 1 ) TOTAL1 = TOTAL1 + DOLLAR
      IF ( KODE .EQ. 2 ) TOTAL2 = TOTAL2 + DOLLAR
      GO TO 10
30    WRITE (6, 40) TOTAL1, TOTAL2
40    FORMAT (1X, 2F10.2)
      STOP
      END
```

g.

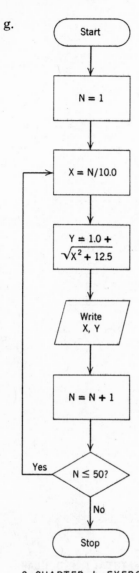

```
C CHAPTER 4 EXERCISE 2G
C
      N = 1
10    X = N / 10.0
      Y = 1.0 + (X**2 + 12.5) ** 0.5
      WRITE (6, 20) X, Y
20    FORMAT (1X, 2F10.2)
      N = N + 1
      IF ( N .LE. 50 ) GO TO 10
      STOP
      END
```

3. TAX = 0.12 * (GROSS - 12.00*DEPEND)
   IF (TAX .LT. 0.0) TAX = 0.0

5. CHARGE = 0.15 * TUITN
   IF (CHARGE .GT. 100.00) CHARGE = 100.00

7.
```
   C CHAPTER 4 EXERCISE 7
   C
         WRITE (6, 10)
   10    FORMAT ('1', 'GOLFER    ACTUAL    HANDICAP    NET'/)
   15    READ (5, 20) ID, NSCORE, NHANDI
   20    FORMAT (3I3)
         IF ( ID .EQ. 0 ) STOP
         NET = NSCORE - NHANDI
         WRITE (6, 30) ID, NSCORE, NHANDI, NET
   30    FORMAT (1X, I5, I8, I10, I9)
         GO TO 15
         END
```

9.
```
   C CHAPTER 4 EXERCISE 9
   C
         READ (5, 10) A, B, C
   10    FORMAT (3F10.2)
         D = A
         IF ( B .LT. D ) D = B
         IF ( C .LT. D ) D = C
         VOLUME = 0.5236 * D**3
         WRITE (6, 20) A, B, C, D, VOLUME
   20    FORMAT (1X, 5F10.2)
         STOP
         END
```

11.
```
   C CHAPTER 4 EXERCISE 11
   C
         READ (5, 10) KODE, SIDE
   10    FORMAT (I1, 8X, F5.0)
         IF ( KODE .EQ. 1 ) GO TO 30
         IF ( KODE .EQ. 2 ) GO TO 40
         WRITE (6, 20)
   20    FORMAT (1X, 'TILT')
         STOP
   30    VOLUME = SIDE ** 3
         GO TO 50
   40    VOLUME = 0.5236 * SIDE ** 3
   50    WRITE (6, 60) KODE, SIDE, VOLUME
   60    FORMAT (1X, I3, 2F10.2)
         STOP
         END
```

Chapter Five

1.
```
   C CHAPTER 5 EXERCISE 1
   C
   10    READ (5, 20) NUMBER, OH, RP
   20    FORMAT (I4, 2F4.0)
         IF ( OH .LT. RP ) WRITE (6, 30) NUMBER, OH, RP
   30    FORMAT (1X, I4, 2F7.0)
         GO TO 10
         END
```

3.
```
   C CHAPTER 5 EXERCISE 3
   C
   C USES THE VARIABLE 'OK' TO 'REMEMBER' IF THERE
   C HAVE BEEN ANY SEQUENCE ERRORS
   C
         OK  = 1
         NPREV = 0
   10    READ (5, 20) N
   20    FORMAT (71X, I3)
```

```
        IF ( N .EQ. 0 ) GO TO 30
        IF ( N .LT. NPREV ) OK = 0
        NPREV = N
        GO TO 10
   30   IF ( OK .EQ. 1 ) WRITE (6, 40)
   40   FORMAT (1X, 'OK')
        IF ( OK .NE. 1 ) WRITE (6, 50)
   50   FORMAT (1X, 'NO GOOD')
        STOP
        END
```

5.
```
C CHAPTER 5 EXERCISE 5
C
   10   READ (5, 20) F1, F2, F3, F4, F5
   20   FORMAT (5F10.0)
        IF ( F1 .LE. 0.0 ) GO TO 40
        IF ( F2 + F3 .LE. F4 ) GO TO 40
        IF ( F5 .EQ. 0.0 ) GO TO 40
        WRITE (6, 30) F1, F2, F3, F4, F5
   30   FORMAT (1X, 5F15.0)
        GO TO 10
   40   WRITE (6, 50) F1
   50   FORMAT (1X, F12.0, '  DID NOT PASS VALIDITY TESTS')
        GO TO 10
        END
```

7.
```
C CHAPTER 5 EXERCISE 7
C
        READ (5, 10) NYEAR, DEER
   10   FORMAT (I4, F3.0)
        NBIGYR = NYEAR
        BIGDR = DEER
   20   READ (5, 10) NYEAR, DEER
        IF ( NYEAR .EQ. 0 ) GO TO 30
        IF ( DEER .GT. BIGDR ) NBIGYR = NYEAR
        IF ( DEER .GT. BIGDR ) BIGDR = DEER
        GO TO 20
   30   WRITE (6, 40) NBIGYR, BIGDR
   40   FORMAT (1X, 'BIGGEST YEAR WAS', I6, '  WITH', F6.0, '  THOUSAND')
        STOP
        END
```

9.
```
C CHAPTER 5 EXERCISE 9
C
        N = 0
        SUM = 0.0
   10   READ (5, 20) SCORE
   20   FORMAT (F10.0)
        IF ( SCORE .LT. 0.0 ) GO TO 30
        SUM = SUM + SCORE
        N = N + 1
        GO TO 10
   30   AVER = SUM / N
        WRITE (6, 40) N, AVER
   40   FORMAT (1X, 'THE AVERAGE OF THE', I4, ' GRADES WAS', F5.1)
        STOP
        END
```

11.
```
C CHAPTER 5 EXERCISE 11
C
        READ (5, 10) A, B, C
   10   FORMAT (3F10.0)
        DISC = B**2 - 4.0*A*C
        IF ( DISC .LT. 0.0 ) WRITE (6, 20)
   20   FORMAT (1X, 'ROOTS IMAGINARY')
        IF ( DISC .LT. 0.0 ) STOP
```

```
          X1 = (-B + DISC**0.5)/(2.0*A)
          X2 = (-B - DISC**0.5)/(2.0*A)
          WRITE (6, 30) A, B, C, X1, X2
    30    FORMAT (1X, 5F10.4)
          STOP
          END
```

13.
```
    C CHAPTER 5 EXERCISE 13
    C
          E = 1.0
          X = 2.0
          FACT = 1.0
    10    E = E + 1.0/FACT
          FACT = FACT * X
          X = X + 1.0
          IF ( X .LT. 10.0 ) GO TO 10
          WRITE (6, 20) E
    20    FORMAT (1X, F10.6)
          STOP
          END
```

Chapter Six

1.
```
    C CHAPTER 6 EXERCISE 1
    C
          DO 20 N = 1, 40
                WRITE (6, 10) N
    10          FORMAT (1X, I5)
    20    CONTINUE
          STOP
          END
```

3.
```
    C CHAPTER 6 EXERCISE 3
    C
```

   a.
```
          NPLUS3 = N + 3
          DO 10 K = 1, NPLUS3
                ...
    10    CONTINUE
```

   b.
```
          NSQ = N ** 2
          DO 10 J = 1, NSQ
                ...
    10    CONTINUE
```

   c.
```
          DO 10 L = 1, 12
                K = L - 1
                ...
    10    CONTINUE
```

   d.
```
          DO 10 K = 1, 100
                XK = K
                X = XL / 10.0
                ...
    10    CONTINUE
```

6.
```
    C CHAPTER 6 EXERCISE 5
    C
          DO 20 J = 1, 101
                C = J-1
                F = (1.8 * C) + 32.0
                WRITE (6, 10) C, F
    10          FORMAT (1X, F5.0, F6.1)
    20    CONTINUE
          STOP
          END
```

7.
```
C CHAPTER 6 EXERCISE 7
C
        DO 20 NUMBER = 1, 20
            X = NUMBER
            SQROOT = X ** 0.5
            WRITE (6, 10) NUMBER, SQROOT
10          FORMAT (1X, I5, F10.5)
20      CONTINUE
        STOP
        END
```

9.
```
C CHAPTER 6 EXERCISE 9
C
        DO 30 K = 1, 2000
            READ (5, 10) QUANT
10          FORMAT (F8.0)
            IF ( QUANT .EQ. 0.0 ) STOP
            IF ( QUANT .GT. 100.0 ) WRITE (6, 20) QUANT
20          FORMAT (1X, F12.4)
30      CONTINUE
        STOP
        END
```

11.
```
C CHAPTER 6 EXERCISE 11
C
    ...
    NERROR = 0
    DO 40 N = 1, 100
        READ (5, 20) GRADE
        IF (GRADE .LT. 0.0 ) GO TO 60
        IF ( GRADE .LT. 40.0 ) NERROR = NERROR + 1
        IF ( GRADE .LT. 40.0 ) GO TO 40
        IF ( GRADE .GT. 100.0 ) NERROR = NERROR + 1
        IF ( GRADE .GT. 100.0 ) GO TO 40
        IF ( GRADE .GT. BIG ) BIG = GRADE
        IF ( GRADE .LT. SMALL ) SMALL = GRADE
        SUM = SUM + GRADE
40  CONTINUE
C
C IF WE FALL THROUGH END OF RANGE, THERE WERE TOO MANY DATA CARDS
C
    WRITE (6, 50)
50  FORMAT ('1', 'THERE WERE TOO MANY DATA CARDS -- JOB STOPPED')
    STOP
60  N = N - NERROR
    AVERAG = SUM / N
    WRITE (6, 70) N, SMALL, BIG, AVERAG
70  FORMAT ('1', 'THERE WERE', I5, '  GRADES, RANGING FROM', F7.1,
   1    ' TO', F7.1/1X, '  WITH AN AVERAGE OF', F8.1)
    STOP
    END
```

13.
```
C CHAPTER 6 EXERCISE 13
C
        DO 30 K = 1, 21
            READ (5, 10) N
10          FORMAT (I5)
            WRITE (6, 20) N
20          FORMAT (1X, I5)
30      CONTINUE
        STOP
        END
```

15.
```
C CHAPTER 6 EXERCISE 15
C
        NSUM = 0
        DO 30 K = 1, 20
            READ (5, 10) N
10          FORMAT (I5)
            WRITE (6, 20) N
20          FORMAT (1X, I5)
            NSUM = NSUM + N
30      CONTINUE
C CHECK FOR SENTINEL
        READ (5, 10) N
        IF ( N .GE. 0 ) WRITE (6, 40)
40      FORMAT ('0', 'THE 21ST CARD WAS NOT A SENTINEL')
        IF ( N .GE. 0 ) STOP
        WRITE (6, 50) NSUM
50      FORMAT (1X, I7)
        STOP
        END
```

17.
```
C CHAPTER 6 EXERCISE 17
C
        NSUM = 0
        DO 30 K = 1, 10000
            READ (5, 10) N
10          FORMAT (I5)
            IF ( N .LT. 0 ) GO TO 50
            WRITE (6, 20) K, N
20          FORMAT (1X, 2I5)
            NSUM = NSUM + N
30      CONTINUE
        WRITE (6, 40)
40      FORMAT ('0', 'THERE WERE TOO MANY DATA CARDS')
        STOP
50      WRITE (6, 60) NSUM
60      FORMAT (1X, I7)
        STOP
        END
```

19.
```
C CHAPTER 6 EXERCISE 19
C
        DO 20 J = 1, 100
            JSQ = J ** 2
            WRITE (6, 10) J, JSQ
10          FORMAT (1X, 2I8)
20      CONTINUE
        STOP
        END
```

21.
```
C CHAPTER 6 EXERCISE 21
C
        NERROR = 0
        DO 30 K = 1, 10000
            READ (5, 10) X
10          FORMAT (F8.0)
            IF ( X .EQ. 0.0 ) GO TO 50
            IF ( X .LT. 0.0 ) NERROR = NERROR + 1
            IF ( X .GT. 0.0 ) WRITE (6, 20) K, X
20          FORMAT (1X, I5, 1X, F12.4)
30      CONTINUE
        WRITE (6, 40)
40      FORMAT ('0', 'THERE WERE TOO MANY DATA CARDS')
        STOP
50      WRITE (6, 60) NERROR
60      FORMAT ('0', 'THERE WERE', I6, '  ERROR CARDS')
        STOP
        END
```

23.
```
    C CHAPTER 6 EXERCISE 23
    C
          NSUMSQ = 0
          READ (5, 10) N
    10    FORMAT (I5)
          DO 20 L = 1, N
              NSUMSQ = NSUMSQ = N ** 2
    20    CONTINUE
          NFUNC = (N**2 + N)/2
          WRITE (6, 30) N, NFUNC, NSUMSQ
    30    FORMAT (1X, 3I8)
          STOP
          END
```

25.
```
    C CHAPTER 6 EXERCISE 25
    C
          NBIG = 1
          READ (5, 10) BIG
    10    FORMAT (1X, F8.0)
          DO 30 L = 2, 10000
              READ (5, 20) X
    20        FORMAT (1X, F8.0)
              IF ( X .EQ. 0.0 ) GO TO 50
              IF ( X .GT. BIG ) NBIG = L
              IF ( X .GT. BIG ) BIG = X
    30    CONTINUE
          WRITE (6, 40)
    40    FORMAT ('0', 'THERE WERE TOO MANY DATA CARDS')
          STOP
    50    WRITE (6, 60) BIG, NBIG
    60    FORMAT (1X, F12.4, I5)
          STOP
          END
```

Chapter Seven

1.
```
    C CHAPTER 7 EXERCISE 1
    C
          DIMENSION A(10)
```

   a.
```
          PROD = A(1) * A(2)
```

   b.
```
          A(3) = ( A(1) + A(3) + A(5) ) / 3.0
```

   c.
```
          IF ( A(10) .LT. 0.0 ) A(10) = -A(10)
```

   d.
```
          DO 10 J = 1, 10
              A(J) = 2.0 * A(J)
    10    CONTINUE
```

3.
```
    C CHAPTER 7 EXERCISE 3
    C
          DIMENSION SAM(35), BEN(35), HALL(35)
          DO 10 J = 1, 35
              HALL(J) = SAM(J) + BEN(J)
    10    CONTINUE
```

5.
```
    C CHAPTER 7 EXERCISE 5
    C
          DIMENSION TOM (5)
          RACHEL = TOM(1) + TOM(2) + TOM(3) + TOM(4) + TOM(5)
```

7.
```
    C CHAPTER 7 EXERCISE 7
    C
          DIMENSION A(15), B(15)
          OK = 1.0
```

```
              DO 10 K = 1, 15
                    IF ( A(K) .LE. B(K) ) OK = 0.0
       10     CONTINUE
              IF ( OK .EQ. 1.0 ) WRITE (6, 20)
       20     FORMAT (1X, 'OK')
              IF ( OK .NE. 1.0 ) WRITE (6, 30)
       30     FORMAT (1X, 'NO WAY')
              STOP
              END
```

9.
```
   C CHAPTER 7 EXERCISE 9
   C
              DIMENSION Q(25)
              DO 20 K = 1, 25
                    READ (5, 10) Q(K)
       10           FORMAT (F10.0)
       20     CONTINUE
              STOP
              END
```

11.
```
    C CHAPTER 7 EXERCISE 11
    C
              DIMENSION NUMBER (400)
              DO 10 J = 1, 400
                    NUMBER(J) = 0
       10     CONTINUE
       20     READ (5, 30) N
       30     FORMAT (I3)
              IF ( N .EQ. 0 ) STOP
              IF ( N .LT. 1 ) GO TO 20
              IF ( N .GT. 400 ) GO TO 20
              NUMBER(N) = 1
              GO TO 20
              END
```

13.
```
    C CHAPTER 7 EXERCISE 13 -- STATEMENTS ADDED
    C
              ...
       40     NSUM = 0
              DO 50 K = 1, 400
                    NSUM = NSUM = NUMBER(K)
       50     CONTINUE
              WRITE (6, 60) NSUM
       60     FORMAT (1X, I6)
              STOP
              END
```

15.
```
    C CHAPTER 7 EXERCISE 15
    C
              DIMENSION NUMBER(400), AMOUNT(400)
              DO 10 J = 1, 400
                    NUMBER(J) = 0
       10     CONTINUE
       20     READ (5, 30) N, DOLLAR
       30     FORMAT (I3, F7.2)
              IF ( N .EQ. 0 ) GO TO 40
              IF ( N .LT. 1 ) GO TO 20
              IF ( N .GT. 400 ) GO TO 20
              NUMBER(N) = 1
              AMOUNT(N) = DOLLAR
              GO TO 20
       40     DO 60 L = 1, 400
                    IF ( NUMBER(L) .NE. 0 ) WRITE (6, 50) L, AMOUNT(L)
       50           FORMAT (1X, I5, F10.2)
       60     CONTINUE
              STOP
              END
```

17.
```
C CHAPTER 7 EXERCISE 17
C
      DIMENSION NYEAR(37), GOVEXP(37)
      NBIG = NYEAR(1)
      BIG = GOVEXP(1)
      DO 10 K = 2, 37
          IF ( GOVEXP(K) .GT. BIG ) NBIG = NYEAR(K)
          IF ( GOVEXP(K) .GT. BIG ) BIG = GOVEXP(K)
   10 CONTINUE
      WRITE (6, 20) NBIG, BIG
   20 FORMAT (1X, I5, '  HAD THE BIGGEST PERCENTAGE,', F8.1, '%')
      STOP
      END
```

19.
```
C CHAPTER 7 EXERCISE 19
C
      DIMENSION NYEAR(37), DISP(37)
      NBIG = NYEAR(1)
      BIG = DISP(2) - DISP(1)
      DO 10 K = 2, 37
          IF ( DISP(K+1) - DISP(K) .GT. BIG ) NBIG = NYEAR(K)
          IF ( DISP(K+1) - DISP(K) .GT. BIG ) BIG = DISP(K+1) - DISP(K)
   10 CONTINUE
      NPLUS1 = NBIG + 1
      WRITE (6, 20) NBIG, NPLUS1
   20 FORMAT (1X, 'THE INCREASE FROM', I6, ' TO', I6, '  WAS GREATEST')
      STOP
      END
```

21. Add an array for the student identification number, call it ID, by an appropriate modification of the DIMENSION. Arrange to read these numbers into the array. Add three statements to do the interchanging of them, along with the grades, just before the CONTINUE having statement number 50. Then in the WRITE include the printing of ID(1) and ID(N).

23. Add an array named, say, NUMBER, having 25 elements. (Or 26, if you want to keep things similar to the program; the last one will always be empty.) Then in the statements just after statement number 50 add a counting statement that adds 1 to the contents of NUMBER(K). Do the zeroing of the NUMBER array somewhere before the DO that is called the program loop.

25.
```
C CHAPTER 7 EXERCISE 25
C
      DIMENSION NUMBER(20), WEIGHT(20), AVER(20)
C ZERO ARRAYS
C
      DO 10 K = 1, 20
          NUMBER(K) = 0
          WEIGHT(K) = 0.0
          AVER(K) = 0.0
   10 CONTINUE
C READ AND STORE DATA
C
   15 READ (5, 20) N, W
   20 FORMAT (I2, F6.0)
      IF ( N .EQ. 0 ) GO TO 30
      IF ( N .LT. 1 .OR. N .GT. 20 ) STOP
      NUMBER(N) = NUMBER(N) + 1
      WEIGHT(N) = WEIGHT(N) + W
      GO TO 15
```

```
C COMPUTE AND PRINT AVERAGES
C
30    DO 50 K = 1, 20
          IF ( NUMBER(K) .NE. 0 ) AVER(K) = WEIGHT(K)/NUMBER(K)
          WRITE (6, 40) K, AVER(K)
40        FORMAT (1X, I2, F10.2)
50    CONTINUE
      STOP
      END
```

Chapter Eight

1.
```
C CHAPTER 8 EXERCISE 1
C
```
  a.
```
      WRITE (6, 10) T, S, R
10    FORMAT (1X, 3F10.2)
```

  b.
```
      WRITE (6, 10) LAST, ARRAY(LAST)
10    FORMAT (1X, I5, F10.2)
```

  c.
```
      WRITE (6, 10) SAMPLE(1), SAMPLE(2), SAMPLE(JOYCE)
10    FORMAT (1X, 3F10.2)
```

3.
```
C CHAPTER 8 EXERCISE 3
C
      WRITE (6, 10) XARRAY
10    FORMAT (1X, 10F8.2)
```

5.
```
C CHAPTER 8 EXERCISE 5
C
      WRITE (6, 10) (GREEK(K), K = 1, 20)

      WRITE (6, 10) (TROJAN(K), K = 1, 99, 2)
```

7.
```
C CHAPTER 8 EXERCISE 7
C
      DIMENSION LINE(20)
      READ (5, 10)LINE
10    FORMAT (20A1)
      WRITE (6, 20) LINE
20    FORMAT (1X, 20A1)
```

9.
```
C CHAPTER 8 EXERCISE 9
C
      DIMENSION WORD(9), UNDER(9)
      READ (5, 10) WORD, UNDER
10    FORMAT (9A1, 9A1)
      WRITE (6, 20) WORD, UNDER
20    FORMAT ('+', 9A1/1X, 9A1)
      STOP
      END
```

11.
```
C CHAPTER 8 EXERCISE 11
C
      WRITE ( 6, 10) SAM
10    FORMAT (1X, F10.2/(1X, 5F10.2))
```

13.
```
C CHAPTER 8 EXERCISE 13
C
      READ (5, 10, END=180) X
10    FORMAT (F10.0)
```

15.
```
C CHAPTER 8 EXERCISE 15
C
      WRITE (12) HARRAY
```

17. You will need another variable, to hold the previous item number. Call it PREVIT, for "previous item." In the initialization section set this to the item number of the first transaction. After reading each item from the transaction file check to see that it is not less than PREVIT and stop if it is. Before going back to read another transaction, set PREVIT equal to the present transaction item number.

Chapter Nine

1.
```
C CHAPTER 9 EXERCISE 1
C
      ANSWER = SQRT(X/12.0) + 12.0
```

3.
```
C CHAPTER 9 EXERCISE 3
C
      GREAT = AMAX1(SAM, BEN, AARON)
```

5.
```
C CHAPTER 9 EXERCISE 5
C
      SMALL = SQRT(AMIN1(X, Y))
```

7.
```
C CHAPTER 9 EXERCISE 7
C
      SUBROUTINE FUNC(A, B, C, SUMSQ, SUMCUB)
      SUMSQ = A**2 + B**2 + C**2
      SUMCUB = A**3 + B**3 + C**3
      RETURN
      END
      .
      .
      .
      CALL FUNC(15.0, 37.0, 89.0, SUMSQ, SUMCUB)
```

9.
```
C CHAPTER 9 EXERCISE 9
C
      SUBROUTINE ZERCNT(ARRAY, NCOUNT)
      DIMENSION ARRAY(100)
      NCOUNT = 0
      DO 10 K = 1, 100
         IF ( ARRAY(K) .EQ. 0.0 ) NCOUNT = NCOUNT + 1
   10 CONTINUE
      RETURN
      END
```

11.
```
C CHAPTER 9 EXERCISE 11
C
      SUBROUTINE SUMMER(ARRAY, TOTAL)
      DIMENSION ARRAY(100)
      TOTAL = 0.0
      DO 10 J = 1, 100
         TOTAL = TOTAL + ARRAY(J)
   10 CONTINUE
      RETURN
      END
```

13.
```
C CHAPTER 9 EXERCISE 13
C
      ...
      DIMENSION GEORGE(100)
      CALL SUMMER(GEORGE, SUM)
      ...
```

Chapter Ten

1.
```
C CHAPTER 10 EXERCISE 1
C
      INTEGER SAM1, GEORGE, DON
      REAL LARRY
```

3.
```
C CHAPTER 10 EXERCISE 3
C
      LOGICAL SAVE
      SAVE = X + Y .GT. 190.0
```

5.
```
C CHAPTER 10 EXERCISE 5
C
      DATA CAT/-12.3/, DOG/12.3/
      DATA CAT, DOG/-12.3, 12.3/
```

7.
```
C CHAPTER 10 EXERCISE 7
C
      DATA KAT1, KAT2, KAT3/3*1/
```

9.
```
C CHAPTER 10 EXERCISE 9
C
      DATA JACK/39*0/
```

11.
```
C CHAPTER 10 EXERCISE 11
C
      COMMON HORSE, COW
```

13.
```
C CHAPTER 10 EXERCISE 13
C
      EQUIVALENCE (SAM(1), GEORGE(21))
```

15.
```
C CHAPTER 10 EXERCISE 15
C
      FUNCTION SUM2(X, Y)
      DIMENSION X(100), Y(100)
      SUM2 = 0.0
      DO 10 K = 1, 100
          SUM2 = SUM2 + X(K) + Y(K)
10    CONTINUE
      RETURN
      END
```

INDEX

FORTRAN STATEMENT PUNCTUATION SAMPLES

Page numbers refer to text discussions of the statements.
Blanks are ignored except within Hollerith fields; statement
spacing is otherwise at the discretion of the programmer.

Page	Statement sample
3	PAY = HOURS * RATE
19	ANSWER = A*B + R1/R2 - E**3
187	ROOT1 = (-B + SQRT(B**2 - 4.*A*C)) / (2.0*A)
117	SUM = SUM + GRADE(INDEX)
180	SWITCH = .TRUE.
180	OK = (K .GT. 0) .AND. (K .LT. N)
187	FUNC(X) = X**3 - 11.5*X**2 + 10.5*X + 45.0
147	BACKSPACE 12
166	CALL TRINGL (HH-3.48, ABC, R, SS)
184	COMMON A, B, K, L
95	CONTINUE
183	DATA A, B, KAT/14.7, 0.0, -12/
183	DATA A/14.7/, B/0.0/, KAT/-12/
184	DATA R, S, T, U, V/5*0.0/
118	DIMENSION ARRAY(10), FORMT(147)
95	DO 80 K = 1, 100
95	DO 200 KLM2 = 2, NPLUS1, 3
181	DOUBLE PRECISION A, B, C, D, E, F, DENOM
6	END
148	END FILE 9
184	EQUIVALENCE (ABC, BCD), (X(51), Z(1))
3	FORMAT (1X, F8.1, F7.2, F10.2)
37	FORMAT ('1', 'HEADING LINE AND PAGE NUMBER', 10X, I3)
39	FORMAT (1H1, 28HHEADING LINE AND PAGE NUMBER, 10X, I3)
146	FORMAT (1X, 4(F8.2, F9.3), F2.1/I4, F5.1)
185	FUNCTION SUM (ARRAY, N)
54	GO TO 20
183	GO TO (200, 100, 80, 300), KPOINT
53	IF (IDNO .EQ. 0) STOP
130	IF ((K .NE. 1) .OR. (KODE .GT. 4)) GO TO 800
182	IF (X - 10.0) 20, 30, 40
179	INTEGER X, YZ, A12233
180	LOGICAL OK, GOOD, I29Z, LOG
147	PRINT 300, G, K
147	PUNCH 400, ARRAY
147	READ 200, Z, X, I
149	READ (9) ARRAY1, ARRAY2
3	READ (5, 100) HOURS, RATE
148	READ (5, 100, END=80, ERR=3000) X, Y, Z
179	REAL INCOME, ESTATE
166	RETURN
148	REWIND 8
6	STOP
166	SUBROUTINE TRINGL (A, B, AREA, HYP)
5	WRITE (6, 200) HOURS, RATE, PAY
141	WRITE (6, 130) (SUZI(L), L = 1, 39, 2)
149	WRITE (9) ARRAY1, ARRAY2